THE CATHOLIC UNIVERSITY OF AMERICA

THE TRADITION OF THE NUN
IN MEDIEVAL ENGLAND

A Dissertation

SUBMITTED TO THE FACULTY OF THE GRADUATE SCHOOL OF ARTS AND SCIENCES
OF THE CATHOLIC UNIVERSITY OF AMERICA IN PARTIAL FULFILLMENT OF
THE REQUIREMENTS FOR THE DEGREE OF DOCTOR OF PHILOSOPHY

BY

SISTER MARY OF THE INCARNATION BYRNE, C. D. P., A. M.,

of the

Sisters of Divine Providence of Kentucky

THE CATHOLIC UNIVERSITY OF AMERICA
WASHINGTON, D. C.
1932

TABLE OF CONTENTS

SELECT BIBLIOGRAPHY [1]

TEXTS

Aelredus, B. Abbas Rievallensis, *De Sanctimoniali de Wattun*, PL 195, cols. 789-796.

—— *De Vita Eremitica*, PL 32, cols. 1451-1474.

Alani de Insulis, *De Arte Praedicatoria*, PL 210, cols. 109-198.

Alcuini, *Opera*, PL 100-101.

—— *Carmina Recensuit Ernestus Duemmler*, MGH, Berlin, 1881, 160-351.

Ambrosii, S., *De Institutione Virginis*, PL 16, cols. 305-334.

—— *De Viduis*, PL 16, cols. 233-262.

—— *De Virginibus*, PL 16, cols. 187-252.

—— *De Virginitate*, PL 16, cols. 265-302.

—— *Exhortatio Virginitatis*, PL 16, cols. 333-364.

Anselmi, S., *Opera*, PL 158-159.

Arnold, T., *Henrici Archidiaconi Huntendunensis Historia Anglorum*, (RS) London, 1879.

—— *Symeonis Monachi . . . Opera Omnia*, vol. 2, (RS) London, 1885.

Assmann, B., *Angelsächsische Homilien und Heiligenleben*, (Bib. d. ags. Pr. 3) Kassel, 1889.

Athanasii, S., *Exhortatio Ad Sponsam Christi*, PL 103, cols. 671-684.

Augustinii, S., *De Civitate Dei, ex recensione Emanuel Hoffmann*, 2 vols. (CSEL 40(1)-40(2)) Vindobonae, 1899-1900.

—— *De Sancta Uirginitate, Recensuit Joseph Zycha*, (CSEL 41) Vindobonae, 1900, 233-302.

Aungier, G. J., *The History and Antiquities of Syon Monastery*, London, 1840.

Babington, C. and J. R. Lumby, *Polychronicon Ranulphi Higden Monachi Cestrensis*, etc., 9 vols. (RS) London, 1865-1886.

Baedae, Venerabilis, *Historiam Ecclesiasticam Gentis Anglorum, Recognovit, etc., Carolus Plummer*, 2 vols. Oxonii, 1896.

Bale, J., *Kynge Johan*, ed. by J. Payne Collier, (CS) London, 1838.

Banks, M. M., *An Alphabet of Tales*, (EETS 126, 127) London, 1904-1905.

---

[1] Over two thousand articles, monographs, and surveys examined by me are not listed here, because they added nothing to my reading of the sources on which their statements are, or are supposed to be, based. The absence here of many works usually found in bibliographies on the Middle Ages does not signify that I did not consult them. I simply did not find them useful. Some works I found to be misleading, but useful as a stimulus to independent conclusions. I therefore include them.

Barbazan, E., *Fabliaux et contes des poètes françois des XI, XII, XIII, XIV et XVᵉ siècles*, vol. 4, 4 vols. Paris, 1808.

Barclay, A., *The Ship of Fools*, ed. by T. H. Jamieson, 2 vols. Edinburgh, 1874.

Bartsch, K. F., *Alte französische Volkslieder*, Heidelberg, 1882.

Birch, W. de G., *Cartularium Saxonicum*, 3 vols. London, 1885-1893.

Blume, C., S. J., *Die Hymnen des 5.-11. Jahrhunderts und die Irische-Keltische Hymnodie aus den ältesten Quellen, Analecta Hymnica 51*, Leipzig, 1908.

Blunt, J. H., *The Myroure of Oure Ladye*, etc. (EETS es 19) London, 1873.

Boeddeker, K., *Altenglische Dichtungen, des ms Harl. 2253*. Berlin, 1878.

Bond, E. A., *Chronica Monasterii de Melsa A Fundatione Ad Annum 1396*, 3 vols. (RS) London, 1866-1868.

Bonifatii, S., *Carmine, Recensuit Ernestus Duemmler*, MGH, Berlin, 1881, 1-23.

Brandeis, A., *Jacob's Well*, (EETS 115) London, 1900.

Breck, E., *Fragment of Aelfric's Translation of Aethelwold's De Consuetudine Monachorum*, Leipzig, 1887.

Brewer, J. S., J. F. Dimrock, and G. F. Warner, *Giraldus Cambrensis Opera*, 8 vols. (RS) London, 1861-1891.

Brewer, J. S. and R. Howlett, *Monumenta Franciscana*, 2 vols. (RS) London, 1858-1882.

Brie, F. W., *The Brut*, (EETS 131, 136) London, 1906, 1908.

Brock, E., *Morte Arthure or The Death of King Arthur edited from Robert Thorton's MS.*, (EETS 8) London, 1871.

Bromyard, J., *Summa Praedicantium*, Basel, 1479.

Brown, W., *The Register of Thomas of Corbridge, Lord Archbishop of York, 1300-1304*, 2 vols. (SS) London, 1925-1928.

——— *The Register of Walter Giffard, Lord Archbishop of York, 1266-1279*, (SS) London, 1904.

——— *The Register of William Wickwane, Lord Archbishop of York, 1279-1285*, (SS) London, 1907.

Bruce, J. D., *Le Morte Arthur*, (EETS es 88) London, 1903.

Bujeaud, J., *Chants et chansons populaires des provinces de l'ouest*, 2 vols. Niort, 1865-1866.

Butler, Dom E. C., (1) *The Lausiac History of Palladius*, (*Texts and Studies 6*) Cambridge, 1904.

Capgrave, J., *The Chronicle of England*, ed by Francis Charles Hingeston, (RS) London, 1858.

——— *The Life of St. Katherine of Alexandria*, ed. by Carl Horstmann, (EETS 100) London, 1893.

Caplan, H., " The Four Senses of Scriptural Interpretation and the Medieval Theory of Preaching ", *Speculum* 4 (1929), 282-290.

Cassiani, Johannis, *De Institutis Coenobiorum et De Octo Principalium*

Vitiorum Remediis—Libri XII, recensuit Michael Petschenig, (CSEL 17) Vindobonae, 1888, 1-231.

—— *Collationum XXIV Collectio,* PL 49, cols. 477-1328.

Clark, A., *The English Register of Godstow Nunnery, Near Oxford, Written About 1450,* (EETS 129, 130, 142) London, 1905-1911.

—— *The English Register of Oseney Abbey by Oxford, Written About 1460,* (EETS 133, 144) London, 1907-1913.

Cockayne, O., *Leechdoms, Wortcunning and Starcraft of Early England,* 3 vols. (RS) London, 1864-1866.

Comper, F. M., *The Life of Richard Rolle together with an Edition of his English Lyrics,* New York, 1929.

Cook, A. S., *The Christ of Cynewulf,* Boston, 1900.

Cooke, M., *Robert Grossetete's Chasteau d'Amour,* etc. (Cax. S) London, 1852.

Coxe, H. O., *Rogeri de Wendover Chronica sive Flores Historiarum,* (RS) Londini, 1861.

Crane, T. F., *The Exempla or Illustrative Stories from the Sermones Vulgares of Jacques de Vitry,* London, 1890.

—— *Liber de Miraculis Sanctae Dei Genetricis Mariae,* Ithaca, 1925.

Cumming, W. P., *The Revelations of Saint Birgitta,* (EETS 178) London, 1929.

Cypriani, S., *De Habitu Virginum, recensuit Guilelmus Hartel,* (CSEL 3(1)) Vindobonae, 1868, 185-205.

Deanesly, M., *The Incendium Amoris of Richard Rolle of Hampole,* New York, 1915.

Dexter, E. F., *Miracula Sanctae Virginis Mariae,* Madison, Wisconsin, 1927.

Du Méril, E. P., *Poésies inédites du moyen âge,* Paris, 1854.

—— *Poésies populaires latines antérieures au douzième siècle,* Paris, 1843.

Dyce, A., *The Poetical Works of John Skelton,* 3 vols. New York, 1864.

Ellis, T. P. and J. Lloyd, *The Mabinogion,* 2 vols. Oxford, 1929.

Erasmi, Desiderii, *Colloquia Familiaria,* Frobenius, Bernae, 1709.

Erbe, T., *Mirk's Festial,* (EETS es 96) London, 1905.

Foerster, W., *Christian von Troyes sämtliche Werke,* 4 vols. Halle, 1884-1899.

Felice, coaevo, *Vita* in *De S. Guthlaco Presbytero, Anachoreta Croylandiae in Anglia,* AA.SS.Boll. Aprilis 2, 38-49.

Fowler, J. T., *The Life of St. Cuthbert in English Verse c. A. D. 1450,* (SS) London, 1891.

Fortunati, Venanti Honore Clementiani, *Opera Poetica, recensuit et emendavit F. Leo,* MGH, Scriptores Rerum Merovingarum 4, Berolini, 1881.

Frenken, G., *Die Exempla des Jacob von Vitry,* (Quellen und Untersuchungen zur lateinischen Philologie des Mittelalters 5) München, 1914.

Furnivall, F. J., (8) *Arthur,* (EETS 2) London, 1869.

—— (7) *Ballads from Manuscripts,* 2 vols. London, 1868-1873.

Furnivall, F. J., (12) *The Chronicles of Robert Manning of Brunne*, 2 vols. (RS) London, 1887.

——— (1) *Early English Poems and Lives of Saints*, Berlin, 1862.

——— (16) *Hali Meidenhad*, (EETS 18) London, 1922.

——— (10) *The History of the Holy Grail Englisht, ab. 1450 A. D., by Herry Lonelich, skynner*, 2 vols. (EETS es 20, 24, 28, 30) London, 1874-1878.

——— (13) *Hoccleve's Works*, The Minor Poems, (EETS es 61) London, 1892.

——— (4) *Hymns to the Virgin and Christ*, (EETS 24) London, 1867.

——— (14) *The Minor Poems of the Vernon MS*. 2, (EETS 117) London, 1901.

——— (15) *Political, Religious, and Love Poems*, (EETS 15) London, 1903.

——— (3) *La Queste del Saint Graal*, (RC) London, 1864.

——— (2) *Roberd of Brunnè's Handlyng synne . . . with the French treatise on which it is founded, Le manuel des pechiez, by William of Wadington*, (RC) London, 1862.

——— (2a) *Robert of Brunne's " Handlyng synne ", A. D. 1303; with those parts of the Anglo-French Treatise on which it was Founded, William of Wadington's " Manuel des Pechiez "*, (EETS 119, 123) London, 1901-1903.

——— (6) *The Stacions of Rome and the Pilgrims Sea-Voyage (Temp. Henry VI) with Clene Maydenhod (5)*, (EETS 25) London, 1867.

Furnivall, F. J. and J. W. Hales, *The Percy Folio of Old English Ballads and Romances*, 4 vols. London, 1905-1910.

Gardner, E. G., *The Cell of Self-Knowledge*, New York, 1910.

Gerbert de Montreuil, *La continuation de Perceval*, éd. by Mary Williams, 2 vols. Paris, 1922-1925.

Giles, J. A., (6) *Anecdota Bedae, Lanfranci, et Aliorum*, (Cax. S) London, 1851.

——— (1) *" De Miraculis Sancti Cuthberti,"* vol. 1, 1-34; *" Vita Sancti Cuthberti,"* vol. 4, 202-356, *The Complete Works of Venerable Bede in the Original Latin*, 12 vols. London, 1843-1844.

——— (4) *Joannis Saresberiensis Opera Omnia, Epistolae*, 2 vols. Oxonii, 1848.

——— (2) *Sancti Aldhelmi . . . Opera Quae Extant*, Oxonii, 1844.

——— (5) *Six Old English Chronicles*, London, 1848.

——— (3) *S. Thomas a Becket . . . Epistolae*, 2 vols. Oxonii, 1845.

Gollancz, I., *Cynewulf's Christ*, London, 1892.

——— *The Exeter Book*, (EETS 104) London, 1895.

Goodwin, C. W., *The Anglo-Saxon Version of the Life of St. Guthlac, Hermit of Crowland*, etc., London, 1848.

Goulburn, E. M. and H. Symonds, *The Life, Letters, and Sermons of Bishop Herbert de Losinga*, 2 vols. London, 1878.

Graesse, J. G., *Jacobi a Voragine Legenda Aurea*, Lipsiae, 1850.

Gregorii, Episcopi Turonensis, *Historia Francorum,* edidit Wilhelmus Arndt, MGH, *Scriptores Rerum Merovingarum,* 1, Hannoverae, 1884.

Gregorii, S., Papae, *Dialogorum Libri Quatuor,* PL 77, cols. 149-430. Liber 2 is in PL 66, cols. 125-214.

────── *Regulae Pastoralis Liber,* PL 77, cols. 13-128.

────── *XL Homiliarum in Evangelia, Libri Duo,* PL 76, cols. 1075 ff.

Greven, J., *Die Exempla aus den Sermones feriales et communes des Jacob von Vitry,* (Sammlung mittellateinischer Texte 9) Heidelberg, 1914.

Griscom, A., *The Historia Regum Britanniae of Geoffrey of Monmouth,* New York, 1929.

Gutch, J. M., *A Lytell Geste of Robin Hode,* 2 vols. London, 1847.

Haddan, A. W., and W. Stubbs, *Councils and Ecclesiastical Documents relating to Great Britain and Ireland,* 3 vols. Oxford, 1869-1878.

Hall, F., *Ane Satyre of the Thrie Estaits . . . by Sir David Lindesay,* (EETS 37) London, 1869.

Halliwell, J. O., *A Selection from the Minor Poems of Dan John Lydgate,* (PS) London, 1840.

Hamilton, H. C., *Chronicon Domini Walteri de Hemingburgh,* 2 vols. Londini, 1848-1849.

Hamilton, N. E., *Willelmi Malmesbiriensis Monachi De Gestis Pontificum Anglorum Libri Quinque,* (RS) London, 1870.

Hardy, T. D., and C.T. Martin, *Maistre Geffrei Gaimar—Lestorie des Engles,* 2 vols., (RS) London, 1888-1889.

Hartland, E. S., *Walter Map's " De Nugis Curialium,"* London, 1923.

Harvey, R., *The Fire of Love and The Mending of Life . . . Englisht . . . by Richard Misyn,* (EETS 106) London, 1896.

Hazlitt, W. C., *Remains of the Popular Poetry of England,* 4 vols. London, 1864-1866.

Hearne, T., *Peter Langtoft's Chronicle,* 2 vols. London, 1810.

────── *Robert of Gloucester's Chronicle,* 2 vols. London, 1810.

Herolt, J., *Sermones de Sanctis, . . . Promptuarium de Miraculis B. M. V.,* Coloniae, 1477.

Herrtage, S. J., *The Early English Versions of the Gesta Romanorum* (EETS es 33) London, 1879.

Hervieux, L., *Les fabulistes latins,* 5 vols. 2nd ed. Paris, 1893-1899.

Herzfeld, G., *An Old English Martyrology,* (EETS 116) London, 1900.

Heseltine, G. C., *Selected Works of Richard Rolle Hermit,* New York, 1930.

Hewlett, H. G., *The Flowers of History By Roger of Wendover,* 3 vols. (RS) London, 1887-1889.

Hieronymi, S., *Epistolae, Recensuit Isidorus Hilberg,* 3 vols. (CSEL 54-55-56) Vindobonae, 1910-1912-1918.

────── *Regula Monacharum,* PL 30, cols. 391-426.

Hingeston, F. C., *Johannis Capgrave Liber de Illustribus Henricis,* (RS) London, 1858.

Hingeston, F. C., *Royal and Historical Letters during the Reign of Henry the Fourth*, vol. 1, (RS) London, 1860.

Holkot, R., *Super librū Sapientie*, Basileae, 1489.

Holt, R., *The Ormulum*, 2 vols. Oxford, 1878.

Holthausen, F., *Vices and Virtues*, (EETS 89) London, 1888.

Horstmann, C., (7) *Altenglische Legenden*, Heilbronn, 1881.

—— (2) "Altenglische Marienlegenden aus Ms. Vernon", *Archiv* 56 (1876), 221-236.

—— (12) *The Early South-English Legendary*, (EETS 87) London, 1887.

—— (3) "Die Evangelien-Geschichten der Homiliensammlung des Ms. Vernon", *Archiv* 57 (1877), 241-316.

—— (10) "*Informacio Alredi Abbatis Monasterii de Rieualle ad Sororem Suam Inclusam*", *Englische Studien* 7 (1883), 304-344.

—— (4) "Die Legende der Eufrosyne", *Englische Studien* 1 (1877), 300-311.

—— (13) *The Life of Saint Werberge of Chester by Henry Bradshaw, Englisht A. D. 1513*, (EETS 88) London, 1887.

—— *The Lives of Women Saints of oure Contrie of England*, (EETS 86) London, 1886.

—— (14) *The Minor Poems of the Vernon MS* 1, (EETS 98) London, 1892.

—— (16) *Nova Legenda Anglie* etc., 2 vols. Oxford, 1901.

—— (8) *Osbern Bokenam's Legenden*, Heilbronn, 1883.

—— (6) "Prosalegenden", *Anglia* 3 (1880), 293-360.

—— (11) "Prosalegenden", *Anglia* 8 (1885), 102-196.

—— (9) *S. Editha sive Chronicon Vilodunense*, etc., Heilbronn, 1883.

—— (5) *Sammlung altenglischer Legenden*, Heilbronn, 1878.

—— (15) *Yorkshire Writers, Richard Rolle . . . and His Followers*, 2 vols. New York, 1895-1896.

Howlett, R., *Historia Rerum Anglicarum of William of Newburgh*, vols. 1-2 of *Chronicles of the Reigns of Stephen, Henry II, and Richard I*, 4 vols., (RS) London, 1884-1889.

Huber, P. M., O. S. B., *Johannes Monachus Liber de Miraculis*, (Sammlung mittellateinischer Texte 7) Heidelberg, 1913.

Hucher, E., *Le saint-graal ou le Joseph d'Arimathie*, 3 vols. Paris, 1875-1878.

Jaffé, P., *S. Bonifatii et Lulli Epistolae*, BRG 3, Berolini, 1866.

James, M. R., *Walter Map, De Nugis Curialium*, Oxford, 1914.

Jeanroy, A., *Les origines de la poésie lyrique en France au moyen âge*, 3rd ed. Paris, 1925.

Jessopp, A., (1) *Visitations of the Diocese of Norwich*, A. D. 1492-1532, (CS) London, 1888.

Joly, A., *Marie de France et les fables au moyen âge*, Caen, 1863.

Jones, D., *Minor Works of Walter Hilton*, London, 1929.

Kaluza, M., *The Romaunt of the Rose . . . Parallel with its Original, Le Roman de la Rose*, London, 1891.

Keller, C., *Die mittelenglische Gregoriuslegende*, New York, 1914.

Kjellman, H., *La deuxième collection anglo-normande des miracles de la saint vierge et son original latin*, Paris et Uppsala, 1922.

Klapper, J., *Erzählungen des Mittelalters*, Breslau, 1914.

——— *Exempla aus Handschriften des Mittelalters*, (Sammlung mittellateinischer Texte 2) Heidelberg, 1911.

Koch, E. A., *Merlin, A Middle-English Metrical Version of a French Romance by Herry Lovelich*, etc., (EETS es 93, 112) London, 1904, 1913.

——— *Three Middle-English Versions of the Rule of St. Benet and Two Contemporary Rituals for the Ordination of Nuns*, (EETS 120) London, 1902.

Kölbing, E., *Arthour and Merlin*, Leipzig, 1890.

Laing, D., *Early Metrical Tales*, Edinburgh, 1826.

Langlois, E., *Le Roman de la Rose, par Guillaume de Lorris et Jean de Meun*, 5 vols. Paris, 1914-1924.

Lawson, A., *The Kingis Quair*, London, 1910.

Le Roux de Lincy, *Le Roman de Brut, par Wace*, etc., 2 vols. Rouen, 1836-1838.

Little, A. G., *Liber Exemplorum ad Usum Praedicantium Saeculo XIII* etc., Aberdonia, 1908.

Liveing, H. G., *Records of Romsey Abbey*, abrg. ed., Winchester, 1912.

Logemann, H., *The Rule of S. Benet, Latin and Anglo-Saxon Interlinear Version*, (EETS 90) London, 1888.

Luard, H. R., *Annales De Wintonia*, 2 vols. (RS) London, 1865.

——— *Annales Monasterii De Waverleia* in vol. 2 of *Annales De Wintonia*, (RS) London, 1865.

——— *Flores Historiarum*, 3 vols., (RS) London, 1890.

——— *Matthaei Parisiensis, Monachi Sancti Albani, Chronica Majora*, 7 vols. (RS) London, 1872-1883.

——— *Roberti Grosseteste Episcopi quondam Lincolniensis Epistolae*, (RS) London, 1861.

Lumby, J. R., *Be Domes Daege*, (EETS 65) London, 1876.

Mabillon, J., *Acta Sanctorum Ordinis S. Benedicti*, 10 vols. Venetiis, 1733-1740.

——— *Annale Ordinis S. Benedicti Occidentalium Monachorum*, etc., 6 vols. Lucae, 1739-1745.

Macaulay, G. C., *The Complete Works of John Gower*, 4 vols., Oxford, 1899-1902.

Madden, F., *Layamons Brut*, 3 vols., London, 1847.

Martin, C. F., *Registrum Epistolarum Fratris Johannis Peckham Archiepiscopi Cantuariensis*, 3 vols. (RS) London, 1882-1885.

Mead, W. E., *The Famous Historie of Chinon of England by Christopher Middleton to which is added The Assertion of King Arthure*, etc., (EETS 165) London, 1925.

Metcalfe, W. M., (*" Barbour's "*) *Legends of the Saints in the Scottish Dialect of the 14th century*, etc., 3 vols., Edinburgh, 1896.

Miélot, J., *Miracles de nostre dame*, (RC) Westminster, 1885.

Morris, R., (6) *The Blickling Homilies of the Tenth Century*, (EETS 58, 63, 73) London, 1874-1880.

—— (2) *Dan Michel's Ayenbite of Inwyt*, (EETS 23) London, 1866.

—— (1) *Early English Alliterative Poems*, etc., (EETS 1) London, 1864.

—— (3) *Old English Homilies and Homiletic Treatises*, First Series, (EETS 29, 34) London, 1867-1868.

—— (5) *Old English Homilies of the Twelfth Century*, Second Series, (EETS 53) London, 1873.

—— (4) *An Old English Miscellany*, etc., (EETS 49) London, 1872.

Morton, J., *The Ancren Riwle*, (CS) London, 1853.

Munro, J. J., *John Capgrave's Lives of St. Augustine and St. Gilbert of Sempringham*, (EETS 140) London, 1910.

Murry, J. A., *The Minor Poems of Lyndesay*, (EETS 47) London, 1871.

Napier, A., *Wulfstan: Sammlung der ihm zugeschriebenen Homilien*, etc., Berlin, 1883.

Nash, D. W., *Taliesin*, London, 1858.

Neuhaus, C., *Adgar's Marienlegenden*, etc., Heilbronn, 1886.

Norman, H. W., *The Anglo-Saxon Version of the Hexameron of St. Basil or Be Godes Six Daga Weorcum. And The Anglo-Saxon Remains of St. Basil's Admonitio ad Filium Spiritualem*, London, 1849.

Pauphilet, A., (2) *La queste del saint graal*, Paris, 1923.

Perry, G. G., *Religious Pieces in Prose and Verse Edited from Robert Thornton's MS.*, enl. and revis ed., (EETS 26) London, 1914.

—— *English Prose Treatises of Richard Rolle de Hampole*, Edited from Robert Thornton's MS., new and revis. text, (EETS 20) London, 1921.

Petri Blesensis, *Epistolae*, PL 207, cols. 1-560.

Plummer, C., *Two of the Saxon Chronicles*, 2 vols., revis. text, Oxford, 1892-1899.

Potvin, C., *Perceval le Gallois; ou, le conte du graal*, 6 vols. in 3, Mons, 1865-1872.

Prudentius Clemens, *Peristephanon Liber*, edidit Ioannes Bergman, (CSEL 61) Vindobonae, 1926, 289-431.

Raine, J., (2) *The Historians of the Church of York and its Archbishops*, 3 vols., (RS) London, 1879-1894.

—— (1) *The Register, or Rolls of Walter Gray, Lord Archbishop of York*, (SS) London 1872.

Raine, J., and J. W. Clay, *Testamenta Eboracensia*, 6 vols, (SS) 1855-1902.

Rhodes, E. W., *Defensor's Liber Scintillarum*, etc., (EETS 93) London, 1889.

Rimbault, E. F., *Cock Lorell's Bote*, (PS) London, 1843.

Rokewode, J. G., *Chronica Jocelini de Brakelonda*, (CS) London, 1840.

Rule, M., *Eadmeri Historia Novorum in Anglia*, (RS) London, 1884.

Schick, J., *Lydgate's Temple of Glas*, (EETS es 60) London, 1891.

Schipper, J., *König Alfreds Übersetzung von Bedae Kirchengeschichte*, (Bib. d. ags. Pr. 4) Leipzig, 1899.

Sedgefield, W. J., *King Alfred's Old English Version of Boethius*, Oxford, 1899.

Sewell, R. C., *Gesta Stephani, Regis Anglorum et Ducis Normannorum incerto auctore, sed contemporaneo*, etc., Londini, 1846.

Skeat, W. W., (2) *Aelfric's Lives of the Saints*, 2 vols., (EETS 76, 82, 94, 114) London, 1881-1900.

───── (3) *The Complete Works of Geoffrey Chaucer*, 7 vols., Oxford, 1899-1907.

───── (1) *The Vision of William Concerning Piers Plowman by William Langland*, (EETS 17, 28, 30, 38, 54, 67, 81) London, 1866-1884.

Skelton, J., *Magnyfycence*, ed. by R. L. Ramsay, (EETS es 98) London, 1908.

Small, J., *English Metrical Homilies*, Edinburgh, 1862.

Smith, L. T., *Les contes moralisés de Nicole Bozon, frère mineur*, (SATF) Paris, 1889.

Sommer, H. O., (1) *Le Morte Darthur by Syr Thomas Malory*, 3 vols. in 2, London, 1889-1891.

───── (4) *The Vulgate Version of the Arthurian Romances*, 7 vols. and index, Washington, D. C., 1909-1916.

Stevenson, J., *Chronicon Monasterii de Abingdon*, 2 vols. (RS) London, 1858.

Stevenson, W. H., *Asser's Life of King Alfred together with the Annals of Saint Neots*, etc., Oxford, 1904.

Stewart, D. J., *Liber Eliensis*, Londini, 1848.

Strange, J., *Caesarii Heisterbaciensis Monachi . . . Dialogus Miraculorum*, 2 vols. Coloniae, Bonnae, et Bruxelles, 1851.

Strunk, W., *Juliana*, Boston, 1904.

Stubbs, W., *Chronica Rogeri de Hoveden*, 4 vols. (RS) London, 1868-1871.

───── *Gesta Regis Henrici Secundi Benedicti Abbatis. The Chronicle of the Reigns of Henry II and Richard I, A. D. 1169-1192; Known Commonly Under the Name of Benedict of Peterborough*, 2 vols. (RS) London, 1867.

───── *The Historical Works of Gervase of Canterbury*, 2 vols. (RS) London, 1879-1880.

───── *Memorials of Saint Dunstan*, etc., Introd. cv, cviii, and *passim*, 71-324, (RS) London, 1874.

───── *Radulfi de Diceto Decani Lundoniensis Opera Historica*, 2 vols. (RS) London, 1876.

───── *Willelmi Malmesbiriensis Monachi De Gestis Regum Anglorum Libri Quinque*, etc., 2 vols., (RS) London, 1887-1889.

Swan, C., *Gesta Romanorum*, translated from the Latin, London, 1906.

Sweet, H., *King Alfred's Orosius*, (EETS 79) London, 1883.

—— *King Alfred's West-Saxon Version of Gregory's Pastoral Care*, (EETS 45, 50) London, 1871.

Tertulliani, *De Cultu Foeminarum*, PL 1, cols. 1303-1334.

—— *De Pallio*, PL 2, col. 1029-1050.

—— *De Velandis Virginibus*, PL 2, cols. 887-914.

Thorpe, B., (1) *Ancient Laws and Institutes of England*, 2 vols., London, 1840.

—— (3) *Florentii Wigorniensis Monachi Chronicon ex Chronicis*, 2 vols., Londoni, 1848-1849.

—— (2) *The Homilies of the Anglo-Saxon Church. The Sermones Catholici or Homilies of Aelfric*, 2 vols., London, 1844-1846.

Uhland, L., *Alte hoch-und niederdeutsche Volkslieder*, 2nd ed., Stuttgart, 1881.

Warrack, G., *Revelations of Divine Love, Recorded by Julien, Anchoress at Norwich*, etc., 5th ed., London, 1914.

Wasserschleben, H., *Die irische Kanonensammlung*, Leipzig, 1885.

Wattenbach and Duemmler, *Monumenta Alcuiniana*, BRG 6, Berolini, 1878.

Wattie, M., *The Middle English Lai Le Freine*, Northampton, Mass., 1929.

Welter, J. T., *Le Speculum Laicorum*, Paris, 1914.

Wheatley, H. B., *Merlin or The Early History of King Arthur*, (EETS 10) London, 1865.

—— *Reliques of Ancient Poetry . . . by Thomas Percy*, 3 vols. London, 1886.

Wright, T., (10) *Alexandri Neckam: De Naturis Rerum*, (RS) London, 1863.

—— (5) *Anecdota Literaria*, etc., London, 1844.

—— (12) *The Anglo-Latin Satirical Poets and Epigrammatists of the Twelfth Century*, 2 vols. (RS) London, 1872.

—— (1) *The Latin Poems Commonly Attributed to Walter Mapes*, (CS) London, 1841.

—— (2) *A Selection of Latin Stories*, (PS) London, 1842.

—— (4) *Three Chapters of Letters Relating to the Suppression of Monasteries*, (CS) London, 1843.

—— (8) *Political Poems and Songs Relating to English History*, etc., 2 vols. (RS) London, 1859-1861.

—— (14) *The Political Songs of England from the Reign of John to that of Edward II*, 4 vols. Edinburgh, 1884.

—— (7) *Songs and Carols*, London, 1856.

Wright, T., and J. O. Halliwell, *Reliquae Antiquae*, 2 vols., London, 1845.

Zupitza, J.—H. Hecht, *Bischofs Waerferth von Worcester Übersetzung der Dialoge Gregors des Grossen*, (Bib. d. ags. Pr. 5) Leipzig, 1900.

—— *Ceremony of the Giving of the Holy Habit and Profession of Perpetual Vows*, (MS.) Sisters of Divine Providence of Kentucky, n. d.

—— *Liber Sextus Decretalium D. Bonifacii Papae VIII*, Romae, 1582.

—— *The Register of Henry of Newark, Lord Archbishop of York*, 1296-1299, in vol. 2 of *Register of John Le Romeyn*.

—— *The Register of John Le Romeyn, Lord Archbishop of York*, 1286-1296, 2 vols. (SS) London, 1913-1917.

—— *Vita S. Cuthberti, anon. auctore Monacho Lindisfarnensi coaevo*, AA. SS. Boll. Martii, 3, 117-124.

STUDIES

Alden, R. M., *The Rise of Formal Satire in England under Classical Influence*, Philadelphia, 1899.

Allen, H. E., (1) " The Mystical Lyrics of the *Manuel des Pechiez* ", *Rom. Rev.* 9 (1918), 154-193.

—— (4) " On the Author of the Ancren Riwle ", PMLA 44 (1929), 635-680.

—— (2) " The Origin of the Ancren Riwle ", PMLA 33 (1918), 474-546.

—— (3) *Writings Ascribed to Richard Rolle*, etc., New York, 1927.

Allen, P. S., *Medieval Latin Lyrics*, Chicago, 1931.

Allen, P. S., and H. M. Jones, *The Romanesque Lyric*, Chapel Hill, 1928.

Andrew, S. O., " The Dialect of Morte Arthure ", *Review of English Studies* 4 (1928), 418-423.

Assmann, B., " Abt Aelfric's angelsächsische Homilie über das Buch Judith ", *Anglia* 10 (1888), 76-104.

Bateson, M., (1) " Archbishop Warham's Visitation of Monasteries, 1511 ", *English Historical Review* 6 (1891), 18-35.

—— (3) " Origin and Early History of Double Monasteries ", TRHS 13 (1899), 137-198.

—— (2) " Rules for Monks and Secular Canons after the Revival Under King Edgar ", *English Historical Review* 9 (1894), 690-708.

Beddie, J. S., " The Ancient Classics in the Medieval Libraries ", *Speculum* 5 (1930), 3-20.

Bédier, J., *Les fabliaux*, 5th ed., Paris, 1925.

—— *Les légendes épiques*, 4 vols. Paris, 1908-1913.

Bell, A., " Gaimar and the Edgar-Aelfðryð Story ", MLR 21 (1926), 278-287.

Bishop, E., " English Hagiology ", *Dublin Review* 13 (1885), 123-154.

Bond, R. W., " The Exemplum in the Early Religious and Didactic Literature of England " (J. A. Mosher, N. Y. 1911) Review, MLR 11 (1916), 235-240.

Brandl, A., " Be Domes Daege ", *Anglia* 4 (1881), 97-104.

Brinkley, R. F., *Arthurian Legend in the Seventeenth Century*, Baltimore, 1932.

Brown, A. C., *The Round Table Before Wace*, Harvard Studies in Philology and Literature 7, Boston, 1900, 183-205.

Brown, C. F., " Cynewulf and Alcuin ", PMLA 18 (1903), 308-334.

Brown, J., *Puritan Preaching in England*, New York, 1900.

Brown, W. E., *The Achievement of the Middle Ages*, London, 1928.

Browne, G. F., *The Importance of Women in Anglo-Saxon Times*, New York, 1919.

Bruce, J. D., " The Composition of the Old French Prose Lancelot", *Rom. Rev.* 9 (1918), 241-268, 353-395.

—— *The Evolution of Arthurian Romance*, 2 vols. Baltimore, 1923.

Brugger, E., " *L'enserrement Merlin* " etc., *Zs. f. fr. Spr. u. L.* 29-30 (1906), 56-140, 169-239.

—— " Neue Arbeiten über den sog. Didot-Perceval", *Zs. f. fr. Spr. u. L.* 36 (1910), 7-71.

Butler, Dom E. C., (2) *Western Mysticism*, London, 1922.

Cabrol, F., " Alcuin ", Article in DACL 1 (1), 1072-1092.

—— *L'Angleterre chrétienne avant les Normands*, Paris, 1909.

Campbell, E. M., *Satire in the Early English Drama*, Columbus, O., 1914.

Campbell, J. M., *The Greek Fathers*, New York, 1929.

Canby, H. S., *The Short Story in English*, New York, 1909.

Chambers, E. K., *Arthur of Britain*, London, 1927.

—— *The Medieval Stage*, 2 vols. Oxford, 1903.

Chambers, R. W., *Beowulf*, Cambridge, 1921.

Chapman, J., " Mysticism ", Article in Hastings, *Encyclopaedia of Religion and Ethics* 9, 90-101.

Charitius, F., " Über die angelsächsischen Gedichte vom Hl. Guðlac ", *Anglia* 2 (1879), 265-308.

Clark, T. B., " Forehead of Chaucer's Prioress ", *Philological Quarterly* 9 (1930), 312-314.

Clay, R. M., *The Hermits and Anchorites of England*, London, 1914.

Coffman, G. R., " A Note on Saints' Legends ", *Studies in Philology* 28 (1931), 580-586.

Cook, A. S., *Judith, An Old English Epic Fragment*, Boston, 1888, lxv-lxvii.

—— " Augustine's Journey from Rome through Richborough ", *Speculum* 1 (1926), 375-397.

Cornelius, R. D., " Corones Two ", PMLA 42 (1927), 1055-1057.

Coulton, G. G., *The Chronicler of European Chivalry*, London, 1930.

—— *Five Centuries of Religion*, vol. 2, 2 vols. Cambridge, 1923-1927.

—— *Life in the Middle Ages*, New York, 1930.

—— *A Medieval Garner*, London, 1910.

—— *Monastic Schools in the Middle Ages*, London, 1913.

—— *Social Life in Britain from the Conquest to the Reformation*, Cambridge, 1918.

Crane, T. F., (5) " Mediaeval Sermon-books and Stories and their Study Since 1883 ", *Proceedings of the American Philosophical Society*, Philadelphia, 56 (1917), 369-409.

—— (2) " Mediaeval Story-Books ", MP 9 (1911), 225-237.

—— (3) " Miracles of the Virgin ", *Rom. Rev.* 2 (1911), 235-279.

Crane, T. F., (4) "Recent Collections of Exempla", *Rom. Rev.* 6 (1915), 219-236.

Cuthbert, F., *The Friars and How They Came to England*, London, 1903.

Dalgairns, J. B., *The Spiritual Life of Mediaeval England*, Introduction to *Walter Hilton's Scale of Perfection*, London, 1870.

Delehaye, H., S. J., (1) *Les légendes hagiographiques*, 2nd ed. Bruxelles, 1906.

———— (2) *Les passions des martyrs et les genres littéraires*, Bruxelles, 1921.

———— (3) *The Work of the Bollandists*, Princeton, 1922.

D'Evelyn, C., "The Middle-English Metrical Version of the Revelations of Methodius; with a Study of the Influence of Methodius in Middle English Writings", PMLA 33 (1918), 135-203.

Dietrich, E., "Abt Aelfrik", *Zeitschrift für die historische Theologie* 25-26 (1855-1856), 487-594, 163-256.

Dodd, W. G., *Courtly Love in Chaucer and Gower*, Boston, 1913.

Einenkel, E., "Eine englische Schriftstellerin aus dem Anfange des 12. Jahrhunderts", *Anglia* 5 (1882), 265-282.

———— "The Life of Saint Katherine", (EETS 80) London, 1884.

———— "Über den Verfasser der neuangelsaechsischen Legende von Katherina", *Anglia* 5 (1882), 91-123.

Emerson, O. F., "Saint Ambrose and Chaucer's *Life of St. Cecilia*", 1912 PMLA 41 (1926), 252-261.

Fansler, D. S., *Chaucer and the Roman de la Rose*, New York, 1914.

Faral, E., *La légende arthurienne*, Paris, 1929.

Fawtier-Jones, E. C., "Les vies de sainte Catherine d'Alexandrie en ancien français", *Romania* 56 (1930), 80-104.

Fischer, R., "Zur Sprache und Autorschaft der mittelengl. Legenden St. Editha und St. Etheldreda", *Anglia* 11 (1889), 175-218.

Förster, M., (2) "Über die Quellen von Aelfric's exegetischen Homiliae Catholicae", *Anglia* 16 (1894), 1-61.

———— (1) *Über die Quellen von Aelfric's Homiliae Catholicae. I. Legenden*, Berlin, 1892.

Fox, J. C., "Marie de France", *English Historical Review* 25 (1910), 303-306.

———— "Mary, Abbess of Shaftesbury", *English Historical Review* 26 (1911), 317-326.

Furnivall, F. J., (9) "Chaucer's Prioress, Her Chaplain and Three Priests", No. 16, 2nd series, in *Essays on Chaucer*, London, 1868-1892.

———— (1) "Chaucer's Prioress' Nun-Chaplain", *Anglia* 4 (1881), 238-240.

Gasquet, F. A., Cardinal, *England Under the Old Religion*, London, 1912.

———— *The Eve of the Reformation*, London, 1900.

Gerig, J. L., "The Mystic Vision in the Grail Legend", etc. (L. A. Fisher, Columbia, O., 1917) Review, *Rom. Rev.* 11 (1920), 87-92.

Gerould, G. H., *Saints' Legends*, New York, 1916.

Giesebrecht, W., "Die Vaganten oder Goliarden und ihre Lieder", *Allgemeine Monatsschrift für Wissenschaft und Literatur* (1853), 10-43, 344-381.

Glöde, O., "Cynewulf's Juliana und ihre Quelle", *Anglia* 11 (1889), 146-158.

Gooch, G. P., *History and Historians in the Nineteenth Century*, New York, 1928.

Gougaud, Dom L., *Ermites et reclus*, Vienne, 1928.

Goyau, L. F., *Christianisme et culture féminine*, Paris, 1914.

Graham, R., *English Ecclesiastical Studies*, New York, 1929.

Greenlaw, E., *The Province of Literary History*, Baltimore, 1931.

Grimm, C., "Chrestien de Troyes's Attitude towards Woman", *Rom. Rev.* 26 (1925), 236-243.

Griscom, A., "The Date of Composition of Geoffrey of Monmouth's Historia", *Speculum* 1 (1926), 129-156.

Günter, H., *Die christliche Legende des Abendlandes*, Heidelberg, 1910.

────── "Legends of the Saints", Article in *The Catholic Encyclopedia* 9, 128-131.

Guiette, R., *La légende de la sacristine*, Paris, 1927.

Gurteen, S. H., *The Arthurian Epic*, New York, 1895.

Haessner, M., *Die Goliardendichtung und die Satire im 13. Jahrhunderts in England*, Leipzig, 1905.

Hamilton, G. L.; R. S. Loomis, "Le Morte Darthur of Sir Thomas Malory and its Sources" (Vida Scudder, N. Y., 1917) Reviews, *Rom. Rev.* 9 (1918), 345-347, 441-447.

Hamilton, G. L., "Saints Legends" (G. H. Gerould, Boston, 1916) Review, MLN 36 (1921), 230-242.

Hanford, J. H., "Medieval Latin Lyrics" (P. S. Allen) Review, *Speculum* 7 (1932), 115-116.

Haskins, C. H., *The Renaissance of the Twelfth Century*, Cambridge, Mass., 1927.

────── "Spread of Ideas in the Middle Ages", *Speculum* 1 (1926), 19-30.

────── *Studies in the History of Mediaeval Science*, Cambridge, Mass., 1924.

────── *Studies in Mediaeval Culture*, Oxford, 1929.

Havens, R. D., *The Influence of Milton on English Poetry*, Cambridge, Mass., 1922.

Hentsch, A. A., *De la littérature didactique du moyen âge s'addressant spécialement aux femmes*, Halle a. S., 1903.

Herbert, J. A., "The Authorship of the 'Alphabetum Narrationum'", *Library*, 6 (1905), 94-101.

Herford, C. H., *Studies in the Literary Relations of England and Germany in the Sixteenth Century*, Cambridge, 1886.

Heuser, W., "Die Kildare-Gedichte", *Bonner Beiträge zu Anglistik*, 14, Bonn, 1904.

────── "Zu Fischer, Sprache . . . der mittelengl. Legenden St. Editha und St. Etheldreda", *Anglia* 12 (1890), 578-584.

Hodgson, G. E., *English Mystics*, Milwaukee, 1922.

────── *The Sanity of Mysticism*, A Study of Richard Rolle, London, 1926.

Holmes, V. T., " New Thoughts on Marie de France ", *Studies in Philology* 29 (1932), 1-10.

Hopkins, A. B., *The Influence of Wace on the Arthurian Romances of Crestien de Troies*, Menasha, Wis., 1913.

Hunt, T. W., *Ethical Teachings in Old English Literature*, New York, 1892.

Hürth, X., *De Gregorii Nazianzeni orationibus funebribus*, Dissertationes Phil. Argentoratenses Sel., XII (1908), 1-160.

J. W. B., " The Influence of Christianity on the Vocabulary of Old English Poetry " (A. Keiser, 1919) Review, MLN 36 (1921), 315-318.

Jenkins, C., " Some Aspects of Medieval Latin Literature " in C. G. Crump and E. F. Jacob's *The Legacy of the Middle Ages*, Oxford, 1926, 147-172.

—— *The Monastic Chronicler*, New York, 1922.

Jessopp, A., (2) *The Coming of the Friars*, 8th ed., London, 1889.

Jirmounsky, M. M., " La survivance littéraire des ' Matières ' de France et de Bretagne au delà du moyen âge ", *Revue de littérature comparée* 9 (1929), 209-222.

Johnson, H., *Gab es Zwei von einander unabhängige altenglische Über-setzungen der Dialoge Gregors?* Berlin, 1884.

Jones, R. F., " Prediger des englischen Barock " (F. Pützer, Bonn, 1929) Review, *Journal of English and Germanic Philology* 30 (1931), 416-417.

Kahle, R., " Das Klosterwesen " in *Der Klerus im mittelenglischen Vers-roman*, Strassburg, 1906, 31-49.

Keenan, Sr. Angela Elizabeth, *Thasci Caecili Cypriani De Habitu Virginum*, Washington, 1932.

Kinard, J. P., *A Study of Wulfstan's Homilies*, Baltimore, 1897.

Kirsch, J. P., " St. Euphrosyne ", Article in *The Catholic Encyclopedia*, 6, 606.

—— " St. Juliana ", Article in *The Catholic Encyclopedia*, 8, 655-656.

Kittredge, G. L., *Chaucer and His Poetry*, Cambridge, Mass., 1927.

Knowlton, E. C., " Notes on Early Allegory ", *Journal of English and Germanic Philology* 29 (1930), 159-181.

Koch, H., " Virgines Christi ", *Texte und Untersuchungen zur Geschichte der altchristlichen Literatur*, 1 (1907), 59-112.

Konrath, M., " Eine übersehene Fassung der Ureisun of Oure Loverde " etc., *Anglia* 42 (1918), 85-98.

Krapp, G. P., *The Rise of English Literary Prose*, New York, 1915.

Lawrence, W. W., *Beowulf and Epic Tradition*, Cambridge, Mass., 1928.

Lea, H. C., *An Historical Sketch of Sacerdotal Celibacy in the Christian Church*, 2nd ed. enl., New York, 1884.

Lecoy de la Marche, A., *Anecdotes historiques*, Paris, 1877.

—— *La chaire française au moyen âge*, 2nd ed., Paris, 1886.

Lehmann, P., *Die Parodie im Mittelalter*, München, 1922.

—— *Pseudo-antike Literatur des Mittelalters*, Leipzig, 1927.

Lenient, C. F., *La satire en France au moyen âge*, 3rd ed., Paris, 1883.

Loomis, R. S., (2) *Celtic Myth and Arthurian Romance*, New York, 1927.

———— (3) "Some Names in Arthurian Romance", PMLA 45 (1930), 416-443.

———— (1) *The Romance of Tristram and Ysolt*, Introduction, New York, 1931.

Lot, F., (2) *Étude sur le Lancelot en prose*, Paris, 1918.

———— *La fin du monde antique et le début du moyen âge*, Paris, 1927.

Lot, M. B., *La femme et l'amour . . . d'après les poèmes de Chrétien de Troyes*, Paris, 1909.

Loth, J., *Les mabinogion*, Introduction, 2 vols., Paris, 1913.

Lowes, J. L., "Simple and Coy ", *Anglia* 33 (1910), 440-451.

Madeleva, Sr. M., *Chaucer's Nuns*, New York, 1925.

Manitius, M., (3) "Philologisches aus alten Bibliothekskatalogen ", *Rheinisches Museum für Philologie* 47 (1892), Ergänzungsheft, v-vi, 1-152.

———— (1) "Zu Aldhelm und Baeda ", *Wiener SB* 112 (1886), 535-634.

Manly, J. M., *Some New Light on Chaucer*, New York, 1926.

Maury, L. F., *Croyance et légendes du moyen âge*, Paris, 1896.

Meyer, P., "Légendes hagiographiques en français ", *Histoire littéraire de la France*, 33 (1906), 328-458.

———— "Versions en vers et en prose des *Vies des Pères* ", *Histoire littéraire de la France* 33 (1906), 254-328.

Mosher, J. A., *The Exemplum in the Early Religious and Didactic Literature of England*, New York, 1911.

Mussafia, A., "Studien zu den mittelalterlichen Marienlegenden ", *Wiener SB* 113, 115, 119, 123 (1886-1890), 917-994, 5-92, 1-66, 1-85.

Neilson, W. A., *The Origins and Sources of the Court of Love*, Boston, 1899.

Neuhaus, C., *Die Quellen zu Adgars Marienlegenden*, Aschersleben, 1882.

Newell, W. W., *King Arthur and the Table Round*, 2 vols. New York, 1897.

———— *The Legend of the Holy Grail and the Perceval of Chretien of Troyes*, Cambridge, Mass., 1902.

Nitze, W. A., "On the Chronology of the Grail Romances ", *Manly Anniversary Studies*, Chicago, 1923, 300-314.

Norden, E., *Die antike Kunstprosa*, vol. 2, Leipzig, 1923.

Nutt, A., *Studies on the Legend of the Holy Grail*, etc., London, 1888.

Ott, J. H., *Über die Quellen der Heiligenleben in Aelfric's Lives of Saints I*, Halle, 1892.

Owst, G. R., *Preaching in Medieval England*, Cambridge, 1926.

Paetow, L. J., "Latin as an International Language in the Middle Ages ", *Annual Report of the American Historical Association*, 1920, 181-186.

Paris, G., "Études sur les romans de la table ronde ", *Romania* 10, 12 (1881, 1883), 465-496; 459-534.

———— *La littérature française au moyen âge*, 3rd ed., Paris, 1905, 92-111.

Paris, G., *La poésie du moyen âge*, 2 vols. 2nd ed. Paris, 1885-1895, vol. 2, 45-74.

——— "Les cours d'amour du moyen âge", *Journal des Savants*, 1888, 664-675, 727-736.

——— "Romans en vers du cycle de la table ronde", *Histoire littéraire de la France* 30 (1888), 1-270.

Paris, P., *Les romans de la table ronde*, 5 vols. Paris, 1868-1877.

Parry, J.J., "Le poème du gral et ses auteurs" (M. Wilmotte, Paris, 1930) Review, *Speculum* 7 (1932), 163-165.

Paul, H., "Brittische Ritterromane", *Grundriss der germanischen Philologie*, 2 vols. in 3. 2nd ed., Strassburg, 1901-1909, 2, 427-430.

Pauphilet, A., (1) *Études sur la queste del saint graal*, etc., Paris, 1921.

Petit-Dutailles, C., "Les prédications populaires" etc., *Études d'histoire du moyen âge dédiées à G. Monod*, Paris, 1896, 373-388.

Pourrat, P., *La spiritualité chrétienne*, 2 vols. Paris (4th ed.) 1919- (2nd ed) 1921.

Power, E., (2) "Madame Eglentyne, Chaucer's Prioress in Real Life" in *Medieval People*, London, 1924, 59-84.

——— "The Position of Women", in C. G. Crump and E. F. Jacob's *The Legacy of the Middle Ages*, Oxford, 1926, 401-433.

Purdie, E., *The Story of Judith in German and English Literature*, Paris, 1927.

Rand, E. K., *Founders of the Middle Ages*, Cambridge, Mass., 1928.

——— "Mediaeval Gloom and Mediaeval Uniformity", *Speculum* 1 (1926), 253-268.

Rashdale, H., *The Universities of Europe in the Middle Ages*, 2 vols., Oxford, 1895.

Reinhardt, K. F., "Fundamental Notions of Mysticism", *The New Scholasticism* 5 (1931), 103-122.

Rey, A., *Skelton's Satirical Poems*, etc., Bern, 1899.

Roger, M., *L'enseignement des lettres classiques d'Ausone à Alcuin*, Paris, 1905.

Rolt-Wheeler, E., "Dame Juliana of Norwich", in *Women of the Cell and Cloister*, London, 1913, 141-174.

Root, R. K., *The Poetry of Chaucer*, New York, 1906.

San-Marte (A. Schulz), *Die Arthur-Sage*, etc., Quedlinburg und Leipzig, 1842.

Schneegans, H., *Geschichte der grotesken Satire*, Strassburg, 1897.

Schönbach, A. E., *Studien zur Erzählungsliteratur des Mittelalters*, Reprint of *Wiener SB* 139, 140 (1898-1899), 1-139, 1-94.

Schröder, E., "Legenda Aurea and Alphabetum Narrationum", *Beiträge zur Geschichte der deutschen Sprache und Literatur* 43 (1918), 545-548.

Scudder, V. D., *Le Morte Darthur of Sir Thomas Malory and Its Sources*, New York, 1917.

Smith, L. T., "English Popular Preaching in the Fourteenth Century", *English Historical Review* 7 (1892), 25-36.

Snell, F. J., *The Age of Transition*, 2 vols. London, 1905.

Tatlock, J. S., "St. Cecilia's Garlands and their Roman Origin", PMLA 45 (1930), 169-179.

Taylor, H. O., *The Classical Inheritance of the Middle Ages*, New York, 1901.

Thrupp, J., *The Anglo-Saxon Home*, London, 1862.

Traube, L., *Textgeschichte der Regula S. Benedicti*, Abhandlungen der historischen Classe der königlichen Bayerischen Akademie der Wissenschaften 21 (1898), 599-735.

Tryon, R. W., "Miracles of Our Lady in Middle English Verse", PMLA 38 (1923), 308-388.

Tucker, S. M., *Verse Satire in England Before the Renaissance*, New York, 1908.

Uhland, L., *Alte hoch und niederdeutsche Volkslieder*, etc., vol. 3, 4 vols. 3rd ed., Stuttgart, 1893.

Underhill, E., (3) *Mysticism*, revis. ed., New York, 1930.

——— (2) *The Mystics of the Church*, New York, 1926.

——— (1) *The Scale of Perfection by Walter Hilton*, London, 1923.

Vollhardt, W., *Einfluss der lateinischen geistlichen Literatur auf einige kleinere Schöpfungen der englischen Übergangsperiode*, Leipzig, 1888.

Walter, H., *English Satire and Satirists*, New York, 1925.

Watenphul, H., *Die Geschichte der Marienlegende von Beatrix der Küsterin*, Neuwied, 1904.

Weston, J. L., (4) *From Ritual to Romance*, Cambridge, 1920.

——— (1) *The Legend of Sir Lancelot du Lac*, London, 1901.

——— (2) *The Legend of Sir Perceval*, 2 vols. London, 1906-1909.

——— (3) *The Quest of the Holy Grail*, London, 1913.

——— (5) "The Relative Position of the 'Perceval' and 'Galahad' Romances", MLR 51 (1926), 385-389.

White, C. L., *Aelfric, A New Study*, New York, 1898.

Willmann, O., *Didaktik als Bildungslehre*, etc., 2 vols. Braunschweig, 1895.

Wilmotte, M., "Marie de France et Chrétien de Troyes", *Romania* 52 (1926), 353-358.

Wünsch, R., "Exemplum", Article in Pauly-Wissowa, *Real-Encyclopädie der Klassischen Altertumswissenschaft* 6, cols. 1586-1588, Stuttgart, 1909.

Wolfe, H., *Notes on English Verse Satire*, New York, 1929.

Wright, T., (9) *A History of Domestic Manners and Sentiments in England during the Middle Ages*, London, 1863.

——— (13) *A History of Caricature and Grotesque in Literature and Art*, London, 1875.

——— (11) *Womankind in Western Europe*, London, 1869.

Zarncke, F., " Zur Geschichte der Gralsage ", *Beiträge zur Geschichte der deutschen Sprache und Literatur* 3 (1876), 304-334.

Zimmer, H., " Histoire littéraire de la France, Tome XXX, 1888, XVIII und 636 S.", *Göttingische gelehrte Anzeigen* (1890) Nr. 20, 785-832.

———— " Bretonische Elemente in der Arthursage des Gottfried von Monmouth ", *Zs. f. fr. Spr. u. L.* 12 (1890), 231-256.

HISTORIES OF MONASTICISM

Allison, T., *English Religious Life in the Eighth Century as Illustrated by Contemporary Letters*, New York, 1929.

Butler, Dom E. C., O. S. B., *Benedictine Monachism*, 2nd ed. New York, 1924.

Cabrol, F., " Bénédictins ", Article in DACL 2 (1), 664-670.

———— " Monasticism ", Article in Hastings, *Encyclopaedia of Religion and Ethics* 8, 781-797.

Dugdale, W., *Monasticon Anglicanum*, 6 vols. in 8, London, 1817-1830. Two additional volumes by J. Stevens, *The History of the Ancient Abbeys*, etc., London, 1722-1723.

Eckenstein, L., *Women Under Monasticism*, Cambridge, 1896.

Gasquet, F. A. Cardinal, *English Monastic Life*, London, 1904.

———— *Henry VIII and the English Monasteries*, 2 vols. London, 1895.

———— *Monastic Life in the Middle Ages*, London, 1922.

———— *Sketch of Monastic Constitutional History*, Introduction to reprint of translation of Montalembert, London, 1896.

Gougaud, Dom L., O. S. B., *Gaelic Pioneers of Christianity*, Dublin, 1923.

Harnack, A., *Das Mönchthum—seine Ideale und seine Geschichte*, 6th ed. Giessen, 1903.

Heimbucher, M., *Die Orden und Kongregationen der katholischen Kirche*, 2 vols. Paderborn, 1896-1897.

Hibbert, F. A., *The Dissolution of Monasteries*, etc., London, 1910.

Montalembert, C. F., *Les moines d'occident . . .* , 7 vols. Paris, 1860-1867.

Murphy, Sr. M. G., *St. Basil and Monasticism*, Washington, 1930.

Power, E., (1) *Medieval English Nunneries*, Cambridge, 1922.

Schaaf, V. T., O. F. M., *The Cloister*, Cincinnati, 1921.

Stenton, F. M., *The English History of the Abbey of Abingdon*, Oxford, 1913.

Zöchler, O., *Askese und Mönchtum*, 2 vols. Frankfurt am M., 1897.

HISTORIES, HISTORIES OF LITERATURE, ETC.

Brandl, A., *Geschichte der altenglischen Literatur*, Sonderausgabe aus der zweiten Auflage von Pauls *Grundriss der germanischen Philologie*, Strassburg, 1908.

Courthope, W. J., *A History of English Poetry*, 6 vols. London, 1895-1910.

De Labriolle, P., *Histoire de la littérature latine chrétienne*, 2nd ed. Paris, 1924.

De Wulf, M., *Histoire de la philosophie médiévale*, 5 éd. revis. Louvain, 1924-1925.

Ebert, A., *Allgemeine Geschichte der Literatur des Mittelalters im Abendlande*, 2 vols. Leipzig, 1880-1889.

Ebert, A., *Geschichte der Literatur des Mittelalters im Abendlande*, 3 vols. Leipzig, 1894 ff.

Gilson, E., *La philosophie au moyen âge*, 2 vols. Paris, 1922.

Gwatkin, H. M., and J. P. Whitney, *The Cambridge Medieval History*, 6 vols. New York, 1911-1929.

Hefele, C. J., *Conciliengeschichte*, 9 vols. 2nd ed. 1873-1890.

Jusserand, J. J., *Histoire littéraire du peuple anglais*, 2 vols. (vol. 1, 2nd ed.), Paris, 1896-1904.

Kirsch, J. P., *Kirchengeschichte*, vol. 1, Freiburg im Breisgau, 1930-31.

Legouis, E. and L. Cazamian, *Histoire de la littérature anglaise*, Paris, 1924.

Lingard, J., *The History and Antiquities of the Anglo-Saxon Church*, 2 vols. 2nd ed. 1858.

Manitius, M., (2) *Geschichte der christlich-lateinischen Poesie*, Stuttgart, 1891.

—— (4) *Geschichte der lateinischen Literatur des Mittelalters*, 3 vols. München, 1911-1931.

Raby, F. J., *A History of Christian-Latin Poetry*, Oxford, 1927.

Sandys, J. E., *A History of Classical Scholarship*, 2nd ed. Cambridge, 1906.

Schröer, M. M., *Grundzüge und Haupttypen der englischen Literaturgeschichte*, 2 vols. (vol. 1, 3rd ed., vol. 2, 2nd ed.) Berlin und Leipzig, 1922-1927.

Seymour, St. John D., *Anglo-Irish Literature 1200-1582*, Cambridge, 1929.

Taine, H. A., *Histoire de la littérature anglaise*, 4 vols. Paris, 1863-1864.

Ten Brink, B., *Geschichte der englischen Literatur*, 2 vols., 2nd ed. Strassburg, 1899-1912.

Ueberweg-Geyer, *Die patristische und scholastische Philosophie*, 11th ed. Ueberweg's *Grundriss der Geschichte der Philosophie*, Berlin, 1928.

Ward, A. W., and A. R. Waller, *The Cambridge History of English Literature*, vols. 1-3, 14 vols. New York, 1907 ff.

Ward, A. W. and others, *The Cambridge Modern History*, vol. 2, 13 vols. New York, 1907 ff.

Wattenbach, W., *Deutschlands Geschichtsquellen im Mittelalter*, vol. 1, 7th ed. Stuttgart und Berlin, 1904.

Wright, T., (3) *Biographia Britannica Literaria*, 2 vols. London, 1842-1846.

BIBLIOGRAPHIES, DICTIONARIES, ETC.

Brown, Carleton F., *A Register of Middle English Religious and Didactic Verse*, 2 vols. Oxford, 1916-1920.

De Douhet, M., *Dictionnaire des légendes du christianisme*, vol. 14 of Migne's *Troisième et dernière Encyclopédie théologique*, Paris, 1855.

Hardy, T. D., *Descriptive Catalogue of Materials Relating to the History of Great Britain*, etc., 3 vols. in 4, (RS) London, 1862-1871.

Hélyot, P., *Dictionnaire des ordres religieux*, vols. 20-23 of Migne's *Encyclopédie théologique* 1st. s.   Paris, 1847-1859.

Kenney, J. F., *The Sources for the Early History of Ireland*, 2 vols.   New York, 1929.

Paetow, L. J., *A Guide to the Study of Medieval History*, New York, 1931.

Parry, J. J., Arthurian Bibliography ,vol. 1.   New York, 1931.

Smith, W. and H. Wace, *A Dictionary of Christian Biography*, 4 vols. London, 1877-1887.

Stephen, L., and S. Lee, *Dictionary of National Biography*, New York, 1885-1900.

Ward, H. L., and J. A. Herbert, *Catalogue of Romances in the Department of Manuscripts in the British Museum*, 3 vols.   London, 1883-1910.

PREFACE

The nun depicted in the pages of modern English and American authors and the nun who lives the conventual life are decidedly different persons. No matter how intimately or how widely one gets to know nuns as individuals, they bear a common stamp that comes from a common training. The novitiate infallibly leaves its mark amid all the infinite variations of personality. The abstraction one makes of them is always being confirmed by the conformity of the individual to the essentials of a type. But the nun of poetry and the drama and romantic prose is different. She too is evidently an abstraction and like the "nut browne mayde" is evidently a tradition, but she differs from the abstraction one draws from living instances. Milton's

> Com pensive Nun, devout and pure,
> Sober, stedfast, and demure,

and Wordsworth's

> The holy time is quiet as a Nun
> Breathless with adoration . . .

and Aubrey De Vere's

> In countenance half a Spirit, half a Nun
> She stood . . .

and the frequent recurrence of tags such as "nunlike," "like a nun", attest to a convention so well established that the brevity of these references is sufficient to recall it—a convention wholly artificial where it is not simply vague; an intangible, mystic quality of elusive femininity that could never come forth from the realities of a novitiate. The discrepancy between the nun of fact and the nun of modern English literature suggests the possibility of a study of the latter. But the presence of a powerful tradition is so evidently informing all modern instances that a study of the source of this tradition is an obvious preliminary task. To this task this dissertation is devoted. It aims first of all to give such a state-

ment of the literary treatment of the nun in medieval England as
can be abstracted from literary remains from the seventh to the
sixteenth century and from pertinent non-literary records in England from the Gregorian mission to Britain until the Reformation.
In doing this it traces the nun-figure as she enters modern literature in Elizabethan England back through Middle English, Anglo-
Norman, and Anglo-Saxon times to patristic Latin forbears on
the Continent.[1]   It happens to be one of those cases in which the
principle of continuity could not easily be over-worked.

I have tried to examine for the purposes of this study all the
records of civilization in England—Poenitentials, Didactic Treatises, Letters, Historical Treatises, Chronicles, Homilies, Epics,
Legends, Anglo-Saxon Translations from the Latin, Apothegms,
Vitae, Songs, Hymns, Ballads, Romances, Satires, Exempla, Records of Episcopal Visitations, Belles Lettres—in Anglo-Saxon,
Anglo-Latin, Anglo-Norman, and Middle English from the first
extant traces until the middle of the sixteenth century. By this time
the several ways of treating the nun are so obviously stereotyped, so
faithful to what has gone before, that these ways are clearly a tradition to be traced out easily and at random in the various genres of
English literature that follow the Reformation.

The Benedictine Rule, of course, is the great, always contem-

---

[1] Others have studied the English nun, but under different aspects.
Montalembert (*Les moines d'occident,* 7 vols., Paris, 1860-1877), as is well
known, rewrote in fluent prose much of Venerable Bede's contribution to
the subject.   Lina Eckenstein in *Woman Under Monasticism,* Cambridge,
1896), has produced a volume that is helpful for a study of nuns in the
West between the sixth and the fifteenth century.   The work is primarily
social.   Not being restricted to English nuns, it is broad in scope.   The
work which touches but does not linger upon a phase of the subject of this
dissertation is *Medieval English Nunneries,* Cambridge, 1922, by Eileen
Power.   In this volume, which is limited to the period between the twelfth
century and the Reformation, and also in a chapter entitled "Madame
Eglentyne, Chaucer's Prioress in Real Life" of a later study of hers,
Medieval People, London, 1924, Eileen Power evinces interest in the
authenticity of some literary representations of nuns.   The weight of her
interest rests, however, upon the social-economic background.   None of
these works follows the line of research which I pursue.   None of them
solves the problem I have undertaken to examine.

porary force making for monastic uniformity throughout the Middle Ages. It is something essentially apart, however, from the literary tradition.

The word "nun" as used in this dissertation is a common designation for a consecrated woman without reference to the rank she may have enjoyed. To distinguish abbesses from nuns without authority, I have employed the somewhat unsatisfactory term, "simple nun" for the latter.

I have used a uniform method of spelling all proper names throughout the text.

I wish here to express my gratitude to the Superiors of the Congregation of the Sisters of Divine Providence, particularly to Reverend Mother M. Lucy and to Mother Celeste Marie, for the opportunity afforded me to pursue this study; to Mrs. Germaine Goettlemann of the Inter-library Loan Department of the Catholic University Library; to Mr. Martin A. Roberts, Superintendent of the Reading Room of the Library of Congress; to Miss Catherine Rich, for her painstaking preparation of the manuscript; to Professor P. J. Lennox, for reading the manuscript; to Dr. Martin R. P. McGuire, for indispensable guidance on medieval and patristic questions and a constructive review of the manuscript; to Dr. H. Edward Cain, for a very careful review of the manuscript and proofs, and to Dr. J. M. Campbell, who directed the dissertation from the beginning and without whose constant and unstinted aid it could not have been completed in its present form.

It will be noted that the style in Chapters II, III, and VI is frequently very heavy. This is due, at least in a measure, to the varying needs of condensation and close paraphrase in these chapters of authors enlisted in proof of the tradition of the nun.

ABBREVIATIONS

AA. SS. Ben.	Acta Sanctorum Ordinis S. Benedicti	Mabillon
AA. SS. Boll.	Acta Sanctorum . . . quae collegit etc. Joannes Bollandus	
Abbr. Chr.	Abbreviationes Chronicorum of Ralph of Diceto	Stubbs
ALSP	Anglo-Latin Satirical Poets and Epigrammatists of the Twelfth Century	Wright
AN	Anno	
An. As.	Annales Asserii in Asser's Life of King Alfred	Stevenson
An. Ord. Ben.	Annale Ordinis S. Benedicti	Mabillon
Anal. Hymn.	Analecta Hymnica vol. 51	Blume
Anc. Laws and Inst.	Ancient Laws and Institutes of England	Thorpe
Ann. Wint.	Annales De Wintonia	**Luard**
Archiv.	Archiv für das Studium der neueren Sprachen und Literaturen	
A.-S. Chr.	Anglo-Saxon Chronicle	Plummer
BAGRH II	Gesta Regis Henrici Secundi Benedicti Abbatis	Stubbs
Bib. d. ags. P.	Bibliothek der angelsächsischen Poesie	Grein-Wülker
Bib. d. ags. Pr.	Bibliothek der angelsächsischen Prosa	Grein-Wülker
BRG	Bibliotheca Rerum Germanicarum	Jaffé
Cax. S.	Caxton Society	
CHEL	Cambridge History of English Literature	Ward and Waller
Chr. Mon. de Ab.	Chronicon Monasterii de Abingdon	Stevenson
Chr. Rog. Hov.	Chronica Rogeri de Hovedon	Stubbs
Chr. W. H.	Chronicon Domini Walteri de Hemingburgh	Hamilton
CM	Matthaei Parisiensis . . . Chronica Majora	Luard
CMH	Cambridge Medieval History	Gwatkin
CS	Camden Society	
CSEL	Corpus Scriptorum Ecclesiasticorum Latinorum	
DCB	Dictionary of Christian Biography	Smith and Wace
De Laud. Virg.	De Laudibus Virginitatis of Aldhelm	Giles
Dial. Mir.	Caesarii Heisterbacensis . . . Dialogus Miraculorum	Strange
DNB	Dictionary of National Biography	Stephen-Lee

EETS	Early English Text Society, original series (es = extra series)	
E S-E Leg.	Early South-English Legendary	Horstmann
Ex. B.	St. Guthlac in the Exeter Book	
FC	Vita S. Guthlac, AA. SS. Boll. April 2	
Fl. Hist.	Flores Historiarum	Luard
Fl. Wig. Chr. C.	Florentii Wigorniensis . . . Chronicon ex Chronicis	Thorpe
Gai. Lest. E.	Gaimar's Lestorie des Engles	Hardy
Ger. Cant. G. R.	Gesta Regum of Gervase of Canterbury	Stubbs
G. P.	Gesta Pontificum of Wm. of Malmesbury	Hamilton
G. R.	Gesta Regum of Wm. of Malmesbury	Stubbs
HCYA	Historians of the Church of York and its Archbishops	Raine
H. E.	Historia Ecclesiastica of Ven. Bede	Plummer
HHH	Historia Anglorum of Henry of Huntingdon	Arnold
HP	Polychronicon of Ralph Higden	Babington
Joc. B. Chr.	Chronica Jocelini de Brakelonda,	Rokewode
L. E.	Liber Eliensis	Stewart
MGH	Monumenta Germaniae Historica, Poetae Latini Aevi Caroli I	Duemmler
MLN	Modern Language Notes	
MLR	Modern Language Review	
MME	Manual of Middle English	Wells
Mon. Franc.	Monumenta Franciscana	Brewer, Howlett
MP	Modern Philology	
NLA	Capgrave's Nova Legenda Anglie	Horstmann
O-E Mart.	Old-English Martyrology	Herzfeld
PL	Patrologia Latina	Migne
PL Chr.	Peter Langtoft's Chronicle	Hearne
PMLA	Publications of the Modern Language Association of America	
PS	Percy Society	
RC	Roxburghe Club	
Rel. Ant.	Reliquae Antiquae	Wright-Halliwell
RG Chr.	Robert of Gloucester's Chronicle	Hearne
RHSP	Royal Historical Society Publications	
Rom.	Romania	
Rom. Rev.	Romanic Review	
RS	Rolls Series	
SD Hist. R.	Symeonis . . . Historia Regum	Arnold
SWC	The Life of Saint Werburge of Chester	Horstmann

Vita S. E. G.	Vita S. Edithae, Gotselino, AA. SS. Ben. 7	
Vita S. W. G.	Goscelin's Life of Saint Werburge in Saint Werburge of Chester, xix-xxvi	Horstmann
Wiener SB	Sitzungsberichte der kgl. Akad. d. Wissensch., Phil-Hist. Kl.	
Zs. f. d. A.	Zeitschrift für deutsches Altertum	
Zs. f. fr. Spr. u. L.	Zeitschrift für französische Sprache und Literatur	

THE TRADITION OF THE NUN IN MEDIEVAL ENGLAND

CHAPTER I

THE PERIOD: SEVENTH TO THE SIXTEENTH CENTURY. A SURVEY [1]

I

The literature of the centuries considered in this study is written in Latin and Anglo-Saxon before the Norman Conquest and in Latin, Anglo-Saxon, Anglo-Norman, and Middle English after that event. Several manuals are available [2] for the reader not a specialist in one or another of these centuries, and while one manual has given way to another as the most authoritative survey of its subject, all of them enjoy a certain vogue here and there, regardless of their relative antiquity. One view in particular is maintained with more or less elaboration by all but one of these manuals, which has a vital bearing upon this study. It leaves an impress— and as I believe—an unwarranted impress upon the minds of students of English literature. I refer to the question of the degree of Christianization to be conceded to the Anglo-Saxon portion of

---

[1] The Christian character of the pre-Conquest centuries is a subject that deserves several monographs. Any survey of it at the present level of scholarship must, therefore, be somewhat superficial. The paragraphs which follow represent a digest of scholarly literature and my own independent reading of all the sources. While my main contentions will probably stand, some of the details must necessarily be merely provisional. They are presented for what they may be worth in lieu of more exact knowledge.

[2] I cite only the more important manuals: Taine, *Histoire de la littérature anglaise*, 4 vols., Paris, 1863-1864; Ten Brink, *Geschichte der englischen Literatur*, 2nd ed., 2 vols., Strassburg, 1899-1912; Jusserand, *Histoire littéraire du peuple anglais*, 2 vols., Paris, 1896-1904; *Schröer*, *Grundzüge und Haupttypen der englischen Literaturgeschichte*, 2 vols., 3rd ed., Berlin, 1927; CHEL, 14 vols., 1907 ff.; Brandl, *Geschichte der altenglischen Literatur*, Strassburg, 1908; Legouis-Cazamian, *Histoire de la littérature anglaise*, Paris, 1924.

1

the pre-Conquest Literature of these centuries. No doubt is expressed about the Anglo-Latin contemporary nor—if Taine be excepted—about the post-Conquest Literature in whatever medium preserved. All of it—to all the critics except Taine—is admittedly informed with Christianity, is Christian in spirit as well as in appearance. But all but one of the manuals which consider the question—despite a progressive approach to what to me seems objectivity—imply where they do not state, or state the contrary so confusedly as to mislead, that the pre-Conquest Anglo-Saxon literature was at best Christian in appearance only, having been thus Christianized by Latin clerics. After examining all Anglo-Saxon literature myself, I have come to the conclusion that such statements are really understatements, that even the Anglo-Saxon part of the pre-Conquest literature of England was Christian in spirit as well as in appearance. Since the pre-Conquest literature in Anglo-Saxon was such a formative force in the development of the literary traditions of England and since my study must, therefore, include the nun whom that literature depicts, the question of its Christian quality has a certain import for the chapters which follow. I therefore consider the question at some length here, though Legouis-Cazamian [3] touches upon it in a way that my study of the sources convinces me is just, so far as it goes. It is scarcely necessary to add that without the considerations which follow, the body of my dissertation stands, and that I am not, of course, interested here in proving the fact of the Christian character of Anglo-Saxon literature so much as suggesting what I believe to be the fact, gathering for the purpose random discoveries of others that seem to bear upon the point plus the testimony of my own independent reading of the remains—all this as a propaedeutic for the reader for the details of the chapters which follow.

I am also interested in this chapter in pointing out specifically and in some detail something which at most can only be inferred even from a work like Legouis-Cazamian, namely, the rôle of the Latin patristic in English literature from the sixth to the sixteenth centuries, and particularly its rôle in the pre-Conquest period. For the purpose of this dissertation the fact needs to be indicated

---

[3] Cf. *op. cit.*, 6-10, 15-16, 28-34.

here rather than to be treated exhaustively. In the following chapters it will be considered in the detail in each instance appropriate.

These two purposes call for a survey, at least in outline, of materials familiar for the most part. Because of the emphasis apportioned to these materials, however, the survey may not be so familiar.

II

I begin with some paragraphs in the history of scholarship. The standard manuals of English literature, if the *Cambridge History* be excluded, have been written by French and German scholars. A comparison of their statements upon the Christian quality of the pre-Conquest Anglo-Saxon literature is most enlightening. Thus Taine in 1863, noting the scarcity of *poésie laïque en Angleterre,* refers to

le reste du courant païen, germain et barbare . . . arrêté ou recouvert, d'abord par l'entrée de la religion chrétienne, ensuite par la conquête des Français de Normandie,[4]

but remaining essentially unchanged;[5] to the Christian hymns as

les chants des anciens serviteurs d'Odin, tonsurés à présent et enveloppés dans une robe de moine; . . . les hymnes chrétiennes continuent les hymnes païennes;[6]

to the pre-Conquest Anglo-Latin of Aldhelm, Venerable Bede, and their followers as an

humble plante qui d'elle-même eût avorté,[7]

the authors of which

sentent eux-mêmes leur impuissance et leur décrépitude;[8]

and to the race in general as

---

[4] Taine, 1, 43.

[5] "Mais ce qui a subsisté suffit et au delà pour montrer l'étrange et puissant génie poétique qui est dans la race, et pour faire voir d'avance la fleur dans le bourgeon."—*Ibid.* Cf. also *ibid.*, 55 and 74-76.

[6] *Ibid.*, 53.

[7] *Ibid.*, 63.   [8] *Ibid.*, note 1.

intacte dans sa grossièreté primitive. La culture (Taine continues) qui lui est venue de Rome, n'a pu ni la développer, ni la déformer. Si le christianisme y est entré, c'est par des affinités naturelles et sans altérer le génie natif.[9]

Even after the Conquest

la race demeure saxonne.[10]

And then in 1877 Ten Brink,[11] writing of the first *volkstümliche Gesänge* in England, avers that

Auch der Schreiber mischte sich selbstdichtend ein . . . da er ja gewöhnlich ein Geistlicher war, um seine christliche Gelehrsamkeit zu zeigen.[12]

But while admitting that the Christian scribe, deleting direct pagan references and altering certain heathen expressions, tampered with the Anglo-Saxon originals, Ten Brink holds that

Die Haltung des Ganzen aber erfuhr dadurch keine Änderung,

and, contradicting Taine, continues

den epischen Helden wurde kein christliches Gewand übergeworfen.[13]

Why there was no need to throw a Christian vestment over the pagan hero of epic song, Ten Brink discloses in the conclusion of his estimate of the pristine Germanic character:

Die tiefe und Nachhaltigkeit der Empfindungen (characteristic of the Teutonic peoples) erscheint hier (in the early English) begleitet von einer gewissen Weichheit des Gemüts, einer Neigung zur Gefühlsschwärmerei, welche der rücksichtslosen Wirklichkeit gegenüber leicht den Charakter der Melancholie annimmt.   Merkwürdig kontrastiert diese Seite ihres Wesens mit dem unbändigen Mannestrotz, der die Gefahr verachtet und dem Tod entgegenlacht; doch entspringt beides schliesslich derselben Wurzel, dem Übergewicht, das die Mächte des Gemüts im innern Leben des Germanen behaupten . . . Kaum zweifelhaft aber scheint es, dass der Keim zu dieser Eigenschaft schon vor der Bekehrung zum Christentum und vor der Niederlassung in Brittannien bei ihm vorhanden war, wenn auch erst das Christentum ihn zur vollen Entfaltung führte.[14]

---

[9] *Op. cit.*, 74.

[10] *Ibid.*, 76.

[11] In his first edition. I quote from the second edition.

[12] *Ibid.*, I; 33.

[13] *Ibid.*, 32.

[14] *Op. cit.*, 9. Ten Brink writes further: " Eine tiefe, ernstsinnige Auf-

In stating the influence of Anglo-Latin Ten Brink again comes into conflict with Taine. Rather than considering Christian Anglo-Latin ineffectual, Ten Brink thinks that

Für dieses ganze Gebiet [15] poetischer Darstellung diente den englischen Dichtern sowohl als Stoffquelle wie als Muster der Behandlung die christlich lateinische Poesie oder die theologische Prosa.[16]

In 1896 Jusserand declares that the Anglo-Saxons were at first but superficially converted; [17] that although a century of Christianity almost achieved their conquest, [18] their literature was but partially changed. Recapitulating the pre-Conquest period, Jusserand writes;

Ainsi va la littérature anglo-saxonne, malgré les efforts de Cynewulf, d'Alfred, de Dunstan et d'Aelfric, se répétant. Poèmes, récits et sermons sont, par places, touchants et grandioses, mais ils sont, pris dans leur ensemble, monotones. Les mêmes notes, peu nombreuses, sont incessamment répétées. Les Angles, les Saxons et les autres conquérants venus de Germanie sont demeurés littérairement intacts au milieu des populations vaincues. Leur littérature est comme immobile. . . . Il manque à cette littérature une greffe; Rome a essayé de la lui donner, mais quelques rameaux seulement et non pas l'arbre ont été vivifiés; le fruit revient le même, chaque année, sauvage, parfois chétif.[19]

Ten years later, in 1906, Schröer,[20] discussing Anglo-Saxon literature, affirms its Christian character. He observes that, since the art of writing was then the exclusive prerogative of the learned,

der Mönche in den christlichen Klöstern, . . . es ist begreiflich, dass diese vor allem für die Zwecke des geistlichen Unterrichts tätig waren.[21]

---

fassung dessen, was den Menschen gross, wenn auch nicht glücklich macht, was seine Pflicht erfordert, zeugt von dem frommen Sinne des englischen Heidentums, das durch die christlichte Lehre allerdings erweicht, jedoch in seinem innersten Wesen nicht umgestaltet erscheint ". *Ibid.*, 34.

[15] Geistliche Epik, geistliche Lyrik, Hymnen, Gebete, moralische Erörterungen, poetische Predigten, Sagen.

[16] *Op. cit.*, 58.

[17] Cf. *op. cit.*, I, 62-63.

[18] Cf. *ibid.*, 64.

[19] *Ibid.*, 94.

[20] I quote from the third edition of 1927.

[21] *Ibid.*, 28.

He recognizes traces of an unwritten heathen literature in the
extant Anglo-Saxon. He writes:

Allerdings sind es geistliche Verse, und diesem Umstande ist es ja auch
zuzuschreiben, dass sie der Aufzeichnung würdig befunden wurden; aber
wenn wir näher zusehen, erkennen wir, dass diese geistliche Dichtung auf
den Schultern einer älteren, weltlichen Volksdichtung steht.[22]

The Cambridge History of English Literature is conservative. Of
this question it states:

The poetry of the Old English period is generally grouped into national
and Christian. To the former were assigned those poems of which the
subjects are drawn from English or rather Teutonic traditions and history,
or from the customs and conditions of English life; to the latter those
which deal with Biblical matter, ecclesiastical traditions and religious
subjects of definitely Christian origin. The line of demarcation is not, of
course, absolutely fixed. Most of the national poems in their present form
contain Christian elements.[23]

Brandl, in 1908, looks upon the Anglo-Saxon period with something akin to esteem. He writes with comparative respect of the
cultural life and literary productivity [24] of the Anglo-Saxons before
the Conquest. Following the customary division of the literature
into Christian and Pagan, he writes:

Aber rein heidnische Denkmäler sind, abgesehen von wenigen Fragmenten,
nicht erhalten. . . . Die Geistlichen brachten ja die eigentliche Schreib-
kunst erst ins Land . . . sie behielten das Schreibmonopol bis herab zu
König Alfred (871-900) und auch nach dieser Ausnahmspersönlichkeit
wieder durch Jahrhunderte, bis endlich mit Chaucer ein Typus gelehrter
Laien einsetzte. . . . Das ags. Christentum war schon in der Geburts-
stunde nationaler geartet, und die englische Literatur hatte davon
dauerndsten Vorteil. Daraus ergiebt sich von vornherein, dass, wenn man
die ags. Denkmäler vor Alfred in heidnische und christliche einteilt, dies
nur als eine verhältnismässige Scheidung zu verstehen ist: dort Dichtungen
mit verwiegend weltlicher Art, aus heidnischer Sitte oder Tradition
entsprungen—hier solche von vorwiegend christlicher Absicht oder Schule.
Ferner: dass die "heidnischen" Denkmäler nicht schlankweg als ältere
vor die christlichen Texte zu setzen sind; jene sind vielmehr in der
Fassung, in der wir sie besitzen, oft gleichaltrig oder jünger als diese und
in den Handschriften nicht selten sogar mit erbaulicher Literatur des
10.-11. Jahrhs. zuzammengeworfen. Nur die Grundlagen jener Erzeugnisse

---

[22] *Ibid.*, 32.   [23] *Op. cit.*, 1; 21.   [24] Cf. *op. cit.*, 1133.

sind älter, ihre Stoffe und Formen deuten auf kontinentale Herkunft, ihre Richtung muss daher als die frühere vorangestellt werden.[25]

Legouis-Cazamian, finally, in 1924, asserts that:

La littérature anglo-saxonne qui nous est parvenue est . . . essentielle-ment chrétienne. . . . (Elle) n'est pas l'expression directe de l'époque païenne. . . . Les rédacteurs n'y ont laissé subsister que ce qui ne leur paraissait pas en opposition formelle avec leur religion. . . . Les plus anciennes lois rédigées témoignent d'une civilisation déjà considérable où l'esprit chrétien a pénétré. . . . Rien n'est donc plus illusoire que de prendre ce que nous avons de littérature anglo-saxonne pour une produc-tion primitive et d'y chercher le reflet direct de la barbarie germanique.[26]

It refers to

la conversion en masse, profonde et fervente, au christianisme . . . qui met les clercs en communion avec la latinité,[27]

and then, corroborating two views expressed in the survey introduc-tory to the body of this dissertation, Legouis-Cazamian adds:

. . . ce que nous appelons littérature anglo-saxonne a subi l'inévitable influence du latin et n'a guère pu subir que celle-là. C'est une littérature où il est rare de trouver et dangereux de chercher l'expression directe et réaliste du génie national pur, tel qu'il était avant d'être modifié par le christianisme.[28]

One fact immediately apparent from a consideration of the pre-ceding statements is that scholarship has come but slowly and con-fusedly to the recognition of the essentially Christian character of the pre-Conquest literature of England written in Anglo-Saxon. It is anticipated in Brandl amid distinctions that bewilder; it is implied in the *Cambridge History;* it is stated forthrightly only in Legouis-Cazamian. While scholarship may be said to recognize this Christian quality today in the work of Legouis-Cazamian, the latter has only partially supplanted the older manuals. The motives of their authors are worth considering, then, because of the influ-ence they have had and still have here and there. All the motives that inform their statements we probably can never recover. But we can see that numerous loyalties are at work in the background, dulling the fine edge of objectivity. A philosophical preconception

[25] *Op. cit.*, 944-945.
[26] *Op. cit.*, 6-7.
[27] *Ibid.*, 8.
[28] *Op. cit.*, 14.

on the general processes of history controls the conclusions of one author; the belief once stoutly held that the northern and non-Christian peoples did not need the civilizing force of the Catholic and Latin South still lurks in the thinking of others; and only one of this earlier group—Taine—seems to have escaped completely the compelling urge of chauvinism. With Taine it is a duty to uphold through thick and thin his favorite thesis that the *donnée,* as he loves to call it, the dominating characteristic of a race, survives and ultimately prevails despite all vicissitudes. For the English race two of these vicissitudes were such Christianization as England received in Anglo-Saxon times and the later, more thorough, Christianization brought in by the Norman Conquest. Each of these events overwhelmed for a time the native *donnée* of the race, but it was finally in the ascendant again in the high-tide of literary excellence that set in with the days of Elizabeth. The excellence which is English literature, therefore, owes nothing of its essential characteristics and none of its essential greatness to Christianity. Ten Brink, Jusserand, and Schröer agree with Taine upon the essentially non-Christian character of the pre-Conquest literature of England written in Anglo-Saxon, but neither do they nor, as it seems to me, does Brandl exhibit Taine's racial detachment on the significance of the Norman Conquest. Jusserand sees in that event the force that civilized the Teutonic barbarian across the Channel, that made him a Christian and a gentleman. To all three of the German authors the Conquest was an accident that merely accelerated, or as Brandl thinks, retarded something already in process; the march of distinctly German qualities to an inevitably high state of cultural development without benefit of clergy, because the qualities recognized as essentially Christian were essentially German also.

The point of interest here is that the several authors have denied, or until Legouis-Cazamian, have not stated clearly, the fact of the essentially Christian character of pre-Conquest Anglo-Saxon. It is quite evident to me—fresh from a study of all sources upon which their statements are supposed to be based—that the motives so obvious from a study of these statements vitiate the authority which they may on many points deserve, particularly on the point which is of primary interest here. In the pages which follow, the Christian quality of Anglo-Saxon literature will be indicated within the limits of my study. Just now I wish to assemble a few facts that bear upon the question by way of introduction.

III

Extant monuments of Anglo-Saxon literature do not ante-date the Benedictine Christianization of Britain (596); neither are there contemporary literary products of the sections of Britain which repelled Christianity longest nor of relapsed kingdoms during the time of their apostasy. What we have has been written by Christians. It is the product of a dual literary tradition; the oral Anglo-Saxon tradition of alliterative form and the academic standard of Latin patristic. The Latin patristic, moreover, where it did not supplant the Anglo-Saxon with replicas of itself, impressed upon it its thought and very often its expression. The literature of this period is decidedly monastic. This is but natural, since Anglo-Saxon learning and letters are monastic productions. The instrument of the Gospel in Southern England had, through the initial force of Saint Gregory's apostolic measures, been Benedictine.[29] A mission inaugurated, as the Anglo-Saxon Chronicle puts it, by a great many monks[30] could be expected to bear the stamp of monasticism. And so it did bear it despite vicissitudes that would have quickly obliterated it, had it not been for the presence in England of what seems to have been a perennial power of monastic renewal. The first episcopal residences of the Roman missioners were, in fact, monasteries.[31] There were also contemporary monasteries for nuns. The religious life appealed strongly to Anglo-Saxon women, offering them, from the historical point of view, a magnificent career in an institution which was to organize and refine early English life.[32]

These monasteries developed rapidly into schools whence educa-

[29] Cf. Sandys, 464 ff.; CMH, 1, 541; Manitius (4) I, 12. Cf. *ibid.*, 11-12, for the debt to the Irish monks.

[30] " mid wel manegum munucum."—A. S. Chr., An. 596, 21.

[31] Cf. H. E., 1; xxvi, 46-47.

[32] Cf. CMH, 1; 542.

tion and literature as well as religion and monasticism emanated.
Anglo-Saxon education was, accordingly, largely [33] a product of
the Roman Benedictine missioners and their successors, although
the Celtic monks of the North assisted during the seventh century
and even later, if a student sought them out in their Irish monasteries.   Monastic learning received a vigorous impetus [34] by the
arrival in 669 at Canterbury of the scholars Theodore of Tarsus
and Adrian of Africa, both monks [35] and both well versed in Greek
and Latin and masters of every science then known.[36]   But the
Danes in the eighth century, having begun their work of depredation in the north at Lindisfarne (793), swept southwards (843)
venting particular fury upon monasteries.   They thus obliterated
much of the fruit of three centuries of monastic cultivation.[37]
Alfred the Great struggled to stem the tide of native illiteracy
consequent upon the Danish occupation.   The result was the Dane-
law, the court school, and the erection and endowment of new
monasteries [38] and through them a general reinvigoration of English intellectual life.   Continued invasion, nevertheless, kept the
country in almost constant turmoil.[39]   With time, however, the
resultant Danish element in the population became Christian and
the tenth and eleventh centuries found Danes as well as natives participating actively in the great Benedictine ecclesiastical and
monastic reform.[40]   The reform was made imperative by the
demoralization attendant upon the horror and desecration with
which their ancestors had waged two centuries of war.[41]   Religious
and social conditions were perhaps equally corrupt.   So active and
widely influential,[42] however, were some ecclesiastics—for the most
part foreign bishops instituted and conducted the reform—that,

[33] Cf. Manitius (4) 1; 9-12.
[34] Cf. H. E. IV, ii, 204.
[35] Cf. *ibid.*, i, 202.
[36] Cf. Manitius (4) 1; 12.
[37] Cf. CMH, 3, 351.
[38] Cf. Fl. Wig. Chr. C. I, 104.
[39] Cf. CMH, 3; 358.
[40] Cf. Bateson (3), 160.
[41] Cf. Thorpe (1), 2, 14, 206, 272; CMH, 3, 372.
[42] Cf. CMH, 3, 363-369.

decadent as it was, the period from the tenth and the eleventh century to the Conquest, might, nonetheless, appropriately be designated the " age of bishops". Like the guiding spirits of the seventh-century florescence of religion, social progress, and general culture, these dominant churchmen were monks. Fresh incursions of Danes, Danish supremacy even, and the return of English rule had made no lasting change in the episcopal-monastic influence except that, as a presage of the Conquest and its shift of prestige, Edward chose as his advisers and as the incumbent of the important see of London not natives but Normans.[43] The literature to which this monastic education and general influence gave rise—and monasticism [44] remained the dominating impulse during the entire epoch—bears the impress of its origin and inspiration; it is inescapably Christian. It is well to point out this impress in the leading authors of the period.

The extant literature of Anglo-Saxon England is on the whole the work of clerics from the seventh to the eleventh century.[45] It began when the Roman missioners, arriving at Kent, brought secular and sacred Latin learning within the reach of the Anglo-Saxons. The next century saw both Latin [46] and Anglo-Saxon literature flourishing in England; the latter, as we know from the familiar story of Caedmon's genius, being cultivated before 680 by the first abbess of Streaneshalch.[47] At the various monasteries there were men inclined to record first in Latin but later in the vernacular both great events and everyday affairs.[48] Monastic recorders of this type have thus provided the bare but never barren chronicles and memorial *vitae,* material in which historical facts and historical figures of these early centuries can be found. The point of interest here is that many of these chronicles came from monastic, and all from Christian, hands.[49]

The first considerable literary figure among English writers of Latin and Anglo-Saxon and the first of whom notably literary

[43] Cf. *ibid.*, 390 and 392-393.
[44] Cf. *ibid.*, 6, 559, and Rashdall, 1, 26.
[45] Cf. Legouis-Cazamian, 6.
[46] Cf. CHEL. 1, 79.
[47] Cf. H. E. IV, xxii, 258-261.
[48] Cf. CMH, 2; 548.
[49] But cf. CHEL. 1; 177.

efforts remain [50] was Aldhelm (d. 709), the pupil of Theodore and of Adrian.[51] He wrote among other works the first extant treatise for nuns, *De Laudibus Virginitatis*,[52] addressed to Hildelid, the abbess of Barking. In it he mentions works of Athanasius, of Evagrius, of Hilarion, of Jerome, of Eusebius, of Gregory, of Cassian, of Rufinus, of Ambrose, of Basil, of Cyprian, and of Augustine.[53] But Aldhelm at the outset of a swift tradition of patristic learning did not cite everyone from whom he borrowed wholesale. *De Laudibus Virginitatis* as well as its companion piece, *De Laudibus Virginum*,[54] a verse treatment of the same subject, is remarkable for ornament, literary allusions, and exhaustive scope. Critics, accordingly, have been interested mainly in the source of Aldhelm's grotesque style. A study of content, however, reveals that some of his most colorful passages are patristic. That which he borrowed, moreover, would imply that at least something of his want of simplicity originates in his embellishment of striking periods and phrases from the Fathers.

A greater scholar than Aldhelm, undoubtedly the greatest scholar of the period, was Venerable Bede (672-735), a monk of Wearmouth and Jarrow, who produced varied and voluminous works in Latin, notably the *Historia Ecclesiastica Gentis Anglorum*.[55]

Among the Anglo-Saxon latinists who were formed in the monastic schools inaugurated by Aldhelm was Saint Boniface (d. 755). To the same group belonged Lul (d. 786), the companion and successor of Saint Boniface as Bishop, or Archbishop, of Mainz. His Latin letters to Anglo-Saxon nuns, like those of Saint Boniface, are typical of the traditional religious didactic tone and patristic phraseology in which Aldhelmian and subsequent monastic writing is couched. Although the correspondence [56] mirrors the activity of the day, discusses, and often promptly decides, questions of conduct,

[50] Cf. DCB, 1; 78. Manitius (4) 1; 134-135.

[51] Aldhelm received his earlier training under Irish teachers at Malmsbury. Cf. Kenney, 226-227.

[52] Ed. Giles, 1-82. Cf. Manitius (4) 1; 138.

[53] Cf. *op. cit., passim.* Cf. also Manitius (4) 1; 12 and 138.

[54] Cf. Giles, 135-202.

[55] Plummer. Cf. Manitius (4) 1; 134.

[56] Jaffé. Cf. Manitius (4) 1; 151-152.

of social conditions, and of ecclesiastical law, it is, nothwithstand-
ing, almost exclusively conventional in expression.

The name and fame of Alcuin of York (740-804), the representative of another great monastic school, are associated principally
with the court of Charlemagne, but Alcuin had passed his fiftieth
year[57] before accepting that monarch's invitation to residence
abroad. Before going to the continent he had attracted numerous
students thence to York.[58] He is, therefore, a representative, and a
brilliant one, of the culture and mentality of the Angles.[59] His
works—all in Latin—include, like those of Venerable Bede, hymns,
narrative verse, scientific treatises, a variety of *carmina*,[60] and letters.[61] His letters particularly are almost without exception of
social and historical value.[62] Besides laying bare Alcuin's markedly
monastic trend of mind, they and his other compositions show how
inseparably religion, monasticism, and learning largely ecclesiastical
were welded together to constitute the culture of the day.[63]

It must be borne in mind, however, that Anglo-Latin, as the
vehicle of instruction in the monastic schools, was primarily conventional. Knowledge of religion and improvement of morals
were the educational objectives.[64] Science was studied,[65] but even
that to a religious end; the exact sciences afforded religious
analogies; the natural, to a great extent, cast pious, etiological
light on history. Theology was the queen of studies. It was recommended to the attention not only of ecclesiastics but also of laymen
and women.[66] It was the end to which other studies were the

[57] Cf. Manitius (4) 1; 273.

[58] Cf. *Vita S. Luidgari*, AA. SS. Ben. Saec. IV, I, 37.

[59] Cf. Manitius (4) 1; 288.

[60] Cf. PL 100-101. Cf. Manitius (4) 1; 273-288.

[61] Ed. Wattenbach-Duemmler, BRG 6.

[62] Cf. Manitius (4) 1; 287.

[63] At this period " Christian poets were read with the same care which
was devoted to Vergil ".—Raby, 156. Alcuin, himself, detailing in his
Poema de Pontificibus et Sanctis Ecclesiae Eboracensis (BRG 6; 127-128)
the works in the library of York, throws light on the learning and the elements of which it was composed. Cf. also Courthope I; 30, Brown, W. C.,
44-45, and Willmann 1; 244-246.

[64] Cf. Willmann 1; 216-217.

[65] Cf. Manitius (4), 14-18.   [66] Cf. Willmann 1; 216-217.

4

means. A literature reflecting these facts can hardly be anything but representative. Anglo-Latin and even Anglo-Saxon literature, directed to an unvarying end and derived from Holy Scripture and the writings of the Fathers, became patterned and stereotyped. Hence, Aldhelm, Venerable Bede, Saint Boniface, and Alcuin, in laying the foundations of English culture, expressed themselves in sentiments that appear wholly impersonal and that, according to the letter, are monotonously alike. But it is the spirit which gives them life, of which more later.

Alcuin, however,—to resume—had hardly organized the court school upon the continent when the depredation of the Danes and Northmen on his native land began to demolish the long and painfully acquired learning of England. Nor was it easily restored. Owing to the scarcity of books and the general illiteracy [67]—the libraries of Lindisfarne, of Wearmouth, of Jarrow, of Canterbury, and of York had not escaped the vandalism of the Danes—Alfred sought means to provide instructive literature in the vernacular. The age, accordingly, became an age of translations, of translations of prose preëminently, a department of the vernacular not extensively represented heretofore, particularly in spiritual subjects.[68] The prose translated by Alfred and by the cosmopolitan group of ecclesiastics [69] gathered at his court consisted of the *Liber Dialogorum* [70] and the *Pastoralis Curae* [71] of Gregory the Great, the *De Consolatione Philosophiae* [72] of Boethius, the *Historiarum libri vvii* [73] of Orosius, and the *Historia Ecclesiastica Gentis Anglorum* [74] and *Martyrology* of Venerable Bede. The inception of the *Anglo-Saxon Chronicle* [75] also belongs to this period.

[67] Cf. Sweet, pref. to *King Alfred's . . . Pastoral Care.*

[68] Vernacular poetry to this date, on the contrary, both that referring to pre-Christian conditions and the larger *corpus* in which the Caedmonian and Cynewulfian compositions loom largest and most representative, was decidedly spiritual. *Beowulf*, as written, moreover, was affected by Christianity. Cf. Chambers, R. W., 54, 72, 112-113, 121-128; Lawrence, 271, 282-284; Chadwick, CHEL I; 29-30; Blackburn, PMLA 12, 204 ff.

[69] Presbiter John of Old Saxony from Corbie; the provost Grimbold; Asser from Wales; the Anglo-Saxon priests, Werewulf and Ethelstan; and Bishops Plegmund of Canterbury and Werfrith of Worcester.

[70] Zupitza.   [72] Sedgefield.   [74] Schipper.

[71] Sweet.   [73] Sweet.   [75] Plummer.

The greatest prose writer in the vernacular before the Conquest, however, was Abbot Aelfric (955-1025), whose eloquent pen was drawn forth to correct disorders and abuses of the late tenth and eleventh centuries, the age of "gloom, iron, and lead". No one had continued Alfred's effort to produce instructive books in the vernacular. Aelfric, consequently, found much theological and moral expounding incumbent upon him. He directed his energies, therefore, to the composition of homilies,[76] didactic letters,[77] and Biblical paraphrases [78]—in a word, to literary coöperation in the contemporary Benedictine Reform.[79] Fired with flaming zeal, he approached the people even more closely than Alfred had done. Intent solely upon one thing, moral reform, he effected two reforms in the domain of style. For the sake of the appeal it would make, he embodied his thought in the alliterative rhythm so dear to the native heart.[80] He thus was the first to compose the vernacular poetic homily and the verse epistle. So forcibly did he write, moreover, that he cast off the *genus dicendi Asiaticum* [81] that had since Aldhelm encrusted even vernacular prose. Yet Aelfric adhered faithfully to tradition; his writings are based firmly on Scripture and the Fathers.[82] So true is he, in fact, to tradition that he might as well be writing in Latin and with the quill of Gregory the Great.

Monasticism revived and learning once more flourished. In the monastery Latin was again studied assiduously. In the monastery and outside it ecclesiastics and the higher social classes were as familiar with the Latin language and Norman court circles now as after the Conquest.[83] For the learned, therefore, the Conquest did not constitute a radical upheaval.

Throughout the five centuries of Anglo-Saxon England the authors and revisers of Anglo-Saxon and the composers of Anglo-

---

[76] Thorpe; Assmann; Skeat.

[77] Assmann, *op. cit.*

[78] *Ibid.*

[79] Cf. Brandl, 1089.

[80] Cf. Dietrich, 2; 186 and 195.

[81] Cf. *ibid.*, 251.

[82] Cf. *op. cit.*, 249. Cf. the source studies by Förster, (1), (2), and Ott.

[83] Cf. CMH, 3; 390-391 and 399; CHEL, 1; 165 and 167.

Latin, being almost exclusively monks and ecclesiastics—Alfred is
the only notable exception—were intent upon a religious purpose.
So imbued were they with the seriousness of their life and work
and so measured was their life to the rule and spirit of the Church,
that, like Shakespeare on the lips of a modern, Scripture or the
Fathers on their quill was not an alien speech but an intimate
expression of what each of them daily thought but none could say
so well. They had shaped their lives to this model; the form, consequently, fit. In one sense their writing shone with a borrowed
light; in another and truer sense the light was their own. It is
necessary, therefore, to distinguish between the trite, conventional
form and the vital content; the former, an expository concatenation
of biblical and patristic citations that seem to say nothing pertinent
and to convey no contemporary message; the latter, material vigor-
ously apposite, abounding in life, meeting the people on the level at
which they lived. The literary level of the age was, as we have seen,
monastic; life and therefore its cultural expression were viewed *sub
specie aeternitatis*. Thought was not shackled, consequently, by the
form; it was rather conveyed thereby in a telegraphic code of
infinite meaning. Failing to note the active spirit informing the
borrowed and seemingly dead letter of the literature of pre-Conquest England, the reader—or even the scholar like Taine, as we
noted above—permits the significance of the entire corpus of Anglo-
Latin and Anglo-Saxon to escape him.

Most of Anglo-Latin and much of Anglo-Saxon, as has been said
of apostolic literature,[84] was not consciously literature. Not indifferent, however, to language, as the Apostolic Fathers were,[85] the
patres ecclesiae anglicanae and their Anglo-Saxon successors
adhered to the consecrated forms and sacred phrases sanctioned by
authoritative use. But like the Apostolic Fathers, the didactic
writers both in Anglo-Latin and in Anglo-Saxon—Aldhelm, perhaps, excluded—were utterly unconscious of contributing to a
literature which would endure. They adopted Christian tradition
and neither "basic Teutonic paganism" nor any extraneous influence disturbed or distorted the Christian character of the pre-
Conquest literature of England. It spoke the conscious mind of

[84] Cf. Campbell, J. M., 15.   [85] Cf. *ibid.*

medieval England and declared it wholly Christian. Indigenous literature written in the vernacular as well as that in Anglo-Latin which would not come under this classification does not exist.

What such a representative body of literature states of the nun must, perforce, have nourished the roots of the forthcoming tradition.

IV

After the Conquest also continental ecclesiastics dominated church and state. Latin became even more generally the literary language. Chronicles grew apace, a species of pseudo-historical composition into which materials of Arthurian romance found their way. The romance developed into the extensive Arthurian Legend which had been given permanent though elastic outlines in the literature of England by Geoffrey of Monmouth (c. 1100-1154). At the same time, religious and didactic treatises, Latin, Anglo-Norman and vernacular *summae, specula,* and *vitae* multiplied, reflecting the intellectual and religious life of the continent, to which England was now more closely linked than ever before.

The post-Conquest centuries saw also the beginnings of political, social, and religious satire. A period of popular gestation and class consciousness such as was the twelfth century formed the proper matrix of satire.[86] Walter Map (d. c. 1210) was among the first to voice this spirit [87] in Anglo-Latin, but there were also Nigellus Wireker (fl. 1190), the Goliards,[88] and the deft and daring writers of fabliaux in Norman-French. Satire ran the gamut in Latin, Anglo-Norman, and Middle English from the twelfth century facetious and irreverent ridicule and parody of things sacred to the drastic, lethal exhalations of Reformation England. Contemporary also was romance, Arthurian, non-Arthurian, and Danish, in which religion gave way to love and adventure as the dominant interest. Nonetheless the transition age from the Conquest to Chaucerian England was still one over which the power of the Church and monastery prevailed.[89]

The Latin religious treatises of clerics like Anselm and his con-

---

[86] Cf. Wright (1), xxi-xxii; Giesebrecht, 14-16, 17-18, 25-26, 381. Cf. Haessner, 9-13; Campbell, 12.   [88] Cf. Giesebrecht, 32.

[87] Cf. Wright, *ibid.*   [89] Cf. CHEL, 1; 246-247.

temporaries helped prepare the way apparently for the mystical vernacular literature of which there is so much in England from the thirteenth century, particularly, to the sixteenth. Thus even didacticism came to feel the light touch of love, and prayer, the " working expression " [90] of mysticism, began to make its way into literature by the exquisite appeal of its intimate tone of personal affection. The communing of the virginal soul with Christ is the bond which unites the various types of the religious literature of southern England—the *Ancren Riwle,*[91] *legenda* of virgin saints, allegorical and homiletic treatises on virginity and on the relation of the consecrated soul to God—with the fourteenth century mystic-ascetical works of the northern recluses; namely, Richard Rolle of Hampole (1300?-1349), Walter Hilton (d. 1396), and Juliana of Norwich (1342-1442?). English literature, however, unlike the continental at this period, is singularly free of that class of lyric, perforce of love, called *chansons de nonnes, Klosterlieder, Nonnen-klagen,*[92] which treats of the nun unwillingly professed or of the maid immured against her will in a convent, where, like a bird in a cage, she beats her wings against the bars [93] or whence after much fluttering, she finally makes her escape.[94] The absence of such lyrics from early English literature, despite their presence in con-temporary romance literature, is not surprising once the integrally and seriously monastic-religious warp and woof of early English history be understood. The sole approach to such a theme in early English literature is found in allegorical works based upon the provençal or general continental [95] concept of a court of love. The *Court of Love,* a piece attributed by some to Chaucer,[96] a pass-age in *Temple of Glas* [97] of John Lydgate (c. 1370-c. 1451), and its counterpart in *The Kingis Quair* [98] of James the First of Scotland

[90] Butler, (2) 189.

[91] Morton.

[92] Cf. Power, (1) 509. Cf. Jeanroy, 189-191; Bujeaud 1, 137-138, 262-264, 323.

[93] Cf. Uhland 1, 666-669; Bartsch, 229-230, 231-232, 234-240.

[94] Cf. Shelley's " Epipsychidion ".

[95] Cf. Neilson, *passim.*

[96] But cf. Skeat, (3) 7; lxxx, 438-439 and 440.

[97] Cf. Schick, 8.   [98] Cf. Lawson, 46.

(1394-1437) represent nuns lamenting their having been in youth forced into the religious life. A very recent theorist, however, on the vernacular emotion informing medieval Latin song suggests the impossibility of denying to medieval England the origin of *planctus monialium* of which but a few anonymous examples survive.[99]

Middle English mystic literature, on the contrary, represents the union of a new delicacy, of a more suavely expressed tenderness with the sturdy, rather blunt tones of Anglo-Saxon instruction taken, matter and form, from the Fathers. From Saint Augustine,[100] Saint Bernard,[101] the Victorines, and Saint Anselm rather than from *amour courtois,* the new melody of personal affection for the Sacred Humanity of Christ, expressed in terms of human love, passes into the vernacular.[102] All of this literature is in praise of virginity, and all of it considers the human soul as the spouse of Christ—two ideas that were inseparable from monastic literature from the third century to the sixteenth. It could not, then, but be inspired with some phase of the nun ideal. Much of the literature, however, was written for anchoresses who, strictly considered, were not necessarily nuns, although some anchoresses were religious. Again, a great part of it was homiletic material applicable to any Christian and some of it was directed to persons living in the world.

While the ruggedly tender mystics of the North and the delicately tender mystics of the South were enamoured of the secret of the king's daughter, Chaucer and John Gower (d. 1408) were observing life with keen and eager eyes. To mention Chaucer and Gower in the same breath with this other-worldly spirituality seems, superficially, to remark strange contemporaries. But fourteenth-

[99] Cf. Allen, P. S., 44, 74-77. But cf. Hanford, *Speculum* 7 (1932), 115-116.

[100] Cf. De Wulf, 122.

[101] But cf. Butler, (2) 245.

[102] A phase of scholarship is concerned with the problem whether or not this literature was composed exclusively for nuns and some of it by nuns. Its feminine sensibility accounts for its being attributed to women and its ardent spirituality associates it especially with the cloistered maid and the recluse in her anchorhold. On this question, cf. p. 56, footnote 254.

century England in its external aspects also presented the age-old, traditional monastic Christianity; there, also, on the lips of the medieval preacher equipped with exempla, new and old, was the nun. Chaucer and Gower, consequently, continue in this respect in the old tradition while they open the way to modern literature. With the close of the fifteenth century the background becomes familiar and land-marks stand out plain. It is but a few steps to Shakespeare where the period of literary origins is clearly remote and modern literature at hand.

V

In surveying critically the English historical and literary field from the seventh century to the verge of the sixteenth, it is impossible to ignore the prevailing ideas of the epoch and not to perceive their effect upon the period which follows. The nun, as a part, and very often a conspicuous part, of the great permanent corporate community, the monastic system, that was the foremost institution in the cultural formation of England and of its literature, was recorded in history and written of idealistically in didacticism and was later presented in satire, romance, and exempla through the eight centuries from Aldhelm to Shakespeare; and this because of the reality of the nun as an English figure and on account of the power of conviction behind the idea of a nun. Which nun is it, the historical or the figure presented in the other literary genres, which has become the nun of English literary tradition? Or what has each contributed to the nun-tradition? And what, ultimately, is the source and origin of the tradition? Before these questions can be answered, each type must be studied separately and its lineage traced to its source. The result of both processes will be to understand English literature the better; to understand how it has given aesthetic expression to an historical figure and spiritual ideal of a definite epoch and to recognize that both the expression and the ideal are, for the most part, a direct heritage from the patristic founders of the literature of Christianity.

CHAPTER II

The Nun in the Didactic Literature, Seventh to Sixteenth Century

I. *Introduction*

Although works studied in this chapter represent a wide variety of literary forms,[1] they are a unit in their purpose. They arise from the most prolific urge of medieval composition—the desire to instruct.[2] As far as conscious motives can be uncovered from documents, they seem to aspire to nothing else. Moral, religious teaching is their chief reason for being. Another bond of unity besides their common purpose is the nun that emerges from their pages. With a single eccentric exception she recurs essentially unchanged throughout the dreary didactic records of pre-Tudor England. A fact so strange on the surface—that, from materials so diverse in form, composed by a variety of authors in a variety of languages, and extending over seven violently changing centuries, the same ideal nun-figure is obtained—is explained in part by the grip of a tradition most powerful in monastic literature as it was powerful in monastic life. This tradition, as we shall see, was patristic in its ultimate source. If this tradition was so dominant in the didactic literature of medieval England and if the didactic motive itself was the most characteristic urge of those centuries, a somewhat detailed examination of this literature for what it says of the nun seems a natural preliminary to similar inquiries among other literary forms. The didactic portrait, in fact, is the typical portrait

---

[1] Admonitory and instructive epistles; prose and verse disquisitions on religious virtues; homilies; hymns; legends; allegorical development of themes pertaining to conventual life, the evangelical counsel of chastity, and general piety. They are written in Latin, in Anglo-Saxon, in Anglo-Norman, and in Middle English.

[2] The division of the medieval literary remains into didactic and non-didactic may seem arbitrary in view of the didactic motive that informs almost all medieval literature. By didactic literature here I mean that the didactic is the dominant conscious purpose of this literature.

for the literature of medieval England,[3] the Middle Ages being what they were and didacticism influencing them as it did.

The earliest of the didactic treatises in England, although by no means necessarily the basis of the rest, is Aldhelm's prose work, *De Laudibus Virginitatis Sive De Virginitate Sanctorum.*[4] Max Manitius, advancing upon previous studies of Aldhelm's sources,[5] after noting his Vergilian phrases [6] and classical turns of expression, observes his more or less general debt for dogmatic thoughts on the subject of virginity [7] to patristic writers. He cites the particular passage in Cyprian, acknowledged generally by Aldhelm, from which the latter borrows his explanation of what he considers the sordid significance of a woman's vain ornaments.[8] He traces to *De Velandis Virginibus* c. 14, of Tertullian [9] the depreciatory interpretation of a wife's attractiveness which Aldhelm uses to exalt the more by contrast the inspiring beauty of a virgin.[10] I myself can state from an examination of commonplaces between Tertullian, Cyprian, and Aldhelm that the large attention given to dress in the last named is almost a verbatim reproduction of Tertullian.[11] Manitius,[12] following a reference in Aldhelm,[13] identifies the passage in Cyprian appropriated by Aldhelm to inveigh against feminine vanity in dyed garments. But Cyprian, in turn, as I have found upon examination, although he does not acknowledge it, borrows the passage in question from Tertullian, in whom the polemic on vanity in dress is launched not against consecrated

---

[3] For the contrary view cf. Eileen Power, *Medieval English Nunneries*, 439, who, unfortunately, did not examine the didactic remains.

[4] Ed. Giles, (2) 1-82.

[5] Cf. " Zu Aldhelm und Beda ", *Wiener SB*, 112;   535-536.

[6] Cf. *ibid.*, 554-558.

[7] Cf. *ibid.*, 603-604.

[8] Cf. *ibid.*, 605-606.

[9] Cf. *ibid.*, 604.

[10] Cf. Giles, (2) 17.

[11] Cf. Tertullian, *De Cultu Foeminarum*, PL 1, cols. 1305-1306; Cyprian, *De Habitu Virginum*, CSEL 3, 197; Aldhelm, *De Laudibus Virginitatis*, 75. For an elaborate treatment of the *De Habitu Virginum* of Cyprian and its sources and influence, cf. Sister Angela Elizabeth Keenan's edition of the work, *The Catholic University of America Patristic Studies*, vol. 34, Washington, 1932.

[12] Cf. *op. cit.*, 605-606.   [13] Cf. *op cit.*, 74.

virgins, but against men and women of the contemporary Roman world.[14] I have also discovered that the allocutions on virginity throughout Aldhelm's treatise and throughout didactic compositions down to the fifteenth century are close reproductions of florid passages in Tertullian, Cyprian, Ambrose, Jerome, Athanasius, Augustine, and Gregory. These points, moreover, constitute the staple of the didactic literature on the nun in England from the early eighth until the late fourteenth century.

Chronologically Aldhelm is the first, as he is by far the most important, writer who concerns us here. He treats in lavish detail the ideal simple nun—the woman undistinguished from other members of the community by the burdens and prerogatives of office, the woman lost to the world without the convent and obliterated among her sisters within, because of perfect conformation to a typical, ideal pattern. He treats of her exclusively, and all the other extant didactic writers treat of her exclusively, with one exception. Alcuin, flourishing almost a century after Aldhelm's *floruit,* holds up the pattern of the abbess. While other didactic writers do not follow him in this, other writers do consider the abbess in non-didactic genres, and she is precisely the abbess of Alcuin in their pages. For purposes of presentation in this inquiry, chronology is here violated in her favor and she is studied first, that the simple nun of Adhelm may be followed without chronological interruption thereafter.

II. *Alcuin's Abbess*

In his correspondence with an Anglo-Saxon abbess,[15] Alcuin writes at length on the necessity of an abbess' extending charity to her community by spiritual advice and temporal solace, by providing them with doctrine as requisite to the nourishment of their souls as food is requisite for the nourishment of their bodies.[16] She must watch over each soul individually, because she will have to render an account for each at the final judgment; the greater

---

[14] Cf. Tertullian, *De Pallio*, PL 2; cols. 1036, 1039; 1043-1045. Cf. also St. Jerome, ep. 22, *Ad Eustochium*, CSEL 54; 185.

[15] Cf. ep. 50, BRG 6; 274-7.

[16] *Ibid.*, 274-275.

her solicitude will have been for her subjects, the greater will be her reward.[17]   Human respect should not deter the abbess from giving her community salutary instruction, graphically illustrated. Going on, not in fear of man but out of love for God, the abbess shall, as occasion demands, admonish this one in all sweetness, and that one correct with her pastoral rod.   The aged monks and nuns she shall honor as fathers and mothers; the young, love as brothers and sisters; and the children, educate as sons and daughters, having care in Christ for all that for each she may have her reward.[18] These souls she must regard as the money of her Lord, which she is to multiply by her diligence and not suffer to diminish through her negligence.   Feast days of the saints she must celebrate fittingly and the poor regale with alms.[19]   So much for her ministration to the needs of others.

Watching and prayer are to be her portion; psalms, not vain words, are to be upon her lips.   Love of God, not worldly ambition, is to fill her heart.   She is to look on all that is amiable in this world as passing and to realize that that alone is enduring which is loved in Christ.[20]

Alcuin then sketches a personal picture of the ideal abbess.   To his mind the abbess should be a woman in herself amiable, serious, and modest in manner, truthful and modest in speech, a nun whose exemplary religious life has lent her a dignity and personal bearing that command the esteem of all and attract the love of many. Aware that her genuine nobility derives from God, her Father, she " so lets her light shine before men " that He may be glorified. His goodness it is that she imitates in the largess that brings her honor, in the mercy that wins her affection.   His Divine Son she copies when she preserves her heart pure and her life simple.   His voluntary poverty ever before her, with lavish alms she resists the temptation to glory and ambition—a temptation perhaps peculiar to an abbess—drawing her to amass wealth, to surround her person with delights, and to insure her posthumous fame by preparing herself a mausoleum of splendid proportions.   Contemning vanishing renown, she labors zealously in her abbatial office in expectation

---

[17] *Ibid.*, 275.
[18] *Ibid.*

[19] *Ibid.*, 275, 276.
[20] *Op. cit.*, 276.

of heaven, where one who has here served Christ with all her being will reign with Him more fully in eternity.[21]

III. *Aldhelm's Nun*

The didactic material with which this chapter is chiefly concerned, begins, however, with *De Laudibus Virginitatis*,[22] a prose treatise on virginity addressed about the close of the seventh [23] or at the beginning of the eighth century by Aldhelm to Abbess Hildelid of Barking, one of the abbesses lauded by Bede in the *Historia Ecclesiastica*.[24] It is the first extant treatise for Anglo-Saxon nuns within this period. It is composed of sixty brief chapters in Latin extolling virginity, explaining the attack made upon it by the eight vices, and depicting its splendor as illustrated in figures from the Old Testament and in saints of the new dispensation. It is followed by another work on the same subject, *De Laudibus Virginum*,[25] but in Latin hexameters. The verse treatment is also addressed to a nun, the abbess Maxima. An analysis of it, however, is obviated by the survey of the prose, for the metrical work merely recapitulates the ideas of the *De Laudibus Virginitatis*. Both the prose and the verse treatments were popular, however, the former being perhaps the " favorite book with our Anglo-Saxon forefathers up to the time of the Norman conquest," [26] and the latter an object of admiration among Aldhelm's contemporaries.[27] As Venerable Bede [28] notes, this dual form was nothing new,[29] although Aldhelm was probably the first among the Anglo-Saxons to employ it, as he was the first among them to express himself in Latin verse.[30]

a. Precepts for Nuns

In a florid and lengthy approach to the subject Aldhelm draws an analogy between the nuns whom he addresses and athletes, comparing the religious' exercise in regular discipline and assidu-

---

[21] Cf. *ibid.*, 276-277.

[22] *Loc. cit.*

[23] Cf. Manitius, (4) 1; 136 and 138.

[24] Cf. HE IV, x, 224-225.

[25] Cf. Giles, (2) 135-202.

[26] Wright, (3) 1; 217.

[27] Cf. Raby, 143.

[28] Cf. HE V, xviii, 321.

[29] Cf. Manitius, (2) 490.

[30] Cf. *ibid.*, 487.

ous study of Sacred Scripture to the gymnast's coursing the
stadium in view of a reward that, unlike the incorruptible crown
to which the nuns aspire, is merely temporal.[31] He then likens the
group of virginal souls industriously drawing the nectar of truth
from the pages of Holy Scripture to bees that suck sweetness from
a field of flowers. Now they pause upon the Gospels, expounded in
the mystic commentaries of the Fathers; then they pass from one
to the other of the quadruple interpretations of the Bible; the historical, the allegorical, the analogical, and the anagogical. Thence
they proceed to less sacred studies—the fables of early historiographers, to chronicles that have preserved the memory of the past,
to grammar, music, chronology, and prosody.[32] Lured thus somewhat far afield, but, in consequence, affording us a survey of the
sacred and profane studies pursued by the Anglo-Saxon nuns, Aldhelm checks himself and turns directly to the theme. The bee, on
account of its peculiar privilege of chastity, is a type of most modest
virginity. Knowing not marriage, plundering the flowers, it produces the sweetest of honey.[33] The bee is also a model of monastic
discipline, regularity, and constancy. No matter how long it has
inhabited its old-familiar dwelling or cherished its humble hut of
graceful osiers or its hive of bark, never does it under any pretext
fly about apart from the swarm on aimless wings—a symbol of the
nun (*vernacula*) who prefers to remain quietly and peacefully in
her cell, hastening back to it as soon as possible, if obedience, for
the time being, has obliged her to leave it.[34] Obedience also is to

[31] Cf. *op. cit.*, 2-3.

[32] Cf. *op cit.*, 4-5.

[33] *Ibid.*, 5. Cf. " Quam te velim, filia, imitatricem esse hujus apiculae
cui cibus flos est, ore soboles legitur, ore componitur! Hanc imitare tu,
filia. Verba tua nullum doli velamen obtendant, nullum habeant **fraudis**
involucrum; ut et puritatem habeant, et gravitatis plena sint."—St.
Ambrose, *De Virginibus* I, viii, PL 16, col. 200. Aldhelm draws the analogy
from the entire chapter viii of *De Virginibus*.

Cf. also " Et tu cave, virgo, illius apiculae modo, ne alarum tuarum
volatum aura mundi hujus extollat ".—St. Ambrose, *De Virginitate*, xvii,
PL 16, col. 293.

[34] *Op. cit.*, 5. Cf. analogous idea in the following: " pura virginitas . . .
etiam foeminarum oculos pati non vult . . . et gaudebit sibi soli et Deo
nota ".—Tertullian, *De Velandis Virginibus*, xv, PL 2, col. 910. " Nullus
sit tuus sine matre processus, quae sit anxia custos pudoris . . . **Considera**

be learned from the bee that hurries to fulfill the orders of its queen and with ready zeal obeys the behests of its superior. Deservedly, then, is the bee contemplated by nuns as a figure of intact virginity and of humble subjection. It manifests the selfless servitude of obedience, and by the surpassing and exquisite sweetness of the fruit of its labor, it illustrates how virginity—to draw the figure finally to an issue—rising above mundane pleasures and spurning earthly luxury and opulence, benefits mankind.[35]

Having finally arrived at the theme, Aldhelm elaborates it, developing or mentioning perhaps almost every patristic idea subsequently advanced by medieval writers of England on virginity and the monastic virtues of women. He outdoes the encomiastic tone of even the passages already summarized, by accumulating figure upon figure to express the excellence of virginity and the rhapsody of its heavenly reward.

The glory of virginity is sister to that of the angels;[36] it is rightly one of the beautiful inhabitants of the supernal city.[37] As honey to the taste transcends every other sweetness, so the prerogative of virginity surpasses in the eyes of God—and in this Aldhelm is careful not to depreciate saints bound by the tie of marriage—every other virtue: it is a special privilege. The fact that the Son of God chose a virgin for His mother is sufficient proof of God's pre-

---

quanta fuerit Maria, et tamen nusquam alibi, nisi in cubiculo reperitur, cum quaeritur (Luc. I, 28). Illa te doceat quid sequaris . . . Docet solitudo verecundiam: et gymnasium pudoris secretum est."—St. Ambrose, *Exhortatio Virginitatis*, x, PL 16, col. 357.

"Semper te cubiculi tui secreta custodiant . . . foris uagentur uirgines stultae, tu intrinsecus esto cum sponso."—St. Jerome, ep. 22, *Ad Eustochium*, CSEL, 54; 178-181.

[35] *Op. cit.*, 5-6.

[36] Cf. . . . "aequales enim sunt angelis Dei . . . quod futuri sumus, iam uos esse coepistis . . . cum castae perseueratis et uirgines, angelis Dei estis aequales".—St. Cyprian, *De Habitu Virginum*, CSEL, 3; 203.

"Nemo ergo miretur si angelis comparentur, quae angelorum Domino copulantur."—St. Ambrose, *De Virginibus* I, cols. 191-192. But cf. "nulla erit rhetorici pompa sermonis, quae te iam inter angelos statuat et beatitudine virginitatis exposita mundum subiciat pedibus tuis."—St. Jerome, ep. 22, *Ad Eustochium*, 146.

[37] Cf. "in coelo profecto est patria castitatis."—St. Ambrose, *De Virginibus* I, 194.

dilection for it.   Another evidence of the divine preference for virginity is the love of Christ for St. John, who, a virgin, was entrusted on Calvary by the Virgin Christ with His virgin mother, and who, at Patmos, rapt into ecstasy, merited to behold the heavenly choir of virgins "following the Lamb whithersoever He goeth" (Apoc. xiv, 4) and to hear them sing the song to which others, indeed, may listen,[38] but which the virgin alone may sing as she moves with the Lamb through the glory of the celestial kingdom.[39]

By heaping up such praises of virginity Aldhelm would not, as he states, lead the nuns into the error of despising marriage.[40] He writes for their benefit, nevertheless, that virginity and matrimony are as mutually remote as East and West.   Virginity, he remarks, quoting one whom he does not name, comes from holy wedlock as gold from the ground, as the rose from the thorn, as the pearl from the mussel.[41]   To show the relative glory of virginity and marriage, Aldhelm observes that silver is not depreciated when gold is preferred, marble is not despised when rubies are selected, nor is wool considered vile because silk gleams more imperially in a regal robe.[42]   Resorting to *De Civitate Dei*,[43] he justifies his comparisons of marriage and virginity, noting that they are of a kind in which the good is not despised, but that

[38] Cf. "nam et illud canticum nouum proprium uestrum dicere non poterit; audire autem poterit et delectari uestro tam excellenti bono. sed uos, qui et dicetis et audietis, quia et hoc quod dicetis a uobis audietis, felicius exultabitis iucundiusque regnabitis . . ."—St. Augustine, *De Sancta Virginitate*, CSEL, 41; 266-267.

[39] Cf. *op. cit.*, 7.

[40] Cf. "Non ego quidem dissuadeo matrimonium, sed virginitatis attexo beneficium."—St. Ambrose, *De Virginibus* I, col. 195.

"Unde . . . sectatrices . . . sacrae virginitatis admoneo, ut bonum suum ita praeferant nuptiis, ne malum iudicent nuptias."—St. Augustine, *De Sancta Virginitate*, 250-251.

Cf. also on the pertinence of this subject in early Christian times, "Les deformations de l'ascetisme chrétien primitif," *L'Encratisme*, Pourrat, 1; 93-96.

[41] Cf. "Laudo nuptias, laudo coniugium, sed quia mihi uirgines generant: lego de spinis rosas, de terra aurum, de conca margaritum."—St. Jerome, ep. 22, *Ad Eustochium*, 170.   But cf. Manitius, *op. cit.*, 604.

[42] Cf. *op. cit.*, 7-8.

[43] Manitius cites liber xxi, 4, 1.   Cf. *op. cit.*, 604.

which is better, is praised.[44] He, therefore, warns the nuns against tepidity and over-security [45] in their higher state; adding that some rest content with their profession, relinquish all effort to improve, and arrogantly look upon themselves as immune from all defilement on account of the prerogative of virginity, although at the same time they do not avoid pride, the ruin of humility.[46] Aldhelm regards pride as the worst of the vices,[47] of course, and humility [48] as one of the fundamental virtues. He makes a great point of the corroding effect of the vice of pride, emphasizing the practice of humility, however, as ancillary to virginity. He, accordingly, referring to the *Collations* of Cassian [49] and the *Libri Moralium* of Saint Gregory, draws out to some length the conflict a religious must sustain with pride, the queen of the eight principal vices, and the evil against which a religious must struggle first and most valiantly. The monster of pride will particularly attack the chastity of the frail mortal. For this reason she must do battle unremittingly and through humility avoid the calamity of being defrauded of her Heavenly Spouse.[50] Although other evils oppose

[44] Cf. *op. cit.*, 9. Cf. "Non est detrahere nuptiis, cum illis uirginitas antefertur. nemo malum bono conparat."—St. Jerome, ep. 22, *Ad Eustochium*, 168.

[45] Cf. ". . . tu te putas securam esse debere? caue, quaeso, ne quando de te dicat deus: uirgo Israhel cecidit; non est, qui suscitet eam."—St. Jerome, ep. 22, *Ad Eustochium*, 150.

[46] Cf. *op. cit.*, 9-10. Cf. "Nolo tibi uenire superbiam de proposito, sed timorem".—St. Jerome, ep. 22, *Ad Eustochium*, 146.

[47] Cf. ". . . Ut omnis superbiae ac jactantiae malum caveas, et humilis ac mitis Christi vivas exemplo."—St. Athanasius, *Exhortatio ad Sponsam Christi*, PL 103, col. 676.

[48] Cf. "Dei ancilla, quid ex his disciplinae tuae conveniat, . . . scilicet humilitatis et castitatis ".—Tertullian, *De Cultu Foeminarum* I, iv, PL 1, col. 1309.

[49] Manitius cites Collat. V, 2. Cf. *op. cit.*, 604. Cf. Cassian, *De Institutis Coenobiorum et de Octo Principalium Vitiorum Remediis*, CSEL, 17, 204-231.

[50] Cf. "Nihil est illi (Deo) carius humilitate, nihil acceptius modestia, nihil perosius gloria . . . Nupsisti enim Christo . . . Incede secundum sponsi tui voluntatem."—Tertullian, *De Velandis Virginibus*, col. 911.

Cf. also "Christus virginis sponsus."—St. Ambrose, *De Virginibus* I, col. 195. "Nam et Christi sponsas virgines dicere ecclesiastica nobis

her, they do so only to betray her into the jaws of pride. Accordingly, Aldhelm takes pains to expound to the virgin every subtle
snare of the vice.[51] He warns her that her state is never secure;
that no apparent truce or peace with this rabid enemy is to be
trusted.[52] Humility alone is her safeguard.[53] Yet, like the queen
*in vestitu deaurato radians et circumamicta . . . varietate resplen-
dens,* she must be radiant with colors symbolic of many virtues.[54]
Should she be so unwise as to confide solely in her purity, thinking
its " unblencht majesty " sufficient for perfection and an exemption
from caution, she would be but a sterile foolish virgin, devoid of
the hundred-fold merit of genuine virginal worth and of the handi-
work of her industry, and carrying a lamp, the flame of which
had fiickered out for want of oil;[55] for not all ten virgins of the
parable found access to the Heavenly Bridegroom, Aldhelm points
out. Those alone were admitted who bore lamps gleaming with

permittit auctoritas; dum in sponsarum modum quas consecrat Domino
velat."—St. Athanasius, *Exhortatio ad Sponsam Christi,* col. 671.

[51] Cf. *op. cit.,* 10, 11-12, 13.

[52] Cf. *ibid.,* 12.

[53] Cf. *ibid.,* 14.

[54] Cf. " Propterea vos, charissimae, quae estis sponsae et filiae regis
aeterni . . . Sedete ad dexteram sponsi in vestitu non exteriori, sed
interiori: deaurato auro charitatis in fimbreis aureis . . . sit undique
vestis circumdata varietatibus: ut jam nihil in ornamentis de virtutibus
desit ".—St. Jerome, *Regula Monacharum,* 416.

" Nihil ergo virginitas sola proficiet, quae coelistis regni gloriam sperat;
. . . Ante ergo omnia pudicitiam integritatemque servantibus, et ejus
remunerationem a Dei aequitate sperantibus mandatorum sunt custodienda
praecepta; ne gloriosae castitatis et continentiae labor in irritum deduca-
tur ".—St. Athanasius, *Exhortatio ad Sponsam Christi,* col. 673.

[55] Cf. " observa, quid dicat: et virgines bonae deficient; quia sunt et
virgines malae . . . perit ergo et mente virginitas. istae sunt virgines
malae, virgines carne, non spiritu, virgines stultae, quae oleum non
habentes excluduntur ab sponso . . . "—St. Jerome, ep. 22, *Ad Eustochium,*
150.

Cf. also " In omni tempore sint vestimenta tua candida, et oleum in
capite non desit, quo faces suas mysticas possit accendere; ut cum venerit
Sponsus, inter illas sapientes virgines (Matth. xxv. 10) coelesti thalamo
digna numeretur, quae devotionis ac fidei suae, gravitatisque lumine munus
sacrae professionis illuminet ".—St. Ambrose, *De Institutione Virginis,*
col. 332. Cf. also St. Ambrose, *Exhortatio Virginitatis,* col. 355.

modesty and burning with the flames of chastity, perseverance in which virtues is obtained from God solely at the price of untiring instancy in prayer.[56] Let her consider that, although the uncontaminated virginity of Mary brought forth the Incarnate Son of God, the consecrated widowhood of Anna prophesied the redemption. She will not, then, presume to depreciate the sixty-fold reward of widowhood in contrast with her promise of the hundred-fold and incur the risk, thereby, of becoming elated by vanity—an evil that can generate the destruction of virginity.[57] Returning again and again to the insidiousness of pride, Aldhelm remarks how a virgin may consider deference her due on account of her dignity and look for precedence in Church, resting content, however, with but the externals of the virtue.[58]

Having indicated into what defects pride can lead the nun, Aldhelm states the kind of virginal life which sheds glory upon virginity. The dignity and prestige of other states in life must, he implies, cede superiority to a sanctified virginal life. Virginity, however, Aldhelm and many of his followers are careful to note, is praiseworthy only when corporal integrity is accompanied by spiritual chastity.[59] His whole endeavor being to indicate the transcendence of divine love over human, Aldhelm hereupon elaborates the comparison drawn in the familiar text: " . . . *Divisa est . . . mulier et virgo innupta cogitat quae sint Domini, quomodo placeat Deo. Nam quae nupta est cogitat, quae sunt mundi et placet viro* (Cor. vii, 33-34). Following the Fathers,[60] whose authority he does not, however, cite at this point, he adapts his argument to the highly associative trait of feminine psychology.

---

[56] Cf. *op. cit.*, 15-17.

[57] Cf. *ibid.*, 14.

[58] Cf. *ibid.*, 15-17.

[59] Cf. " continentia uero et pudicitia non in sola carnis integritate consistit, sed etiam in cultus et ornatus honore pariter ac pudore, ut secundum apostolum quae innupta est sancta sit et corpore et spiritu ".—St. Cyprian, *De Habitu Virginum*, I, 190.

" Virgo erat (Cf. St. Augustine, lib. iv, de Doct. Christ., c. 21) non solum corpore, sed etiam mente."—St. Ambrose, *De Virginibus*, II, col. 209.

[60] Cf. Tertullian, *De Velandis Virginibus*, iv, col. 893-894; St. Cyprian, *De Habitu Virginum*, v, 191; St. Jerome, ep. 22, *Ad Eustochium*, 174-175, and St. Augustine, *De Sancta Virginitate*, 254.

The wife, he avers, rejoices in carnal love, desires necklaces of pearl, and to have her fingers begemmed with rings. The virgin rejoices in the assurance that she will be a companion of the angels. She also wishes to gleam, but with the most beautiful splendor of modesty, to glisten with golden virtue, and to wear the pearls of blameless merit. Aldhelm, like the Fathers, does not leave it to the nuns, however, to pursue the parallels further. But Aldhelm —again as do the Fathers—works out the analogy in detail. The wife curls her hair with an iron, darkens her eyelids with antimony, and rouges her cheeks; the virgin, unconcerned about the appearance of her hair, carries the palm and bears upon her brow the crown of virginity. The pomp of the wife can be as baneful as it is beautiful, debasing those who behold it; the appearance of the virgin, on the contrary, invariably lifts the mind to heavenly desires.[61] Virginity, Aldhelm continues, is difficult, but it is a grace that endures; it is like a rose that never withers; it preserves

[61] Cf. *op. cit.*, 17. Manitius traces the thought of the degrading character of the wife's adornment to Tertullian, *De Velandis Virginibus*, XIV.

Cf. "Quodsi Christum continentia sequitur et regno Dei uirginitas destinatur, quid istae cum terreno cultu et cum ornamentis, quibus dum hominibus placere gestiunt, Deum offendunt . . . caeleps cogitat ea quae sunt Domini, etc. . . . uirgo non esse tantum sed et intellegi debet et credi: nemo cum uirginem uiderit, dubitet an uirgo sit . . . neque enim uirginem fas est ad speciem formae suae comi aut de carne et de eius pulchritudine gloriari . . ."—St. Cyprian, *De Habitu Virginum*, 190-191.

Cf. also *ibid.*, 199-200.

Cf. analogous passages in Tertullian, *De Cultu Foeminarum*, II, and "Habitus foeminae duplicem speciem circumfert, cultum, ornatum. Cultum dicimus, quem mundum muliebrem vocant; ornatum, quem immundum muliebrem convenit dici. Ille in auro, et argento, et gemmis, et vestibus deputatur; ista in cura capilli, et cutis, et earum partium corporis, quae oculos trahunt. Alteri ambitionis crimen intendimus, alteri prostitutionis: ut jam hinc prospicias, Dei ancilla, quid ex his disciplinae tuae conveniat, quae de diversis institutis censearis, scilicet humilitatis et castitatis."—I, col. 1309.

"In illum enim delinquunt, quae . . . genas rubore maculant . . . Displicet nimirum illis plastica Dei, in ipsis redarguunt, reprehendunt artificem omnium . . . Quantum autem a vestris disciplinis et professionibus aliena sunt, quam indigna nomine christiano faciem fictam gestare, quibus simplicitas omnis indicitur.—*Ibid.*, II, col. 1321.

"Quid enim tanta ornandi capitis operositas ad salutem subministrat?

the joy of perpetual youth. And, although it surpasses marriage, yet on account of its difficulty, it is counseled, not prescribed.[62]

Then taking up another thought frequently referred to in subsequent monastic treatises, Aldhelm with what he calls *verbosa garrulitas aut garrula verbositas* goes into detail to distinguish the relative value of the three states of life. He calls the states *virginitas, castitas,* and *jugalitas*.[63] Virginity is gold; widowhood, silver; matrimony, bronze. Virginity is wealth; widowhood, competence; matrimony, poverty. They are respectively, peace, redemption, captivity; the sun, the moon, darkness; the day, the dawn, the night; a queen, a lady, a servant; the home-land, a port, the wide sea; man, something but half animate, a body; royal

Quid crinibus vestris quiescere non licet . . . ? Aliae gestiunt in cincinnis . . . Deus vos velari jubet, credo."—*Ibid.*, II, cols. 1323-1324.

"Projiciamus ornamenta terrena, si coelestia optamus."—*Ibid.*, II, col. 1332.

"Vestite vos serico probitatis, byssino sanctitatis, purpura pudicitiae. Taliter pygmentatae Deum habebitis amatorem."—*Ibid.*, II, col. 1334.

Cf. St. Jerome, ep. 107, CSEL, 55; 296.

Cf. "Iam quanto pretio opus est, ne etiam pulchra displiceat! Hinc pretiosa collo dependent monilia, inde per humum vestis trahitur aurata. Emitur igitur haec species, an habetur? Quid, quod etiam ad odorem variae adhibentur illecebrae! Gemmis onerantur aures, oculis color alter infunditur. Quid ibi remanet suum, ubi tam multa mutantur? Sensus suos amittit mulier, et vivere posse se credit? Vos vero, beatae virgines, quae talia tormenta potius quam ornamenta nescitis: quibus pudor sanctus verecunda suffusus ora, et bona castitas est decori."—St. Ambrose, *De Virginibus*, I, col. 197.

Cf. also "Ipse habitus et uestitus doceat eam, cui promissa sit. caue, ne aures perfores, ne cerussa et purpurisso consecrata Christo ora depingas, ne collum margaritis et auro premas, ne caput gemmis oneres, ne capillum inrufes et ei aliquid de gehennae ignibus auspiceris. habet alias margaritas, quibus postea uenditis emptura est pretiosissimum margaritum."—St. Jerome, ep. 107, CSEL, 55; 296.

Cf. also "Munda collum, ut non aurea reticula capillus portet, et suspensa monilia, sed illa potius ornamenta circumferat, de quibus Scriptura dicit . . ."—St. Athanasius, *Exhortatio ad Sponsam Christi*, col. 678.

[62] Cf. *ibid.*, 17-19. Cf. "quare ergo non habet domini de uirginitate praeceptum? quia maioris est mercis, quod non cogitur et offertur, quia, si fuisset uirginitas imperata, nuptiae uidebantur ablatae et durissimum erat contra naturam cogere angelorumque uitam ab hominibus extorquere et id quodam modo damnare, quod conditum est."—St. Jerome, ep. 22, *Ad Eustochium*, 171.   [63] *Ibid.*, 19.

purple, linen, wool. Virginity is borne in the carriage of a ruler; widowhood rides in a cart drawn by mules, and matrimony goes on foot.[64] Then follows the classic comparison, repeated almost invariably by monastic moralists; virginity merits an hundred-fold, widowhood a sixty-fold, and matrimony, a thirty-fold reward.[65]

Aldhelm turns then to illustrious examples of virginity. First he cites figures from the Old Testament. Then he mentions Apostles, Popes, Fathers, and monastic models and authorities. Next he appends compact *vitae* of men and women, virgin saints.[66] Among the latter whom Aldhelm, guided in his choice by Eusebius[67] and Jerome,[68] mentions as models for the nuns, and who are often treated in the subsequent literature of the type very much in the same fashion, are Saints Basilissa, Cecelia, Agatha, Lucy, Eugenia, Agnes, Tecla, Eulalia, Scholastica, and Eustochia.[69] They are written of in glowing terms that re-echo in later literature, the reply of Saint Agnes to the judge, for instance, being included in some rituals of religious investiture and profession of nuns even today.[70] Epithets, symbolic expressions, and stock ideas current

---

[64] Cf. *op. cit.*

[65] Cf. *ibid.*, 20. Cf. "centesimus et sexagesimus fructus . . ."—St. Jerome, ep. 22, *Ad Eustochium*, 163. Cf. "uirginalis uita in centeno fructu sit, in sexageno vidualis, in triceno autem coniugalis."—St. Augustine, *De Sancta Virginitate*, 290.

[66] Cf. *op. cit.*, 20-70.

[67] Cf. *ibid.*, 36.

[68] Cf. *ibid.*, 64.

[69] Cf. *ibid.*, 46-65.

[70] Cf. ". . . Quia jam ab alio amatore praeventa sum, qui me annulo fidei suae subarravit . . . cui Angeli serviunt, cujus pulchritudinem Sol et Luna mirantur."— *op. cit.*, 60.

"The professed sister, having received the ring from the bishop, says aloud, ' I have become the Spouse of Him unto Whom the Angels minister and of Whom the Sun and the Moon admire the everlasting Beauty.

The Novices having been invested in the religious habit, the choir sings, " Gaudens gaudebo in Domino, quia induit me vestimentis salutis sicut sponsam ornatam monilibus suis . . . "—*Ceremony of Profession of Perpetual Vows of the Sisters of Divine Providence of Kentucky*, MS. 24, 26.

in later literature of this kind abound: *sponsa*,[71] *castissima virgo*,[72] *virgo Christi*,[73] *virgo sacratissima*,[74] *beata virgo*,[75] *sancta virgo*,[76] *vernacula*,[77] *devota Christi virguncula*,[78] *tyruncula Christi*,[79] *coronatam et floridae virginitatis vexillo armatam*,[80] *coronam castitatis*,[81] *virginitatis palma*,[82] *virgines sapientes cum limpidis lampadibus*,[83] *cum Virginitatis palma . . . paradisi praemia possessurae, et cum CXLIV milibus Virginalem melodiam modulaturae ad Christum pariter perrexerunt;*[84] the nobility of despising earthly riches and pleasure for the preservation of virginity;[85] the superiority of the interior beauty of the soul to that of the external beauty and vain adornments[86] of body; and the sublimity of the privilege of being numbered, after a virginal life, among the one hundred and forty-four thousand who, singing the song the virgin alone may sing, follow the Lamb whithersoever He goeth;[87] and mystic terms[88] applied to the Blessed Virgin, who is held aloft in

[71] Cf. *op. cit., passim.* [76] *Ibid.,* 68. [81] *Ibid.,* 63, 65.

[72] Cf. *ibid.,* 55. [77] *Ibid.,* 57. [82] *Ibid.,* 67.

[73] Cf. *ibid.,* 65. [78] *Ibid.,* 61. [83] *Ibid.,* 63.

[74] Cf. *ibid.,* 54. [79] *Ibid.,* 56, 64. [84] *Ibid.,* 67.

[75] *Ibid.,* 56, 67. [80] *Ibid.,* 58.

[85] Cf. *op. cit.,* 65. Cf. St. Cyprian, *De Habitu Virginus*, I, 192-196.

[86] *Ibid.,* 47. Cf. Tertullian, *De Cultu Foeminarum*, II, cols. 1319-1320.

[87] *Ibid.,* 67. Cf. St. Cyprian, *De Habitu Virginum*, IV, 189-190. A typical passage àpropos this idea is the following:

" Sanctifices eam (Virginem) in veritate, in virtute confirmes, in charitate connectas, atque ad illam pudicitiae et intergritatis coelestem gloriam, *coronam illibatam*, immaculatamque divino tuo favore perducas; ut illic *Agni sequatur vestigia . . .* nec in grege sodalium incedat; sed agnis tui admixta, sine offensione versetur comes virginum, pedisseque Mariarum (Apoc. xiv. 4; Cant. 1. 6)."—St. Ambrose, *Exhortatio Virginitatis*, col. 333.

Cf. also " gaudia propria uirginum Christi non sunt eadem non uirginum, quamuis Christi; nam sunt aliis alia, sed nullis talia. ite in haec, sequimini agnum."—St. Augustine, *De Sancta Virginitate*, 264.

Cf. also the elaborate description for the heavenly reward for virginity in St. Jerome, ep. 22, *Ad Eustochium* (c. 41), 209-211, especially the following: " Tunc centum quadraginta quattuor milia in conspectu throni et seniorum tenebunt citharos, et cantabunt Canticum novum et nemo poterit scire canticum illud, nisi numerus definitus . . . virgines . . . hi sunt, qui secuntur agnum, quocunque vadit."—*Ibid.,* 210.

[88] *Virgo perpetua, hortus conclusus, fons signatus, sponsa et foelix ver-*

this treatise, as in most of those that follow, as the model par excellence of religious [89]—all these become the details of the spiritual make-up of the traditional nun. Replete with the connotation of their patristic context and familiar from constant repetition, they become auto-suggestive and in later literature carry their message without the need of long or minute explanation.

Having cited the pertinent facts of the lives of these virgin saints —emphasizing the chastity of Basilissa,[90] the interior joy and praise of Saint Cecelia; [91] the trials endured by Saint Agatha, Saint Lucy, Saint Agnes, Saint Tecla, and Saint Eulalia to preserve their virginity; [92] the monk-disguise of Saint Eugenia; [93] the powerful prayer of Saint Scholastica; [94] the learning of Eustochia to whom Saint Jerome directed renowned instruction [95]—Aldhelm (who seems to have forgotten for a time his addressees in the lengthy paragraphs on the virgin saints) reverts to the first theme.[96] He cautions Hildelid and the nuns of Barking to observe that the integrity of virginity is distinguished not by the charm of exterior beauty, but by the interior beauty of religious chastity,[97] an observation opening the way to a reproach about nuns' extravagances in dress. These remarks—which are obviously in imitation of patristic models [98] in which rhetorical convention plays an important part—have provided commentators upon early Anglo-Saxon conventual life with what they [99] accept as documentary evidence of the worldliness and luxury of the late seventh-century or early eighth-century nuns. Supporting his statements by the authority of the Fathers,[100] Ald-

nacula, regina, columba.—*Op. cit.*, 54.   Cf. St. Ambrose, *De Institutione Virginis*, PL 16, col. 321.

[89] Cf. " Quo virgines acrius impellantur ad Mariae imitationem."—St. Ambrose, *De Institutione Virginis*, 326-327; and *De Virginibus*, II, 208-211, and " nos meliorum exempla sectemur. propone tibi beatam Mariam. . . ."—St. Jerome, ep. 22, *Ad Eustochium*, 203. Cf. also St. Augustine, Sermo LI, 26, PL 38, col. 343.

Cf. Pourrat, 1; 376, and H. Koch., 92-94.

[90] Cf. *op. cit.*, 47.   [93] Cf. *ibid.*, 58-59.   [96] Cf. *ibid.*, 73.
[91] Cf. *ibid.*, 54.   [94] Cf. *ibid.*, 61-62.   [97] Cf. *ibid.*
[92] Cf. *ibid.*, 55-61.   [95] Cf. *ibid.*, 64.

[98] " De peplorum amiculo rhetoricamur."—*Op. cit.*, 78. Cf. p. 37 ff. for evidence.

[99] Cf. Thrupp, 227, 232, 233; Wright, (11) 86.

[100] Cf. *op. cit.*, 74-75.

helm inveighs against the vanity and folly of nuns, fashioning for themselves worldly garments like those of seculars. If the exterior be worldly, he avers, in vain do religious labor at acquiring or perfecting interior beauty. In no way can the forbidden ornaments of the world—violet garments, robes dyed with the tincture of precious purple, contrary to apostolic and ecclesiastical decrees as they are—be considered fitting or becoming the cloistered maiden, the virgin of Christ.[101] He then cites Scripture,[102] Saint Gregory,[103] and Saint Cyprian,[104] on the subject. He borrows, as he acknowledges in part, from the last literally and at great length, endeavoring by very slightly adapted passages from the *Liber de Habitu Virginum* [105] (which in turn are borrowed from Tertullian) to lend

[101] Cf. *op. cit.*, 73-74.
[102] Cf. *ibid.*, 74.
[103] Cf. *ibid.*
[104] Cf. *ibid.*, 74, 75.
[105] Cf. Manitius, (1) 605-606. But cf.:

ALDHELM	CYPRIAN	TERTULLIAN
De Laud. Virg., pp. 74-75.	*De Habitu Virg.*, pp. 191-197.	*De Cultu Foem., I, viii*, col. 1312.
" Neque enim **Virginem** fas est ad speciem formae suae comi, aut de carne, et ejus pulchritudine gloriari, c u m Apostolus dicat, Mihi autem absit gloriari, nisi in cruce Domini n o s t r i Jesu Christi; nulla sit illis magis quam adversus carnem colluctatio et vincendi corporis ac domandi obstinata certatio ".—p. 74. " Nunquid ille conditor ac creator omnium Deus hirsutas bidentum lanas et setosa vervecum vellera, non potuit rubro conchilii sanguine aut c r u e n t o bacciniorum succo inficere, seu certe, purpureis tincturae mu-	" neque e n i m uirginem fas est ad speciem formae suae comi aut de carne et de eius pulchritudine gloriari, cum nulla sit illis magis quam aduersus carnem conluctatio et uincendi corporis ac domandi abstinata certatio. Paulus forti ac sublimi u o c e proclamat: mihi autem, etc.: et uirgo in ecclesia de specie carnis ac de corporis pulchritudine gloriatur. . . . " sericum et purpuram indutae Christum induere non possunt, auro et margaritis et monilibus adornatae ornamenta cordis ac pec-	" Proinde et vestium de coloribus honorem servi etiam eorum terunt. Sed et parietes tyriis et hyacinthinis et illis regiis velis, quae vos operose resoluta transfiguratis, pro pictura abutuntur. Vilior est apud illos purpura, quam rubrica. Quis enim est vestium honor justus de adulterio c o l o r u m injustorum? Non placet Deo, quod non ipse produxit, nisi si non potuit purpureas et aerinas oves nasci jubere. Si potuit, ergo jam noluit; quod Deus noluit; utique non licet fingi. Non ergo natura optima sunt ista, quae a Deo non sunt,

weight to his words. Again he quotes Saint Cyprian virtually verbatim to convince the nuns of the hidden danger in making themselves attractive, a danger, if not for themselves, for those whom they attract.[106]

ALDHELM	CYPRIAN	TERTULLIAN
De Laud. Virg., pp. 74-75.	*De Habitu Virg.*, pp. 191-197.	*De Culta Foem.*, I, *viii*, col. 1312.

ricibus naturaliter colorare, si hoc nostris usibus commodum e t utilitati profuturum solerti praescientia praevidisset, ut illud veraciter impletur, quod per Ironiam a Poeta foeliciter cantum est:
Nec varios discet mentiri lana colores:
Ipse sed in pratis aries jam suave rubenti
Murice, jam croceo mutavit vellera luto,
Sponte sua sandix pascentes vestiet agnos.
Et quasi ille de quo dictum est; Qui vivit in aeternum, creavit omnia simul, c u m conderet orbem originaliter creare nequiverit. Nunc mortalium industria stolidis ac superfluis adinventionum argumentis addere et amplificare contendat. Unde inclytus item Cyprianus Punicorum Pontifex inquit: Neque enim Deus coccineas, aut purpureas oves fecit, aut herbarum succis et conchiliis tingere, et colorare lanas docuit."

toris perdiderunt. . . . Neque enim Deus coccineas aut purpureas oues fecit aut herbarum sucis et conchyliis tinguere et colorare lanas docuit nec distinctis auro lapillis aut margaritis contexta serie et numerosa conpage digestis monilia instituit, quibus ceruicem quam fecit absconderet, ut operiatur illud quod Deus in homine formauit, et conspiciatur id desuper quod diabolus inuenit. . . ."

auctore naturae, sic a diabolo esse intelliguntur, ab interpolatore naturae. . . ." Cf. also ibid. I, ii, cols. 1305-1306

Cf. also St. Jerome, *Regula Monacharum*, xxxi, cols. 417-418.

[106] Cf. *op. cit.*, 75 with *De Habitu Virginum*, 194. Cf. Manitius (1), 606.

Rare dyes of various hues would indeed seem to us to have subtly fascinated Anglo-Saxon religious women, did we not perceive that the equally colorful and fantastic line of reasoning employed by Aldhelm is itself a passage as old as Tertullian,[107] and irresistible to the admonitory writer on this subject, rhetorically inclined. *Neque enim Deus,* Aldhelm writes, taking the words from Saint Cyprian,[108] *coccineus, aut purpureas oves fecit, aut herbarum succis et conchyliis tingere, et colorare lanas docuit."* [109]   He reminds the nuns that Judith, whom later moralists also select as a model for virgins, put off her queenly robes when she, like a lily blooming in chastity, retired from the world to live secluded among her maidens.[110]   He then passes to the famous description of rich and colorful garments which he condemns severely as a garb for religious.   Yet, like most of Aldhelm's ideas expressed here, this also, apart from the question of its applicability, seems attributable rather to a desire to write in the tenor of the Fathers than to an effort to face an actual situation.

Not only nuns, he begins, but clerics also should eschew bold adornment.[111]   He becomes explicit, however, about the clothing of the former.   Nuns should avoid the luxury of those who wear double tunics of scarlet or hyacinth, hoods and flowing sleeves of silk, made with long points and edged with fur; of the vanity of those who, with a curling iron, Aldhelm is meticulous to state, curl their hair about the brow and then arrange their tinted veils

606. But this idea also is originally Tertullian's. Cf. ". . . primo quod non de integra conscientia venit studium placendi per decorem, quem naturaliter invitatorem libidinis scimus; quid igitur in te excitas malum istud. . . ." *De Cultu Foeminarum* 1, col. 1317. Cf. also ibid., col. 1319.

[107] Cf. note 105, pp. 37-38.

[108] *Ibid.*

[109] *Op. cit.,* 75.

[110] Cf. *ibid.,* 76. Cf. also St. Ambrose, *De Viduis,* I, PL 16, col. 246.

[111] Cf. "certe . . . stolam fundere, comam struere, cutem fingere, speculum consulere, collum demulcere, aurem quoque foratu effoeminatus. . . . Tertullian, *De Pallio,* 1, col. 1041. Cf. also "sunt alii—de mei ordinis hominibus loquor—qui ideo ad presbyterium et diaconatum ambiunt . . . omnis his cura de uestibus, si bene oleant, si pes laxa pelle non folleat. crines calamistri uestigio rotantur, digiti de anulis radiant et, ne plantas umidior uia spargat, uix inprimunt summa uestigia."—St. Jerome, ep. 22, *Ad Eustochium,* 185.

to charming effect, fastening them so with fillets that they drape gracefully to the ground; who point their nails to talons like the hawk's or, at least, like those of the night owl—birds of prey, to which such claws are a necessity, since they are fitted by nature to pounce upon their food.[112]

Fearing, perhaps, that the nuns whom he addresses may be taken somewhat aback, Aldhelm employs all the rhetoric in his power, apparently, to appease them.[113]   He then apologizes for his virulence with the adage, " Better are the wounds of a friend than the kisses of an enemy," and exculpates himself from any personal allusion to Hildelid or to her community by stating that the severity of his remarks is for no one in particular, that an entire convent cannot be condemned in which each member is blameless.[114] He promises them a metrical version of the theme; [115] begs their prayers; [116] and closes with a tribute to nuns as sublime as it is pregnant with all the poetry and mystic symbolism that the literary convention and tradition then forming in England ever after employed to catch the elusive significance of the ideal nun-figure: " Farewell, O flowers of the Church; adieu, my monastic sisters, my pupils, pearls of Christ, jewels of Paradise, and inhabitants of the celestial fatherland." [117]

---

[112] Cf. *op. cit.*, 77. Cf. also ". . . Tunc abjectio vestium, cujus taedet mulierculas fatuas, vos delectabit. Tunc rusticanus et abjectus pannus, purpurae praeponetur et bysso. Tunc crassa et rudis velamina capitis aestimabuntur ex sericis. Certe tanta erit deformitas in melotis, tanta grossities in cucullis, caputia tam rudi artificio praeparata, quod si hic forent, saecularium indumenta, artificum panni brevi tempore periret omnis industria.

Ista, charissimae, decent monachas: non strictis manicis, pretiosis et compositis pannis, subtili velamine velatis superciliis, cor meretricum non tam praetendere quam habere. Non tales existimo monachas, sed pessimas meretrices, et scortum vilissimum."—St. Jerome, *Regula Monacharum*, 417.

[113] Cf. Bede's witness to the fervor and regularity at Barking at this time: *H. E.*, IV, ix, 224-225.

[114] Cf. *ibid.*, 77-78.

[115] Cf. *ibid.*, 80.

[116] Cf. *ibid.*, 81-82.

[117] *Ibid.*, 82. Cf. also "flos est ille ecclesiastici germinis, decus adque ornamentum gratiae spiritalis."—St. Cyprian, *De Habitu Virginum*, 189.

b. Portrait of the Ideal Nun

The foregoing ideas of Aldhelm on the ideal nun are found one after another throughout the *De Laudibus Virginitatis*. There are two passages, however, in the treatise in which, taken together, Aldhelm sums up all that he has stated and implied on the subject. These two passages (Chapters VI and XIV)[118] form a personification of the theories or principles scattered throughout the disquisition, and while they are not repeated precisely verbatim in the subsequent literature, they are repeated in other words: they are a convenient summary of the whole question. They draw the personal picture of the ideal man—the embodiment of the moral lessons advanced in detail in the rest of the work. The personification applies and vitalizes the abstractions presented throughout the treatise. It not only sums up concretely the various qualities treated in the abstract, but, through constant repetition of the figure and of the details apart from the figure, it comes about that the mention of anyone of these details calls up automatically all the others as summed up in Aldhelm's personification.

This nun-figure, derived at the opening of the treatise from the symbol of the bee [119] and the illustration of the perfect virginal life,[120] is an ideal embodiment of virginity and of monastic decorum. Aloof from the world, she is modestly retiring. She cherishes the solitude of her cell. She is docilely obedient and studious. Urged on by the flames of divine love burning within her, she presses on tremulously, longingly, toward heaven. Impatient of the trammels of the flesh and " breathless with adoration ",[121] in anticipation of her heavenly occupation,[122] she breaks forth alternately

[118] For convenience, the composite passage may be designated vi-xiv, for it is from these two sections of *De Laudibus Virginitatis* that the personification is drawn.

[119] Cf. *op. cit.*, 3-6.

[120] Cf. *ibid.*, 14-15.

[121] Cf. " The holy time is quiet as a Nun
      Breathless with adoration. . . ."—Wordsworth, (Sonnet, 1802).

[122] Cf. *op. cit.*, 14-15. Cf. also " . . . non propter praesentem huius saeculi uitam, sed propter futuram, quae in regno caelorum promittitur, perpetuam continentiam deligendam."—St. Augustine, *De Sancta Virginitate*, 256.

into deep sighs and snatches of sacred song and psalmody.[123]   She cannot hide her tears; they well up from the depth of compunction burdening her heart.   Sweetly satiated with the delight and regaled with the nectar of the contemplative life, this " unblemish'd form of Chastity " finds nothing on earth comparable to her virginal joy.[124]   This figure constitutes Aldhelm's most complete picture of the ideal simple nun.

Recapitulating the prominent ideas of the treatise, we see that the following are outstanding: the peerless excellence of the virginal state; its superiority to other states of life, if it is preserved interiorly as well as exteriorly, buttressed by other virtues and protected by humility; the bane of pride; the folly of a virgin's confiding in chastity alone; the distinction between the virgin and the wife, particularly between the ornaments proper to each and the quality of their respective delights; the degree of merit accruing to virginity, to widowhood, and to marriage.   The apocalyptic reward of the first, the example of the Blessed Virgin and the virgin martyrs; the ignominy of a nun's wearing worldly and colorful garments; the evil of her rendering herself attractive; the example of Judith's simplicity in dress and retirement of life, and finally, the allusion to the five foolish and five wise virgins, and the composite sketch in chapters vi-xiv of the ideal nun-figure.

The piece is plainly a literary exercise, a demonstration of the author's acquaintance with classical and patristic thought, and of his skill in combining a multiplicity of ideas in one fairly unified and coherent disquisition, decorated with—as it seems—every rhetorical ornament at his command.   Medieval literature was under the weight of a literary tradition, and religious-didactic literature particularly was under the influence of Latin patristic.   But the

---

[123] Cf. " . . . tu una de virginibus . . . tu, inquam, in cubili tuo, et nocturno tempore constituta, semper meditare Christum, et ejus adventum omnibus sperato momentis.

" Si tardare tibi videtur, exsurge . . . tardare videtur, cum vocem non excitas psalmis." (Cf. the entire chapter.)   St. Ambrose, *De Virginitate*, col. 283.   Cf. also " Cum psalmum dicis, cujus verba dicis agnosce; et in compunctione magis animi quam in tinnulae vocis dulcedine delectare. Lachrymas enim psallentis Deus magis quam vocis gratiam comprobat." —St. Athanasius, *Exhortatio Ad Sponsam Christi*, col. 684.

[124] Cf. *op. cit.*, 14-15.

unvarying conformity of Aldhelm's ideas and very often of their expression in this treatise with the early Christian writings on virginity indicates his studied imitation. He seems obviously to have had in mind the creation of a composition for contemporary nuns such as Saint Cyprian, Saint Ambrose, or Saint Jerome directed to virgins of their period. The Aldhelmian literary school was, again, distinguished for florid, pompous style. But Aldhelm's extreme figures; his lengthy excursions into traditional topics, followed by apologies for verbosity and garrulousness bespeak writing especially for the writing's sake. The promise, moreover, further to adorn the treatise by turning it into verse also indicates Aldhelm's rhetorical purpose. Although the enduring popularity of the *De Laudibus Virginitatis* was of itself sufficient to propagate all the ideas contained in the treatise, they are not found *in toto* and in detail again in any work of a subsequent author within this period. Saint Boniface touches upon almost every one of the points in his various compositions. All of them, however, are repeated again and again by one writer after another down to the fifteenth century.

IV. *Repetitions of the Materials Found in Aldhelm*

a. Precepts for Nuns

The supreme excellence of the state of virginity is repeated for the benefit of nuns by Boniface [125] and by Aelfric.[126] It is implied in works which, if not addressed directly to nuns, form the staple of their extra-Scriptural reading.[127] It is declared in a twelfth century Anglo-Saxon poem addressed to a nun,[128] in a contemporary letter of Peter of Blois (1130 - c. 1203) to another nun,[129] and in an admonitory epistle [130] of the same cleric—both letters

---

[125] Cf. " *Bonifatii Carmina,*" MGH 1; 8-9; and ep. 86, BRG 3; 234.

[126] Cf. "Natale Omnium Sanctorum," Thorpe (2) 1; 546 (and in many other places).

[127] Cf. the various *vitae,* p. 52 below.

[128] Cf. " Versus Serlonis Parisiacensis ad Muriel sanctimonialem," Wright, (12) 2, 233-240. Cf. also 240-241.

[129] Ep. 36. *Ad Christianam Sanctimonialem,* PL 207, col. 115.

[130] Cf. *ibid.,* ep. 234, 535.

being couched in the traditional didactic phraseology and repeating nearly every patristic praise of virginity. Thus the mystic literature from the twelfth to the fifteenth century also emphasizes this virtue but not with precisely the same development as that found in Aldhelm and the pre-mystic writers who follow him. The supremacy of virginity is explained in the *Ancren Riwle*.[131] It is detailed succinctly but traditionally in an early thirteenth-century dialogue, the *Vices and the Virtues*,[132] and in a closely contemporary homily.[133] It is the whole message of *Hali Meidenhad*.[134] This treatise, while thoroughly traditional in its ideas and development, intensifies, if anything, the customary superlative praise of the virginal state. It is addressed to young women, and it depicts for them the glories of virginity so exultantly and the miseries and cares of marriage so lugubriously and so realistically [135] that it is the climax of its weary theme in the literature of England during this period. The treatment of virginity in *The Pearl* [136] is the secret of the much prized beauty of the poem, every line of which strives to set forth the beauty of the bride of Christ. The superiority of virginity is expounded at length in the familiar details in the *Ayenbite of Inwyt* [137] and constitutes the underlying thought of the whole, and is the exclusive subject of one stanza of Thomas of Hales' versified treatise,[138] *A Luue Ron*.[139] The same is true

[131] Cf. *op. cit.*, 164.

[132] Cf. *op. cit.*, Holthausen, 120.

[133] Cf. Morris (5) 2, 45.

[134] Cf. *op. cit.*, Furnivall, (16) 10-14.

[135] Even through the crudities which render the expression of the ideas on marriage as contrasted with the life of virginity seemingly unique and original here, it is easy to discover the sane and moderate statements of Saint Ambrose on the respective attractions of the two states. Cf. *De Virginibus*, 195-197.

[136] Cf. *op. cit.*, Morris (1) 13 ff.

[137] Cf. *op. cit.*, Morris (2) 227-235, 267-268.

[138] The term "versified treatise" is employed advisedly. Ten Brink, it is true, has described the composition as *eine kontemplative Lyrik* and has stated that its author *verfügt über poetische Ideen und besitzt Ohr und Phantasie des Lyrikers.* (*Gesch. d. Eng. Litt.* 1; 246). Its ideas, however, are those familiar to the traditional literature of virginity and its tone is the usual moralizing, didactic one of the conventional writer on this subject.   [139] Cf. *op. cit.*, Morris (4) 93-99 and stanza 2, 98.

of a very similar group of verses on the same subject and entitled *Of Clene Maydenhod.*[140] It is lauded in the traditional tone in Robert Holkot's *Super Librum Sapientie* [141] (ante 1349). The superiority of the state of virginity is, in fact, the burden of all the didactic literature on the subject of virginity.

Not only do followers of this literature after Aldhelm repeat Aldhelm as to the superior excellence of the virtue, but in varying degrees of faithfulness the authors repeat the ideas with which he amplifies his statement. Thus virginity is called sister of the angels by Boniface; [142] the virginal life is compared to that of the angels by Aelfric; [143] it is likened to them by Peter of Blois,[144] and by the authors of the *Ancren Riwle,*[145] *Hali Meidenhad,*[146] *A Luue Ron,*[147] and *Ayenbite of Inwyt* [148] respectively. It is stated specifically as an inhabitant of heaven by Aelfric,[149] and is designated as the highest earthly state [150] by the latter, who identifies its perfection with the life of a nun.[151] God's predilection for it, as indicated by His selecting a virginal mother for His Son, is repeated in *Vices and Virtues;* [152] while the superiority of the virgin to the wife is implied in an admonitory epistle of Peter of Blois,[153] in *A Luue Ron,*[154] and in *Of Clene Maydenhod.*[155] The concept is elaborated with unsparing emphasis in *Hali Meidenhad.*[156] The ninth-century Anglo-Saxon version of Gregory's *De Cura Pastorali,* while again advancing the superiority of virginity to marriage, nevertheless reminds virgins that the married, faithful to their vows, surpass them, if the virgins exalt themselves. Virgins are admonished

[140] Cf. Furnivall (14) 464-468 and stanza 2, 468.
[141] Cf. *op. cit.,* Lectio xl, col. 2.
[142] Cf. MGH 1; 8. Cf. also ep. 10, BRG 3; 61.
[143] Cf. *Thorpe* (2) 1; 547.
[144] Cf. Ep. 234; PL 207, col. 536.
[145] Cf. *op. cit.,* Morton, 102.
[146] Cf. *op. cit.,* 5, 6, 16, 20.
[147] Cf. *op. cit.,* 97.
[148] Cf. *op. cit.,* 227.
[149] Cf. Thorpe (2) 1, 547; Cf. Assmann, 41.
[150] Cf. Assmann, 39.
[151] Cf. *ibid.,* 33.
[152] Cf. *op. cit.,* 119.
[153] Cf. *op. cit.,* 536.
[154] Cf. *op. cit.,* 94-97.
[155] Cf. *op. cit.,* 465-467.
[156] Cf. *op. cit.,* 32-58.

to elevate the state of virginity and to keep in mind the fact that, should they fail to observe their vows of chastity, they are far inferior to the married.[157]   Aelfric, in citing the excellence of the virginal state, goes further.   He warns nuns not to despise their mother, because, unlike them, she became a wife.[158]   *Hali Meidenhad* also warns the virgin not to condemn widowhood and matrimony,[159] and the *Scale of Perfection* of Walter Hilton explains that many a wife and "worldly woman" may far surpass the virgin in the love of God, and so receive a greater reward in eternity.[160]   The *Ayenbite of Inwyt* also refers to the need of the interior as well as of the exterior virtue.[161]   Nearly every writer upon this subject stresses the transcendence of virginal and divine love over earthly and human love,[162] and the superiority of the virtues and other adornments of the virgin over jewels and human beauty.[163]   The hundred-, the sixty-, and the thirty-fold merit respectively of virginity, widowhood, and marriage is also repeated.[164]   Aelfric explains the degrees in great detail,[165] but only a twelfth-century homily on the Epiphany approaches Aldhelm's catalogue of metaphors illustrating the relative excellence of the three conditions.   Here the three kings who followed the star signify maidenhood, "spousehood", and widowhood, for he who lives his particular life rightly is a king.   The three gifts also, the gold, the "recheles", and the "mirre" are, respectively, maidenhood, marriage, and widowhood.[166]

[157] Cf. *op. cit.*, Sweet, 409.

[158] Cf. Assmann, 37.   Aelfric here accommodates St. Ambrose *De Virginitate*, PL 16, col. 273.

[159] Cf. *op. cit.*, 61.

[160] Cf. *op. cit.*, Underhill (1) 150-151.

[161] Cf. *op. cit.*, 229.

[162] Cf. Boniface MGH 1; 8; Peter of Blois, ep. 36, 115; *Hali Meidenhad*, 8-9; *Ancren Riwle*, 98, 103, 396-400; *A Luue Ron*, 98; *Of Clene Maydenhod*, 445-446; *On Ureisun of Oure Louerde*, Morris (3) 185-186.

[163] Cf. Boniface, *ibid.* and ep. 86, 234; Peter of Blois, ep. 55, 167, 168; ep. 234, 535; Aelred of Rievaulx, *De Vita Eremitica*, PL 23, col. 1462; *Ayenbite of Inwyt*, 228, 229.

[164] Cf. *Hali Meidenhad*, 32; *Ayenbite of Inwyt*, 234.

[165] Cf. Thorpe (2) 148; Assmann, 21, 39.

[166] Cf. Morris (5) 45.

The futility of the externals of the virtue without counter-balance of the interior spirit is likewise repeated as a salutary check upon the high praises of virginity. An eighth-century Anglo-Saxon inter-linear of *Defensor's Liber Scintillarum,* in two chapters devoted to *Be forlaetendum worulde* [167] and *be faemnhade,*[168] stresses this phase of the nun ideal. It states the necessity of cleanness of mind for " faemnhade " and the insufficiency of a chaste body, if the mind be defiled. Aelfric also alludes to this point.[169] It is brought up again in the *Vices and Virtues,*[170] in the *Ayenbite of Inwyt* [171] and in *Ego dormio,*[172] written by Richard Rolle of Ham-pole " to a certain nun of Yedingham." [173] The great danger of a virgin's becoming proud [174] of her lofty state and, consequently, her essential need of the virtue of humility [175] are implied in the often repeated warnings above mentioned against a virgin's elevating herself above others. Usually, as in *De Laudibus Virginitatis,* the caution is sounded either after the relative merits of the states of virginity, of widowhood, and of matrimony have been eluci-dated—unavoidably to the prejudice of the latter and last—or after the first has been highly exalted. It takes ordinarily the form of salutary advice not to contemn the less meritorious states. Aelfric does this in the homily *De Sancta Virginitate,*[176] in the epis-tle *Be þaere halʒan claennysse,*[177] and in the story of Judith.[178] In *De Sancta Virginitate,* to the statement of the degrees and the ne-cessity of humility in the highest vocation, he adds—perhaps uncon-

[167] Cf. *op. cit.,* Rhodes, xi, 57-64.

[168] Cf. *ibid.,* xiii, 68-71.

[169] Cf. Assmann, 21.

[170] Cf. *op. cit.,* 120.

[171] Cf. *op. cit.,* 229.

[172] Cf. Horstman (15) 1; 50.

[173] Cf. Allen (3) 250.

[174] Cf. Aelred of Rievaulx, *op. cit.,* xxix, col. 1461; *Hali Meidenhad,* 57, 58-60.

[175] Cf. Alcuin, ep. 280, 859; Assmann, ep. 136, 39-40, 114; Aelred of Rievaulx, *op. cit.,* xlvii, cols, 1465-1466; Peter of Blois, ep. 136, 115, ep. 234, 536; *Ancren Riwle* 148, 276; *Hali Meidenhad,* 19, 62-63; John of Bromyard, *op. cit.,* 56, col. 4, art. ix.

[176] Cf. Assmann, 39-40.

[177] Cf. *ibid.,* 21.   [178] Cf. *ibid.,* 102-116.

sciously bringing Aldhelm's [179] and Gregory's [180] increasingly concise statements to a focus—

> Betere bið þaet wif, þe wunað on sinscipe,
> ʒode a ʒehyrsum to his halʒum bebodum
> and eadmod on heortan, . . .
>
> . . . .
> þonne þaet maeden beo, þe modiʒ bið on heortan
> and ʒode unʒehyrsum. . . .[181]

The reason Aelfric gives is that the obedient wife has two goods, matrimony and humility; the proud virgin has two, chastity and pride, one a great good and the other a great evil. The lesser good with another inferior good is more laudable a possession than a great good and a great evil, especially if the evil be pride, from which all other vices derive.[182] In *Be þaere halʒan claennysse* Aelfric observes that the hundred-fold will be the virgin's, if to virginity in the service of God she adds humility.[183] He cites many authorities [184] for the statement and appeals finally to the example of the numerous monks and nuns who lived chastely for Christ in the depth of the desert.[185] Consistent with the lessons expounded in the works just cited, Aelfric makes much, in the homily on the Book of Judith, of humility as a companion virtue to virginity. He constitutes Judith a model for religious women,[186] appending to the swift and compelling narrative of her heroic deed, forty-two [187] lines of moralizing, seventeen of which are directed explicitly to a nun whom Aelfric addresses as " min swustor." [188] In these lines Aelfric notes particularly the union of humility and purity in Judith in order to deduce therefrom a lurid lesson for nuns. It was humility which brought the queenly Judith to her knees to beg God's aid and to solicit the prayers of her people that success be hers over the enemy.[189] It was the combination of these two vir-

---

[179] Cf. p. 29, above.

[180] Cf. pp. 45-46, above.

[181] *Op. cit.*, 40.

[182] Cf. *op. cit.*

[183] Cf. *ibid.*, 21.

[184] Basil, Jerome, Augustine, Martin, Gregory, Cuthbert, Bede. Cf. *op. cit.*, 22.

[185] Cf. *ibid.*, 23.

[186] Cf. p. 39, note 110 above.

[187] Cf. *op. cit.*, 115.

[188] Cf. *ibid.*

[189] Cf. *ibid.*, 109-110.

tues that enabled her to undo Holofernes. Aelfric thus presents in Judith the ideal union of lowliness and chastity—the former being a protection of the latter—a union which he and others advocate for the man, but which no one within this period has yet dwelt upon at such length as he. The virtue is advocated in later treatises.[190] Humility, of course, as a virtue recommended nuns and recluses, is a commonplace in the Middle English mystic literature, particularly in the *Ancren Riwle* [191] where, moreover, Judith is again presented as a model of retirement and of an industrious life.[192] The attack of pride and the other capital vices upon the virginal soul is, also, described in the *Ancren Riwle* in a figure strikingly reminiscent of Aldhelm's presentation of the vice and its seven subsidiary evils. Intimately connected with the viciousness of pride and the virtue of humility in a nun is a point of special interest to early English history, a point, in fact, in didactic material for the nun that needs the light of history to give it significance. Aldhelm adverted to the possibility of a nun's expecting to be shown deference and given precedence in church solely on account of her profession, while she neglects the interior virtue.[194] Bede casts light on this subject when in a homily [195] he remarks that in the procession [196] of the Greater Litanies to Saint Peter's the nuns follow third in rank, the clerics first, the abbots and monks second. A few lines from a metrical homily by Aelfric come ready to hand to illustrate again the rank of nuns in ecclesiastical society and incidentally to indicate how persistently, even in what appears to have been a merely casual expression, the idea of virginity attached itself as a matter of course to the religious. In this

---

[190] Cf. p. 47 above. Cf. the exemplum on the abject humility of a nun, p. 205 below.

[191] Cf. *op. cit.*, 148, 276.

[192] Cf. *ibid.*, 126-128, 130, 136.

[193] Cf. *ibid.*, 198-210.

[194] Cf. p. 31 above.

[195] Cf. Homilia xcvii " De Majora Litania ", PL 94, col. 499.

[196] On the subject of ecclesiastical processions in early Britain, cf. Cook, " Augustine's Journey from Rome through Richborough ", *Speculum* 1, (1926) 393-394. Cf. also " Die Litaniä oder Rogationes (Bittgänge) sollen von dem ganzen Clerus und Volke mit grosser Ehrfurcht begangen werden. " Council of Cloveshoe ", Hefele, 3; 564.

homily Aelfric summons up, as it were, a procession of saints from various ranks of clerical and religious life.   He mentions in order

> . . . halige bisceopas . . .
> and wise maesse-preostas . . .
> and manega munecas on mycelre drohtnunge.

As in Bede, the next in line are the virgins. Yet it is not the adjective " holy " or " wise ", or the phrase " of excellent conduct " that Aelfric employs to describe them.   They are, conventionally and traditionally,

> . . . claene maedenu þe criste þeowodon,
> on gastlicre drohtnunge for heora drihtnes lufan.

Impelled, no doubt, by force of literary association, he then adds,

> and ða synd nu ealle on ðam ecan wuldre
> for heora claennysse mid criste wunigende.[197]

The heavenly reward of virginity, consequently, is another idea expressed in Aldhelm and repeated faithfully in connection with the nun by the religious didactic writers.   The reward is depicted in terms of Apocalypse xiv, 3-4.   Venerable Bede uses it in *De Die Iudicii* [198] where a few lines witness to the medieval nun tradition, although they do not mention the nun specifically.   *Be Domes Daege,* the Anglo-Saxon version of the poem, is much later than the dates of Venerable Bede.[199]   It indicates, accordingly, the continued prominence of the idea.[200]   In his hymn for the feast of Saint Agnes, virgin-martyr, Venerable Bede again brings out the same idea—the heavenly reward for virginity according to the Apocalypse.   He refers in the hymn to the " virginal throng ", to being united with the " Lamb ", to the " new sons ".[201] Saint Boniface mentions this reward in his verses on virginity [202] and Alcuin uses it to encourage a religious in her trials.[203]   A ninth-century

---

[197] Cf. Skeat (2) 2, " Spel loca hwaenne mann wille," 350-352.

[198] Cf. PL 94; 637.   Cf. Legouis-Cazamian, 42.

[199] Cf. *op. cit.*, Lumby, vi.   For the quality of the translation.   Cf. Brandl in *Anglia* 4, 97 ff.

[200] Cf. Lumby, 18.

[201] Cf. *op. cit.*, PL 94; 626.

[202] Cf. *op. cit.*, MGH 1; 8-9.

[203] Cf. ep. 229, BRG 6; 738.   Cf. also ep. 279, 858-859.

anonymous Latin hymn on virgins [204] treats of practically the same subject. Aelfric, like Aldhelm [205] and Saint Augustine before him, extends the text after perfervid praise of the virgin's privilege to concede to others in heaven the pleasure at least of listening to the song that virgins alone can sing. But Aelfric sees a difficulty here. If those who have not lived as virgins on earth can participate in the bliss of the celestial song, they would seem to be the favored ones both in time and in eternity, for without having made the sacrifices of a life of virginity on earth, they enjoy without the effort involved in singing, the beauty of the melody in heaven. Aelfric finds a naïve solution of the problem, and with it reinstates virgins in their position of precedence. Virgins, he quickly adds, "have no labor in thus singing, but with ease and without effort reign in bliss during the heavenly song".[206] The Apocalypse text is elaborated in *Sawles Warde*,[207] a thirteenth-century allegory suggestive of the literature of the nun, but not necessarily such. It is referred to in *De Vita Eremitica* [208] and in two letters [209] of Peter of Blois in the twelfth century; in *Vices and Virtues;* [210] it is enlarged upon in *Hali Meidenhad*,[211] cited in the *Ayenbite of Inwyt*.[212] So identified with the idea of the religious life does the text become that, even in a staid chronicle, the phrase to "follow the Lamb" is employed to record a king's determination to relinquish the world and become a monk.[213]

Virginity, though its reward be glorious, entails, as Aldhelm points out, struggle. Both Alcuin [214] and Aelfric [215] repeat the thought, and it is rarely absent from the mystic ascetic litera-

---

[204] *Ymnis de Virginibus,* from a ninth-century *MS Aethelwoldi Episc. in Cod. Cantebrigien, LI, 1. 10 (pars ii),* Blume, *Anal. Hymn.* 51: 314-315.

[205] Cf. p. 28 above.

[206] Cf. Assmann, 43. Cf. also *ibid.,* 18-19.

[207] Cf. Morris (3) 261.

[208] Cf. *op. cit.,* col. 1459.

[209] Cf. ep. 35, 114; ep. 234, 535.

[210] Cf. *op. cit.,* 119.

[211] Cf. *op. cit.,* 21, 25, 30-31.

[212] Cf. *op. cit.,* 228, 267-268.

[213] Cf. Howlett, William of Newburgh's *Historia Rerum Anglicarum,* I; 77.

[214] Cf. ep. 229, 738.

[215] Cf. Assmann, 36.

ture [126] in Middle English. Alcuin observes that *certari est virgini,* if she is to be a worthy spouse of Christ, singing daily, *Dilectus meus mihi et ego illi, qui pascitur inter lilia,* that is, amidst the dazzling whiteness of virginity. He mentions another thought employed by Aldhelm and many followers [217] in allusion to faithful and to negligent religious: the parable of the wise and the foolish virgins with their lighted and their extinguished lamps.[218] Aelfric, basing his remarks on Saint Jerome, calls the life of one consecrated to God a martyrdom, and religious, " Christ's martyrs, victims not of one stroke, but of the daily battle which is required by the self-denial of monastic life ".[219] In conformity with this view, and in the tradition of the Fathers,[220] didactic writers keep before the eyes of nuns the *vitae* of the virgin martyrs as well as of the saints who were virgins but not martyrs of blood. Those cited in *De Laudibus Virginitatis* are the *vitae* commonly repeated, although *Juliana* as presented in the Cynewulfian epic-legend and in later versions [221] of the saint's life, the *vitae* of Saint Katherine and of St. Margaret are perhaps even more exclusively associated with literature written primarily to exalt virginity. The recurring account of Saint Ursula and the eleven thousand virgins is also pertinent. But rather than didactic literature about the nun, these hagiographical legends and pseudo-historical records are more correctly, literature read, perhaps, by the nuns [222] or, at least, heard by them as by the rest of the faithful, when delivered as homilies. Venerable Bede writes of the heavenly triumph of Saint Agnes.[223] He greatly enlarges upon Aldhelm's brief mention of Saint Scho-

[216] Cf. *Ancren Riwle,* 178 ff., 368 ff.; þe *Wohunge of Ure Lauerd,* Morris, (3) 275.

[217] Cf. Boniface, ep. 86, 234; Peter of Blois, ep. 234, 535; *Ayenbite of Inwyt,* 232-233; John of Bromyard, *Summa Praedicantium,* 55, col. 4; Lydgate, Poems, 178.

[218] Cf. ep. 229, 738.

[219] Assmann, 35-36, 39.

[220] Cf. St. Jerome, ep. 130, *Ad Demetriadem,* CSEL 56; 179; St. Ambrose, *De Virginibus,* I, 194. Cf. Bede, PL 94, col. 626; Aelred of Rievaulx, *De Vita Eremitica,* 1459-60; *Hali Meidenhad,* 64.

[221] On sources and later versions cf. Strunk, xxiii-xxix, xliii-xliv.

[222] Cf. *Ancren Riwle,* 244, 370.

[223] Cf. PL 94; 626.

lastica,[224] going to the source [225] for a detailed account of this saint, whose exemplary religious life was ever kept before the mind of every Benedictine nun. The source itself was translated into Anglo-Saxon [226] by Waerferth, one of the literary associates of Alfred the Great. Aelfric refers to her in a homily on Saint Benedict.[227] Aelfric's *Lives of the Saints* [228] also includes these representative *vitae* from the martyrology of the early Church and repeats many of the points mentioned in the analysis of this portion of the *De Laudibus Virginitatis* as contributory to the traditional nun-ideal.[229] They are found again in the fourteenth century collection of *Legends of the Saints in the Scottish Dialect*.[230] The Blessed Virgin is consistently given, as in Aldhelm, as the supreme model. Venerable Bede, presents her in the poem, *De Die Iudicii*,[231] as she is shown century after century, reigning over the courts of heaven where the resplendent virgins throng. Boniface represents her so.[232] In the *Christ* [233] of Cynewulf and again in *Hali Meiden-had*,[234] in *The Pearl*,[235] and in the *Ormulum*,[236] the Blessed Virgin is exalted as the first among women to consecrate her virginity to God. Alcuin refers to her as leading the virginal celestial choir.[237] Aelfric finds in each successive stage of Mary's earthly life a particular example and model for maidens, who, for Christ's love, have chosen to live in virginity.[238] He depicts innumerable virgins, following in her footsteps in this life, living purely, renouncing marriage, and binding themselves solely to Christ.[239] Peter of

[224] Cf. *In Die Festa Sanctae Scholasticae Virginis, ibid.*, cols. 480-489.

[225] *Liber Dialogorum* II, PL 66.

[226] *Übersetzung der Dialoge Gregors des Grossen*, Bib. d. ags. Pr. 5, xxxiii-xxxiv, 167-169.

[227] Cf. Thorpe, (2) 2; 182-184, 189.

[228] Cf. Skeat, (2) 1; 24-50, 90-114, 170-218; 2; 334-354.

[229] Whether Aelfric's and others' accounts of Saint Euphrasia or Eugenia and those also of Marina belong to the literature of the nun or of the monk is a nice question. Were it not that these women lived their religious life as monks, they would be considered as simple nuns.

[230] Cf. Metcalfe, 2, 47; 121-151, 346, 358, 368, 387, 424, 442.

[231] Cf. PL 94; 637.

[232] Cf. MGH I; 8.

[233] Cf. Cook, 11-12.

[234] Cf. *op. cit.*, 19-20.

[235] Cf. *op. cit.*, 14.

[236] Cf. *op. cit.*, I, 79-80.

[237] Cf. ep. 229, 738.

[238] Cf. Assmann, 32-33.

[239] Cf. *ibid*.

Blois refers in three different letters [240] to her as the model of virgins; *Hali Meidenhad* exalts her as such,[241] as does John of Bromyard later in the *Summa Praedicantium*.[242]

Fortifying nuns with the example of the martyrs against the difficulties of the virginal life, didactic writers, as Aldhelm did, ordinarily repeat the fact that the vow of chastity is not a precept, but a counsel. Aelfric becomes very explicit on this point—one extremely pertinent to later continental literature particularly and not utterly irrelevant to that of England. Virginity, he states definitely, is to be vowed to God only of one's free choice; a constrained or involuntary vow is not pleasing to God.[243] *Hali Meidenhad* brings out the liberty of choice between virginity and marriage, and although the entire thesis of the treatise is the superiority of the former state, the author explains unmistakably that virginity is only a counsel, and that what is counseled is not commanded.[244]

Aldhelm's elaborate and highly rhetorical condemnation of rich and gaudy clothing for nuns, however, is not repeated in the religious didactic [245] works of Anglo-Saxon and Middle English literature. The conventional comparison of the virgin with the wife, nevertheless, ordinarily leads to the suggestive remark that the former disregards vain adornment to give her attention to the acquisition of virtue. It is to be expected, however, that in a work like the treatise *De Vita Eremitica* [246] *ad Sororem* of Aelred of Rievaulx (1109-1166) and the *Ancren Riwle*,[247] addressed to

[240] Cf. ep. 36, 115; 55, 167; 234, 536.

[241] Cf. *op. cit.*, 19, 63-64. In the *Ancren Riwle*, the Blessed Virgin is mentioned as the model of silence (Cf. p. 66) and of solitude (Cf. p. 160).

[242] Cf. *op. cit.*

[243] Cf. Assmann, 34, 44.

[244] Cf. *op. cit.*, 18-20, 27.

[245] Although Ven. Bede records an abuse closely akin to this subject as prevailing for a time in the monastery of Coldingham, and St. Boniface, writing from the continent, mentions his fear lest the extravagant fashions of the world invade the cloister, and inspires legislation on the subject at the Council of Cloveshoe (747 A. D.) and although ecclesiastical legislation is repeatedly directed against religious' vanity in dress, the subject is strangely absent from the literature written deliberately for the instruction of nuns. Cf. p. 74 below.

[246] Cf. *op. cit.*, xx, col. 1458, and Horstmann, (10) 304-344.

[247] Cf. *op. cit.*, 418-420.

women of means, seeking a definite rule of life, simplicity of garb
should be enjoined. No regulation of this nature, however, can be
looked upon as a repetition of Aldhelm's flamboyant periods. This
part of Aldhelm's treatise is, moreover, the only one not carried
on by subsequent writers into the later didactic literature relative
to the nun.

b. Portrait of the Ideal Nun

Let us now consider Aldhelm's Chapters VI and XIV as the
materials occur in the later literature, for although the faithful and
constant repetition of one or the other scattered characteristics
suffices of itself to summon up the whole figure in the literature
after Aldhelm, some writers not only develop detached statements
but also repeat in their own words a complete picture of the whole
figure.

Alcuin, for instance, in prescribing the ideal to a nun,[248] accu-
rately depicts the outward decorum, interior occupation, and palpable impression of holiness created by Aldhelm's personification.
The points are—and their conformity to those of Chapters VI and
XIV is obvious—prayer, broken by study; constant attention to
the presence of God; sobriety [249] in manner; modesty and veracity
in word; probity and chastity of deed; edification of others by a
devout and regular life, a life looking, at every hour and at every
moment, toward death and eternity, not fearfully, but with ardent
affection, in expectation of Him Who during her life has been the
object of all her love.[250] Aelfric, also, in the course of a homily,
Natale Omnium Sanctorum,[251] presents the nun as one living most
purely, renouncing marriage, attaching herself to her Heavenly
Bridegroom with steadfast mind, holy conduct, and humble mien
and garb.[252]

The nun figure of vi-xiv repeatedly reappears in more or less

---

[248] Cf. ep. 46, 268-269. According to Wattenbach-Duemmler (BRG 6,
268) she was a nun pure and simple. Cf. " Ergo Hundreda monacha fuit,"
note 3, deduced from " regularis vitae devotio " in context. But cf. PL 100,
note C, col. 470.

[249] A word that in Middle English often is translated in this connection
by " sad ", creating thereby in the modern mind a mistaken impression of
the nun. Cf. p. 135 below.   [251] Cf. Thorpe, (2) 1; 546.

[250] Cf. *op. cit.*, 268.   [252] Cf. *op. cit.*

detail in subsequent didactic writings down to the thirteenth century.[253]   At this time the didactic writings take a new turn. The mysticism which has gradually been gaining way in English pious works since the time of Saint Anselm and Saint Bernard [254] becomes a determinative factor in the didactic writings of the thirteenth and fourteenth century.   From now on the writings in the vernacular are with few exceptions addressed to the anchoress rather than to the nun in the monastery, to the woman seeking mystical union with God in this life as well as a spiritual union with Him in the next.   The same details of advice are given in the mystical didactic writings as in the pre-mystical: many of the points addressed to Aldhelm's ideal nun are faithfully repeated, but now for the most part they are addressed to the anchoress; now the objective of the life of renunciation is changed; now the symbolical language of the earlier literature gives way to more specific aspirations, rendered, as it would seem from their expression in the vernacular, more simple and direct.   At least as represented in the earlier didactic literature, the nun merely sighed and panted for a spiritual union to be consummated only in the next life; [255] therefore, all was relatively vague when expressed in terms

[253] Cf. Aelred of Rievaulx, *De Vita Eremitica*, particularly cc. iii-iv, on retirement; cc. xxi-xxii on solitude for the protection of virginity; c. xxix on over-security and timorousness; c. xxxiii on pride, and c. xlvii on the delight of the virgin in contemplation, PL 32; 1451-1466. Cf. also Peter of Blois, ep. 234, PL 207; 535-537. Cf. the *Ormulum*, 1; lines 6303-6308, 218 and lines 6356-6357, 220 for general but suggestive features. Cf. also the virtues personified by the simple nuns in *The Abbey of the Holy Ghost*, Horstman, (15) 1; 323-325, 327, 329, 330, 332.

[254] Cf. Ueberweg-Geyer, 2; 149; Pourrat, 2; 12, 20, 29, 98. On the arguments and ramifications of this subject, see: Morris, (3); Einenkel, (2) 265; Vollhardt, 34, 46, 47, and *passim;* Deanesly, 38; Allen, (1) 138 ff., 186-187; Konrath, 85-98; Pourrat, 2, 245; Butler, (2) 245; 106, 127, 129, 138, 179-192 and (3) 89; Underhill, (2) 110-132; M. M. E., 529; Allen, (3) 201, 202, 210-211, 291, 292; Comper, xii, 139, 142, 150, 154-155, 156; Chapman, 94-95.

[255] Cf. p. 42 above. Of course, the monasticism of the time could not have been successful unless very definite objectives, such as the rewards that come from living the life of holiness, were realities for the nun of the time. The monastic literature of the times simply does not record these earthly rewards, being, to some extent, rhetorical exercises devoutly repeated from the Fathers.

of this earth. The anchoress can be more specific simply because she has an objective in view which is obtainable even in this life. For her, too, virginity is emphasized and its eternal reward extolled. She too abstains from all carnal intercourse, but she aspires to a mystical union with Our Lord on this earth as well as to a spiritual union hereafter.[256] Therefore, symbolism is dropped and its place taken by metaphors borrowed directly from the field of human love.[257] To one who knows nothing of the mystical life such metaphors might seem *a priori* as vague and shadowy as the symbolism of the pre-mystical didactic writings are stereotyped and artificial. But he has only to compare the mystical literature with the pre-mystical to note the greater precision of aspiration in the former and also the new tone of familiar, intimate personal affection for Christ.[258] Thus in the *Ancren Riwle*,[259] in the anonymous Middle English mystic literature, in the works of Richard Rolle, of Walter Hilton, of Juliana of Norwich, the details of Aldhelm's ideal simple nun are applied to anchoresses, but the anchoress in each instance is aspiring to a partial reward [260] here as well as to a complete reward hereafter.

V. *Additions Made By Later Writers to the Materials Found in Aldhelm*

Additions to the ideas expressed in *De Laudibus Virginitatis* are, on the contrary, comparatively meager and of minor importance. Venerable Bede seems to be the first to have utilized the patristic device [261] of personifying the active and the contemplative life—soon identified, however, with the secular and the religious—

[256] Cf. Horstman, (15) 1; *þe forme of Livyng*, 3-49, and *ibid.*, *Ego dormio*, 59.

[257] Cf. *Ancren Riwle*, 98, 100, 102, 103, 120, 218, 291, 388-392, 396-400; *On Ureisun of Oure Louerde*, 183-189; *þe Wohunge of Ure Lauerd*, 269-287; *Of Clene Maydenhod*, 466-467; *Incendium Amoris*, *Ego dormio*, Horstman, (15) 1, 58-59; *ibid.*, *þe forme of Livyng*, and poems of love, 71-82. Cf. also *Cell of Self-Knowledge*, Margery Kempe of Lynn, 55; *Scale of Perfection*, *passim*. Cf. on this subject Butler, (2) 160-161; Underhill, (3) 138.

[258] Cf. *ibid*.   [259] Cf. *ibid*.   [260] Cf. Underhill, (3) 428.

[261] Cf. Origen, Hom. xi, PG 13. It is common after him. Cf. St. Jerome, ep. 22, 177-178.

by the sisters, Martha and Mary.[262]   The device has carried over even into the literature proper where Mary's choice of the " better part " usually indicates the religious life of a nun.[263]   He also it is who in this period first stresses the reticence and restraint, if not timorousness, recommended the nun in presence of men [264] and later elaborated in the *Ancren Riwle* [265] and associated with the ideal nun as a literary figure.   Bede also is perhaps the earliest English homilist whose works are extant to use the text " *Et omnis qui relinquerit domum, vel fratres. . . .* " (Math. xix, 29) in connection with the religious life.[266]   Aelfric again employs the text [267] to effect, explaining in one place that the " *hundred-fold* " consists in spiritual parents and brethren in place of the natural ones relinquished, and in another, that the reward will be " above sons and daughters ".[268]   *Hali Meidenhad* [269] expresses the same idea.   Bede also is probably the first in England to give lyric expression [270] to the heavenly reward of virgins, a subject, as we have seen, upon which didactic writers [271] become dithyrambic.   Within this period Saint Boniface is the first to use in connection with the nun another Scriptural text which is conventionally [272] employed to designate the spiritual significance of the nun's vocation and God's love for her virginal virtue.   It is *Audi, filia, et inclina aurem tuam et obliviscere populum tuum, et domum patris tui, quia concupivit rex speciem tuam* (Ps. 44, 11-12).[273] *Alanis de Insulis* (1128-1203)

---

[262] Cf. Pseudo-Bede, *Homilia in Die Assumptionis Mariae*, PL 94, 420-421.

[263] Cf. L. E., II, 109; Aelred, *De Vita Eremitica*, xli, 1464; *Ancren Riwle*, 414-418; Hilton, *Scale of Perfection*, 109-110; Jones, *Mixed Life*, 10-11.

[264] Cf. *Homilia, In Feria Quarta Quatuor Temporum*, PL 94; 325.   Cf. also *ibid.*, 480-489.   Cf. Aelred de Rievaulx, *De Vita Eremitica*, 1451-2; 1458-9, and Peter of Blois, ep. 35, 114.

[265] Cf. *op. cit.*, 56-58, 174.

[266] Cf. *Homilia, In Natali Sancti Benedicti Episcopi*, PL 94; 226-228.

[267] Cf. Thorpe, (2) 1; 398.

[268] Cf. Assmann, 41.

[269] Cf. *op. cit.*, 25.

[270] Cf. *De Die Iudicii*, PL 94, cols. 633-638.   Cf. Lumby, *Be Domes Daege*, v-vi, and PL 94, col. 626.

[271] Cf. p. 50 above.

[272] Cf. the opening of St. Jerome's epistle on virginity to Eustochius, 22, 143-144.   [273] Cf. ep. 86, 234.

also employs the text, a commonplace in treatises on virginity.[274] Peter of Blois writes of it in letters [275] to nuns, and Walter Hilton in the *Scale of Perfection* [276] utilizes the text to voice a call from the world and distraction to a life of retirement and union with Christ. Boniface also is apparently the first writer in England to mention the virgin's " verdant crown ".[277] The figure of the virginal crown of flowers recurs in the correspondence of Boniface [278] and in *Hali Meidenhad*.[279] *The Pearl* depicts the bride of Christ as " coronde clene in vergynte " [280] and as crowned in heaven as a queen.[281] The virgin's crown is alluded to again in the *Ayenbite of Inwyt*.[282] Boniface also in a letter to a nun stresses the necessity and merit of patience in tribulation [283] An anonymous letter [284] in his collected correspondence—the style points to Lul as author—contains an idea expressed by Venerable Bede in the *Historia Ecclesiastica*,[285] by Alcuin,[286] and by many later writers in the historical genre, to denote the prestige of the religious as spouse of Christ. It is that greater nobility derives from religious life than from noble or royal birth.

Throughout all the religious didactic literature after Aldhelm it is implied, where virginity is mentioned as praiseworthy, that it be virginity preserved, as Cynewulf puts it, " unto the Lord ".[287] *The Ormulum* refers to this fact.[288] Aelfric, in addition, con-

---

[274] Cf. *"Ad Virgines"*, *Summa de Arte Praedicatoria*, xlvii, PL 120, col. 194.

[275] Cf. ep. 35, 113; 55, 167.

[276] Cf. *op cit.*, 121.

[277] Cf. MGH 1; 8, and St. Jerome, ep. 22, *Ad Eustochium*. Cf. Emerson, 252-261; Cornelius, 1055-1057; Tatlock, 176.

[278] Cf. ep. 14, 66.

[279] Cf. *op. cit.*, 31. Cf. Chaucer's use of the figure in " The Seconde Nonnes Tale ", *Canterbury Tales*, Skeat, (3) IV.

[280] *Op. cit.*, 23.

[281] Cf. *ibid.*, 13.

[282] Cf. *op. cit.*, 234-235.

[283] Cf. ep. 87, 235-236; 90, 240.

[284] Cf. ep. 95, 242.

[285] Cf. p. 86 below.

[286] Cf. ep. 21, 179.

[287] Cf. *The Christ*, 12. Cf. also " Memoriae nostrae puella dudum nobilis in saeculo, nunc nobilior Deo, cum . . . ad sacrosanctum altare confugit."—St. Ambrose, *De Virginibus* II, x, PL 16, col. 206, and " quia uirginitas est, sed quia deo dicata est, honoratur . . . "—St. Augustine, *De Sancta Virginitate*, viii, 241-242.

[288] Cf. *op. cit.*, 1; 79-80.

fronted with contemporary social disorders which affect cloister as
well as home, condemns religious abuses that, long after, enter into
the theme of literary works, first having been registered in historical
records [289] of later Medieval England. Having stated the worthless-
ness of a constrained vow,[290] Aelfric turns to the opposite extreme.
Apparently in an effort to present the seriousness and responsibility
of pronouncing a vow and to prevent its being taken lightly, he
observes that a maiden who has voluntarily assumed the obligation
of a vow of chastity and then violates it is grievously guilty before
God. Never again, as the *Ancren Riwle* [291] and *Hali Meidenhad* [292]
also explain, may that consecrated one call herself " virgin " or hope
for the " hundred-fold " and the rewards peculiar to chastity.[293]
She may, of course, return to God by penance,[294] but the " white
robe " of the " maiden throng " " with blossoms hung " is relinquished forever. Not satisfied with implying the possibility of this
event, Aelfric, in the moral appended to *Judith,* plainly states the
existence of nuns who live scandalously and as bluntly reveals their
future punishment in hell. But lest the nuns to whom he is
directing the moral lose confidence in their power to resist evil
as Judith had resisted it, he explains to them, among other ideas
already cited, a point that Milton makes the theme of *Comus,* i. e.
that maidenhood and purity contain in themselves very great
might.[295] When we recall that England at the time is infested with
Danes as inimical to cloistral virtue as the leader of the enemy
encamped upon the plains of Esdralon was to the virtue of the
magnificent Judith and that secular persons are making lamentable
inroads upon monastic privacy; [296] that monasticism itself is greatly
degenerate, Aelfric's drastic pictures and plain speech are not so

[289] Cf. p. 125 ff. below.

[290] Cf. p. 54 above.

[291] Cf. *op. cit.,* 164.

[292] Cf. *op. cit.,* 14-15.

[293] Cf. Assmann, 21-22; 33-34; 115. Cf. " suscitare uirginem non potest
post ruinam."—St. Jerome, ep. 22, *Ad Eustochium,* 150.

[294] Cf. *op. cit.*

[295] Cf. *ibid.,* 115.

[296] Cf. the practically contemporary homilies of Wulfstan, particularly
Larspell, Napier, 269 and 271. Cf. also Kinard, 56-57, and Map, *De Nugis
Curialum,* 209-210.

surprising—unusual as they are in this material. In Aelfric is found mention of another abuse that has made its impress upon literature as well as upon history. Some parents, he states, to their discredit, wish to commit their most unpromising child to the Church.[297] Leaving the consequences of such a practice undeveloped, Aelfric is satisfied with condemning it and with reminding his readers that to God only the best should be offered.[298]

Finally to the virtues of the nun shown in *De Laudibus Virginitatis* Alcuin adds charity,[299] not indeed specifically recommended before him in this literature, but certainly necessarily implied. Peter of Blois adverts to it;[300] and Middle English mystic literature, of course, recognizes it as the prime requisite—an essential like humility—for union with God.[301] Aelfric adds the obligation to practice the eight beatitudes;[302] to eschew malicious words and bitter thoughts.[303] The *Ayenbite of Inwyt* also states the need of good works.[304] The *Ancren Riwle,* of course, expounds in detail a complete rule of perfection and the particular virtues and practices obligatory upon a recluse. Þe *Wohunge of Ure Lauerd,*[305] Rolle's *Ego dormio,*[306] *The Amending of Life, the Commandment,*[308] and the *Abbey of the Holy Ghost,*[309] in conformity with the purpose and the tender sentiments of mystic literature, would have the soul living in union with Christ practice poverty because He was poor, and in delicate sympathy constantly meditate upon His sorrowful passion.[310]

[297] Cf. Assmann, 35.

[298] Cf. *ibid.*

[299] Cf. ep. 229 and 279, 738, 858. Cf. "Haec enim docet humilitatem, qua et adquirat et custodiat caritatem."—St. Augustine, *De Sancta Virginitate,* xxxi, 269.

[300] Cf. ep. 36, 115, and 234, 535.

[301] Cf. Hilton, *The Scale of Perfection,* xxiv, and 150-151. Cf. St. Augustine, *ibid.*

[302] Cf. Assmann, 45-47.

[303] Cf. *ibid.,* 46-47.

[304] Cf. *op. cit.,* 227.

[305] Cf. *op. cit.,* 277, 279.

[306] Cf. *op. cit.,* 92-100.

[307] Cf. Heseltine, 117.

[308] Cf. Heseltine, 6-7.

[309] Cf. Horstman, (15) 1; 322.

[310] Cf. Aelred of Rievaulx, *De Vita Eremitica,* xxxix, 1463; *Ancren Riwle,* 258-260; 18, 34-38, 108, 136, 188, 404-406, þe *Wohunge of Ure Lauerd,* 279, 281, 283, 285; *Cell of Self Knowledge,* 53, etc.

7

VI. *Summary*

The examination of the religious-didactic works of England during the period of origins until the approach of the fifteenth century, i. e., the works of Aldhelm, the non-historical works of his late contemporaries, Venerable Bede and Saint Boniface, the Cynewulfian poems, the works of Alcuin and of the anonymous writers in the eighth and the ninth centuries, the Anglo-Saxon translations emanating from the School of Alfred the Great, the works of Aelfric and his contemporaries; treatises and correspondence of the following centuries; the *Ancren Riwle,* the homilies, allegorical compositions, prayers, and spiritual works associated with the mysticism of the thirteenth and fourteenth centuries;— a study of all these reveals that the ideal nun-figure presented in the *De Laudibus Virginitatis* of Aldhelm, written at the close of the seventh or in the early eighth century, persists intact and with the acquisition of very few additions throughout the entire period.

In *De Laudibus Virginitatis* the time-honored patristic points are set down. In grotesqueness of expression and ideas Aldhelm does not usually go beyond his patristic sources, which he here and there acknowleges, but he does frequently outdo them in elaborate treatment [311] of details. The other didactic writers do not reflect the elaborateness of Aldhelm's treatment, but they do repeat, with all the florid patristic rhetoric, the ideas found in him and in the Fathers. Out of these repetitions evolves the simple nun of Anglo-Saxon and Middle English literature. Aldhelm practically exhausts the subject for the medieval mind. He completely exhausts the arsenal of medieval rhetoric on the simple nun. A late contemporary of his school, Saint Boniface, has very many of the ideas of Aldhelm on the subject. It is to be noted that with the passage of time the repetitions of these materials tend to become more selective, more precise, and specific. There are some slight additions in ideas to the *De Laudibus Virginitatis* in the following centuries, but not one of them is so striking or so independent as not to be a possible development or corollary of some passage in that work.

[311] The highly rhetorical statements have their effect upon the non-didactic literature. Cf. pp. 94 ff. and 118 ff. below.

Moreover, everyone of them, I believe, is also a patristic borrowing. This is true even of an epistolary treatise that stands out from the other didactic writings of later times because of its comparatively independent treatment, namely, Alcuin's description of an ideal abbess, in which details are added to the traditional material in Aldhelm on the ideal simple nun. Aelfric, writing amid the hard realities of Danish occupation and Benedictine Reform of the tenth and the eleventh centuries, discourses simply and directly upon the subject of the ideal nun. He is stating and correcting monastic abuses current in his time and not merely expressing the rhetorical diatribes of the traditional literature before him. His tone, accordingly, is somewhat clearer and more penetrating than that of his predecessors and of his followers, but he reiterates, nevertheless, the traditional language and ideas of Aldhelm on the ideal nun.

The process of selection and tendency toward greater precision continues down to the fifteenth century. When we come to the Middle English mystic-ascetic literature, many of the detailed elaborations of the *De Laudibus Virginitatis* are dropped. Virginity alone of the time-honored points is left. From now on the sublimity, the superiority of virginity, the means of preserving it, its heavenly reward are emphasized even more than in the past, in harmony with the mystic note that enters English literature at this time from another patristic source, i. e. Saint Augustine, through Anselm, Saint Bernard, and the contemporary mystic philosophers.

From Aldhelm's time, however, virginity is emphasized in this literature far more than the two other evangelical counsels. It is singled out for almost exclusive attention in literature on the ideal nun, because of the hold tradition has upon the genre. In early Latin patristic writings from which this material derives, virginity was the great Christian antithesis to paganism;[312] it became a synonym for Christian asceticism.[313] " Even later, when monasticism arose and monastic organization made feasible the practice of perfect Poverty, and even still later, when it made obligatory the practice of perfect Obedience, the ascetical life was still looked upon as a life of continence. . . . In that day a profession of

[312] Cf. Pourrat, 1; 58, 57-64.   [313] Cf. Murphy, 30.

Chastity upon entrance into a monastery was a profession of monasticism itself." [314] Didactic writers, other than authors of religious rules, wherein both poverty and obedience are enjoined according to the nature of the institute, were men bound by a literary convention. When they wrote, they turned to a model; borrowing its content, they repeated Scripture and patristic; imitating its style, they continued an established mode of symbolism.

This symbolism was so widely accepted that phrases from it, which are almost meaningless to us without elaborate study, had immediate connotation for the medieval mind regardless of the presence or absence of a context. I refer to the snatches of ascetic and monastic principles and the fragments of scriptural texts that turn up now in isolation and again in what to us would seem meaningless profusion and confusion throughout the religious didactic literature of England. Each isolated detail is rich in personal connotation and association. Each detail, from constant repetition with the same significance, has become so familiar and its connotation so established and unerring in the impression which it makes, that, of itself, it both suggests the entire picture of the ideal nun and creates the peculiar literary symbolistic milieu in which she moves. Each part suggests the whole. This power of suggestion and wealth of association is the result of two circumstances. The first: that, in the patristic source of these details there is a concrete characterization,[315] a sketch of the ideal nun—the consecrated virgin, a summing up of all the details in a personal illustration of their perfect practice. Details and picture, occurring together so frequently in such authoritative contexts, become inseparably associated, so that the personal picture represents a perfect synthesis of the details. The literary art of the patristic authors, nevertheless, has created in these pictures so definite an impression of unity and of authentic human personality that the medieval mind, even while analyzing them into their component didactic factors, does not recognize a mere mechanical collection of moralizing items, but a living embodiment of monastic perfection.

[314] *Ibid.* Cf. also Pourrat, 1; 64.

[315] Cf. St. Jerome, *Regula Monacharum*, xxix, PL 30; 416; St. Ambrose, *De Virginibus*, PL xvi, 200.

Even the pictures of the antithesis of the ideal which are found in these treatises contribute toward the defining and intensifying of the personality of their foil. The second circumstance from which the effectiveness of each separate detail derives is the fact that each has reference, in turn, to the personification. So long and so constantly have the details been reiterated that—to repeat—each item, such as those traced here throughout the religious didactic literature of early England, automatically calls up the ideal nun. The fact that the *De Laudibus Virginitatis,* the first treatise on the subject of virginity in the literature of England, employs both isolated details and concrete picture exactly in the manner of the Fathers merely strengthens the tradition and spurs it on through centuries of insular literature.

A mere allusion to the " hundred-fold " or to " the white-robed throng following the Lamb " suffices, consequently, to suggest the whole tradition and to conjure up the presence of the ideal nun as pictured therein. Such items, moreover, have become symbols. One who knows the literature of religious didacticism needs but the slightest suggestion of one of them to be reminded of all of them and also of the ideal nun with whom they are invariably associated. Of such details is the literary tradition formed. Each detail has in itself the power and suggestion of all the rest. With such impress and tenacity, moreover, has the literary symbolism of the ideal nun fastened upon medieval didactic thought and expression that its vocabulary and phraseology and idealogy have carried over therefrom into other literary genres. Historiographers and hagiographers, as well as authors of official ecclesiastical documents and epistles, when writing, respectively, of nuns or to them, invariably clothe their thought in this traditional garb. Their ideas become the conventional ones of religious didacticism on the nun.

The force, then, of a seemingly mere cliché, like "with lamp in hand ", is so important in the creation of the literary tradition of the nun that if its significance is not understood, not only is the significance of that particular idea lost, but lost also is the significance of the constant repetition of that idea throughout the religious didactic literature of England. Two points, therefore, are essential to an understanding of the genesis of the literary tradition of the nun in English literature: the original patristic denotation and connotation of these details and the recognition of the purpose of their persistent repetition with this same denotation and connotation throughout the early literature of England.

Aldhelm's treatment happens to be the first chronologically in a long and literal and, in many respects, verbatim tradition. That Aldhelm was the source for any or all of those that follow him cannot be shown, for the patristic forerunners upon whom Aldhelm seems to have leaned so heavily were also available for all the writers who followed him.[316]

The ideal nun-figure, moreover, traditional in this literature, is, with the exception of the ideal abbess depicted by Alcuin, that of the simple subject-nun depicted first by Aldhelm in the extent literature of Anglo-Saxon England. The analysis of the materials has shown the figure to be essentially a personification, a composite of patristic symbols for the virtue of virginity and of the simple monastic virtues of obedience, studiousness, and retirement, as ancillary to virginity. Humility protects her virginity. Prayer (articulate after the thirteenth century), ardent love, and contempt for the vanity of the world make of her a figure suggestive of beauty more of heaven than of earth. She becomes a mediate source of the quasi-romantic form, "half a spirit, half a nun", familiar in later English literature.

By the fourteenth century, at least, the ideal nun-figure, as traced from Aldhelm on, is already fully launched in literature proper. John Gower in the *Mirour de L'Omme*,[317] but particularly in *Vox Clamantis* presents a figure suggestive of that in Aldhelm's chapters VI and XIV. The passage in *Vox Clamantis* on the ideal

---

[316] Cf. Manitius, (3) v-vi.

[317] Cf. *op. cit.*, Macaulay, lines 16830; 16838-16848, p. 195; 16852-16882, p. 196; 16972, 17010-17011, 17012, 17020-17023; 16998-17000, p. 197; 17053-17055, p. 198; 21160-21161, p. 239. By this time even the most-quoted lines,

> " O tresgentile dame, simple et coie
> Des graces et des vertus replenis ",

of one of Gower's balades to his lady suggest the now-formed literary nun-figure. Cf. *ibid.*, 346.

nun [318] conforms closely to Aldhelm's composite picture and that on the supremacy of virginity [319] not only repeats much of the actual phraseology but at the same time incorporates many of the isolated statements on virginity found in *De Laudibus Virginitatis*. From Gower's time, at least, Aldhelm's nun-figure is one of the traditional figures in English literature.

[318] Cf. *op. cit.*, Macaulay, lines 637-638 and 639-646, p. 184.
[319] Cf. *ibid.*, lines 547-576, pp. 184-185.

CHAPTER III

The Nun in the Historiographical Literature, Seventh to Sixteenth Century

I. *Introduction*

The earliest references to nuns in the extant historical records of England are found in four *vitae;* three, of the life of Saint Cuthbert and one, of the life of Saint Wilfrid by Eddius. They were written at various times in the last two or three decades of the seventh century or the first two or three decades of the eighth.[1] While we cannot be precise about their dating, we can arrange, on the basis of their interdependence, the order of their appearance. And a further study of content reveals that all of them preceded by various intervals the publication of Bede's *Historia Ecclesiastica,* two of them being earlier compositions of Bede himself, and the other two serving as sources for his pages.[2]

The abbess, not the simple nun, appears in the pages of these *vitae.* To her and to her various gifts and experiences considerable space is given in these brief versions. Outstanding in the three *vitae* of Saint Cuthbert, two of which were written by Venerable Bede, is the figure of the royal Abbess Elfleda of Whitby. A guest at her monastery, Saint Cuthbert reveals his knowledge of future and distant events. On another occasion at her request and against his wont, he meets the abbess and, conceding to her tearful importunity, foretells how long her brother will reign and who will suc-

---

[1] The earliest of the four was written by an anonymous monk of Lindisfarne who was a contemporary of St. Cuthbert (d. 687). Plummer (1; cxlvi, cxlviii) dates the metrical and the prose versions of Bede's *vitae* of St. Cuthbert " Before 705 " and "About 721 ", respectively. The *vita* of St. Wilfrid by Eddius, the last of the four, was written, according to Raine, (2) 1, xxxii, not long after 710.

[2] The *vita* by the anonymous monk of Lindisfarne was used by Bede in both his *vitae* of St. Cuthbert; Eddius' life of St. Wilfrid is a source for H. E. V. xix, of Bede. Cf. Plummer, 2; 315.

ceed him upon the throne.[3] These instances of the intercourse of
the saintly ecclesiastic with the royal abbess are repeated as late as
the fifteenth century.[4] Only two of the abbesses of whom Eddius
treats in his life of Saint Wilfrid concern us here. And even of
these two, only one incident in the life of each calls for specific
mention. All else to the point—and there is little else such—is
found, with much besides, in the pages of the *Historia Ecclesiastica*
in that detail and emphasis characteristic of later historiographical
accounts.

One of the incidents that becomes traditional in later versions,
although somehow unmentioned by Bede, either in the *vitae* or in
the *Historia Ecclesiastica,* has to do with the statesmanlike Abbess
Elfleda at the time of the Synod on the Nid in 705. As told in
Eddius's *Vitae Wilfridi Episcopi,* she is present with another
abbess at the death-bed of King Ecgfrid, her brother, bitter enemy
of Wilfrid. The dying king expresses the wish that his successors
live in concord with Wilfrid. Elfleda becomes the posthumous mes-
senger of his wish. In 705, in conformity with a mandate of the
Holy See, the Synod of the Nid is convened and to it repair the
King, princes, and various high-placed ecclesiastics to restore harmony between Wilfrid and the other dignitaries of church and state.
Elfleda is the spokesman of the late king and in delivering her message she brings the assembly to a decision.[5] The role of the Abbess
Elfleda here recalls the similar part played by the Abbess Hilda in
the Synod of Whitby as related by Bede in the *Historia Ecclesiastica* and by Eddius in his *Vita Wilfridi* and reported so often in
English medieval historiography. From Eddius and not Bede,
however, the statesmanship of Elfleda enters the medieval chronicles of England to swell the English conception of the typical
Anglo-Saxon abbess.[6]

[3] Cf. anon. *Vita,* S. C. AA. SS. Boll., Martii 2; 121-123; Bede, Metrical
Vita, ed. Giles, 1; 18-19, 22, 24; Prose *Vita, ibid.,* 4; 284-290, 294-296,
312-316.

[4] Cf. Aelfric's homily, *Depositio S. Cuthberti Episcopi,* Thorpe, (2) 2;
146, 150; NLA, 1; 225-230. Cf. Fowler, *Life of St. Cuthbert* (c. 1450),
77, 83, 94-96.

[5] Cf. *op. cit., Raine,* (2) 1; 88-92.

[6] Cf. *Vita, S. Wilfridi,* Fridegoda, Raine, (2) 1; 144-145; G. P., 234,
242-243.

The sole other incident contributory to the tradition of the abbess which is independent of the touch of Bede is the story of the wayward queen who became an exemplary abbess, Her name was Ermenburg. She was the sister-in-law of Abbess Elfleda, as Eddius tells us, and the second wife of King Ecgfrid. Bishop Wilfrid had been so influential with the King and his first wife that the latter, under Wilfrid's direction, had separated from the King and had become a nun. With the King, Wilfrid's prestige continued, and in opposition to his influence Ermenburg was become his implacable enemy. Finally she poisoned the King against him; caused him to be cast into prison, and flaunted his sacred relics as ornaments of her person. *Arrepta a daemone,* in the language of Eddius, and seized with an attack of violent pain while sojourning at the monastery of Abbess Ebba, the aunt of the King, the Queen recovers only when, upon the advice of the abbess, the King promises to release Wilfrid.[7] On the death of the King, this Queen, as the *Vita* puts it and later Chronicles record,[8] *de lupa . . . agna Domini, et perfecta Abbatissa, materque familas optima commuta est.*[9]

From Bede rather than from his predecessors—so far as extant literature can tell the story and except for the two passages of Eddius' life of Saint Wilfrid above referred to—arise those traits and the incidents illustrative of traits so faithfully repeated of nuns by English medieval chronicles. It is not merely that they emphasize the same traits as he and in the same way, but they tell the same stories which he tells to fill out the picture. Many references to nuns in the chronicles are, however, of an incidental, barren, and utterly isolated character. These, of course, are not taken into consideration here. Only those that have entered into literature either directly by providing literary material, or indirectly by shaping or helping to shape a type or that contradict a type are cited. Apart from these negligible records, nevertheless, so closely do later historiographers adhere to the *Historia* in the monastic

---

[7] Cf. Raine (2) 1; 50, 55-56.

[8] The following works repeat the incident: *Vita S. Wilfridi,* Fridegoda (c. 950), Raine, (2) 1; 132; G. P. 232—12th century; An. Ord. Ben. 1; 533—12th century; CM, I, 290—13th century.

[9] Raine (2) 1; 34.

essentials as presented by Bede, so little do they add to or subtract from these dominant traits, that only a searching scrutiny of their works reveals deviations in detail. These deviations consist chiefly in abbreviating the words of Bede as the alluvial accretion of each generation of chroniclers swells the total deposit to be carried on, and in the inevitable changes of nomenclature, as the new chronicler adds stories of his own time to the annals which he has received, or, after the eleventh century, in elaborations borrowed from the didactic writings. Bede's *Historia Ecclesiastica,* so far as we know, was the first chronicle of Anglo-Saxon England down to 731. It is the sole authority for us of its period, except for the scanty *vitae* mentioned above. Probably it was the sole authority, with the same scanty exceptions for subsequent chroniclers. They either go back to the *Historia Ecclesiastica* or to some lost hypothetical work which both followed most loyally. What Bede relates, they relate before adding their individual contributions and what he emphasizes, they ordinarily emphasize and develop according to his pattern in those parts of their accretions which are original. A somewhat detailed study of the *Historia Ecclesiastica,* therefore, is the inevitable approach to the centuries that follow and, because of the repetitious features of English chronicles, is at the same time a digest and unavoidable anticipation of most of the significant historiographical materials of pertinence to this study.

In the *Historia Ecclesiastica* Venerable Bede refers with more or less elaboration to twenty-four distinct nuns,[10] and on another occasion he treats of the nuns of an entire community *in globo*.[11] Some of these references extend over as much as four chapters of the *Historia*.[12] Nuns are so prominent a feature in his work because the leaders among them were prominent features in the life of the times of which he treats. These leaders—all but two[13] of whom are designated as abbesses—are named and dated; their

[10] Cf. *op. cit.*, I, III, viii, 142-144; xi, 149-150; xxiv, 178-179; xxv, 183; IV, vi, 218-219; vii, 219-220; viii, 220-221; ix, 221-224; x, 224; xvii, 243-246; xviii, 247-248; xxi, 252-258; xxii, 258-262; xxiii, 262-266; xxiv, 267-268; V, iii, 285-286.

[11] Cf. *ibid.*, IV, xxiii, 262-266.

[12] Cf. *ibid.*, III, xxiv-xxv; IV, xxi-xxii, 177-189, 252-262.

[13] Cf. *ibid.*, III, viii, 142-144, and IV, xxi, 253.

ancestry is traced when significant, and their influence upon reigning sovereigns is told. Their remarkable monastic virtues are brought to the fore, reinforced by accounts of the miracles performed during their earthly or posthumous careers. Bede's accounts of the abbesses are, in truth, eulogies.

Nine [14] of the nuns mentioned by Bede in the *Historia* are drawn into the narrative merely as witnesses to the marvelous or glorious in the life, death, or posthumous career of the abbess. They are simple religious women without high position in the community and without recorded impress upon their times. But they have a considerable influence upon subsequent English literature and at least they exemplify for the first time in the extant literature of England that nun who sums up in herself the religious, monastic perfection expounded by the Fathers of the Church and that abstract of virtues which is found in the didactic literature contemporary and subsequent to Bede and which is repeated so often in creative literature down to our own day. The only impressive difference between Bede and Bradshaw here is the striking interval of time which separates them.

In fact, even in the *Historia Ecclesiastica* these simple nuns constitute a type. Each being the witness or in some manner connected with an account of a supernatural manifestation and presented always within the intimacy of the cloister's seclusion and apart from the official administrative activity of the monastery, gives, in Bede's treatment, the impression of radiant spirituality,[15] of modest retirement,[16] of simplicity,[17] of a character untouched by guile and devoid of worldliness. She is represented as something childlike—docile,[18] genial in obedience,[19] attractive to children,[20] and exhibiting at all times a loyal affection [21] for the

[14] Cf. *ibid.*, 1) III, xi, 150; 2) IV, viii, 220-221; 3) *ibid.* 221; 4) IV, ix, 221-224; 5) *ibid.* 222-223; 6) IV, xxi, 257; 7) *ibid.* 8) *ibid.* 258; 9) V, iii, 285-286.

[15] Cf. *op. cit.*, IV, viii, 221; ix, 223-224; xxi, 257, 258.

[16] Cf. *ibid.*, III, xi, 149, 150.

[17] Cf. *ibid.*, IV, ix, 222-223; V, iii, 286.

[18] Cf. *ibid.*, IV, ix, 223, for two instances.

[19] Cf. *ibid.* and III, xi, 149-150.

[20] Cf. *ibid.*, IV, viii, 220-221.

[21] Cf. *ibid.*, IV, xi, 222; 223; xxi, 257; 258.

Mother Abbess. Even when no longer young [22] she creates the impression of simplicity and childlike docility. These points, hinted at in the *Historia Ecclesiastica,* become very concrete in the works that hold up the type of the ideal nun.

The abbess, in Bede's treatment, inevitably produces a different impression upon the reader. She is not a witness to the marvelous exclusively, shut off from the currents of the world. She is a matter-of-fact, workaday, responsible person. In Anglo-Saxon England she is a great force even beyond the walls of the monastery.[23] Compelled by circumstances, she plays a statesman's role.[24] The historian, therefore, must present her, and must present her in connection with problems which she helped to solve. The abbess, too, then, becomes a type, but forged from the everyday realities of her actual career in Anglo-Saxon England. Without the example of the patristic writings, she must have become what she did become in Bede's treatment.

So definitely crystallized do the two distinct types become, moreover, that by the eleventh century at latest they are used to describe successive portions of the same monastic career. The story of the pre-abbatial career of a given religious conforms to Bede's pattern of the simple nun; that of the abbatial, to the traditional abbess type. The respective portions of such *vitae* must, necessarily, be considered separately and as distinct in a study fashioned on the lines of this dissertation.

II. *The Abbess*

1. In the *Historia Ecclesiastica* of Venerable Bede

The abbesses in the *Historia Ecclesiastica* are all, with one exception,[25] mentioned as women of high social station—the sister of distinguished abbots and bishops;[26] near relatives of ruling

[22] Cf. *ibid.,* IV, ix, 223; 223-224; IV, xxi, 257.

[23] Cf. Cabrol, 206.

[24] Cf. H. E. III, xxv, 183, and Raine (2) 88-92.

[25] Of one abbess the station is not mentioned. Cf. *op. cit.,* V, viii, 285-286.

[26] Cf. *ibid.,* III, ix, 149; IV, vi, 218.

sovereigns;[27] princesses;[28] queens.[29] Abbatial dignity enhances their prestige, for beyond remaining intimate with their royal relatives and friends, they become as abbesses the advisers of kings and princes. Why this is so is explained by Bede in the *Historia* in the case of one abbess only, namely, that she herself had an excellent corps of counsellors.[30] Presumably the position of abbess gave its incumbent opportunity for exhibiting those statesmanlike qualities and the executive capacity that had raised her to the abbatial rank.

In referring to their government of monasteries Bede emphasizes their prudence [31] and wisdom.[32] Placed at the head of a newly-founded or of an extensive double monastery, they devote themselves to the establishment or maintenance of regular discipline, themselves setting the example by their edifying conduct and conformity to rule.[33] One instance given by Bede does not persuade us of the administrative virtues of the abbess. It is the case of a monastery whose members have lost their ideals *in toto;* and yet the abbess is for a long time unaware of the fact.[34] Although this would seem inexcusable in any superior and inexplicable in a wise and prudent one, Bede concentrates in his story of her upon her saintliness as a religious and does not seem to feel that he is called upon to state anything as to her abbatial qualities.

As superior of a community the abbess' great care is directed to the provision of all that her subjects need;[35] hence, both in a spiritual and in a material sense the abbess merits the title, Mother, a term of affection and reverence applied frequently to the abbesses of whom Bede writes. One, he remarks, is mother not only to her vast community but mother to all who know her,[36] so all-embra-

---

[27] Cf. *ibid.*, IV, xvii, 244; IV, xvii, 243; IV, xxi, 252.

[28] Cf. *ibid.*, III, viii, 142; III, xxiv, 178-179; IV, xxiv, 267-268.

[29] Cf. *ibid.*, III, viii, 142; IV, xvii, 243.

[30] Cf. *ibid.*, III, xxi, 153; IV, xxii, 260.

[31] Cf. *op. cit.*, IV, xxi, 254.

[32] Cf. *ibid.*, IV, xxi, 253.

[33] Cf. *ibid.*, IV, vi, 219; IV, ix, 222; IV, x, 224; IV, xvii, 244; IV, xxi, 253; 254.

[34] Cf. *ibid.*, IV, xxiii, 262-266.

[35] Cf. *ibid.*, IV, viii, 219; IV, x, 224.

[36] Cf. *ibid.*, IV, xxi, 255. Whether or not " Mother " was an official

cing is her devotion and solicitude.[37]   Nuns call the abbess " My
most dear Mother " [38] and Venerable Bede describes one as " A
careful Mother ",[39] the " Mother and nurse of consecrated
women " ; [40] another, " The virgin Mother of many nuns ".[41]
So genuine, reverent, and ardent is the filial affection which the
abbess wins that it seems no less spontaneous than that enjoyed
by one abbess who is actually [42] the mother of one of her nuns.[43]

The abbess in Bede is a person of many tasks, monastic and
extra-monastic.   Sometimes she erects new monasteries,[44] she is
greatly concerned about the reverent interment of the dead and
about selecting the proper location [45] for the community cemetery
—a hallowed spot and one that figures largely in Bede's account as
the scene of supernatural phenomena.[46] Again she sets the brothers [47] of the monastery to work at rearing a stately church.[48]
Twice [49] it is mentioned to an abbess' praise that she has the bodies
in the over-crowded community cemetery removed to a more suitable location.   Three instances are given wherein at the instigation
of the living abbess the remains of a specially venerated predecessor
are exhumed and reinterred more honorably.[50]

The abbess is presented not only as taking an active interest
and influential part in the life of the laymen about the monas-

designation for a religious superior at that time is aside the point.   The
context of the term in Bede implies in the case of all these women a tribute
to their mother-like solicitude.

[37] Cf. *ibid.*

[38] *Op. cit.*, IV, ix, 223.

[39] *Ibid.*, IV, vii, 219.

[40] *Op. cit.*, IV, vi, 219.

[41] *Ibid.*, IV, xvii, 244.

[42] Cf. *ibid.*, V, iii, 285-286.

[43] The bond of nature, however, is evident in this case, for the abbess
looks forward to her daughter's succeeding to her office.

[44] Cf. *ibid.*, III, xxiv, 179; IV, xvii, 244; IV, xxi, 257.   Cf. Giles (2)
112, 116.

[45] Cf. H. E., IV, vii, 219; IV, x, 224; IV, xvii, 244.

[46] Cf. *ibid.*, III, viii, 144; IV, vii, 219-220; IV, x, 224; 224-225.

[47] Cf. *ibid.*, III, viii, 144.

[48] *Ibid.*

[49] Cf. *ibid.*, IV, x, 224; xvii, 244.

[50] Cf. *ibid.*, III, viii, 143; 144; IV, xvii, 244-245.

tery,[51] but also as controlling the education and ecclesiastical training of the monks.[52] In one instance, moreover, she is held personally responsible by the bishop for the medical treatment given the
sick [53] and in another is shown hastening at night out of the monastery proper to the guest house where a visitor lies suddenly
stricken.[54] It is enlightening to observe that it is the abbess herself who responds to the late summons at the monastery door;[55]
that it is she of whom the attendant is first in search and that it
is only when matters have been submitted to her that the priest
is called,[56] the abbess herself and her attendant nun going to the
monks' residence in the monastery on the errand.[57] She it is also
who, when exorcism and all remedies fail, decides what is to be
done to relieve the possessed man, and who, finally, has recourse
to the application of a relic which she has sent the nun back to
the monastery to procure.[58] It is patent that all—nuns, monks,
and priests—defer to her. Within the monastery she has supreme
power.

Because of the enormous reach of monastic institutions, the
abbess was inevitably a power in political and economic as well
as social life. In virtue of this power she participates in a synod
of national and ecclesiastical import and there with her followers
is a noteworthy factor within a party.[59] An abbess is seen visiting
another monastery there to converse with a visiting queen.[60] Kings
and princes visit her and seek her counsel [61] and dignitaries and
learned men give her the benefit of their wisdom.[62] The abbess as
Venerable Bede portrays her in the *Historia Ecclesiastica* is a
woman eminent in church and state.

But it is virtue [63] that Bede stresses as the distinguishing quality of the abbess. Her elevated worldly station he seems to consider as a matter of course, but her sanctity he repeatedly specifies

---

[51] Cf. *ibid.*, IV, xxi, 255; IV, xxii, 260.

[52] Cf. *ibid.*, IV, xxi, 254-255.   [57] Cf. *ibid.*

[53] Cf. *op. cit.*, V, iii, 285.   [58] Cf. *ibid.*, 150.

[54] Cf. *ibid.*, III, xi, 149.   [59] Cf. *ibid.*, III, xxv, 183.

[55] Cf. *ibid.*   [60] Cf. *ibid.*, III, xi, 149.

[56] Cf. *ibid.*   [61] Cf. *ibid.*, IV, xxi, 254.

[62] Cf. *ibid.*, 253; IV, xxiv, 267-268; V, iii, 285-286.

[63] Cf. *op. cit.*, III, viii, 142; *ibid.*, 143; *ibid.*, 144; IV, vii, 219; *ibid.*,
IV, ix, 222; IV, x, 224; IV, xvii, 244-245; IV, xxi, 254; IV, xxiii, 265.

as proper historical subject-matter. In fact, of the very first
abbesses of whom he treats Bede states definitely that it was on
account of their virtue [64] that they were raised to that lofty position.

The "glory of virginity" he lauds most. The sole occasion
upon which Venerable Bede breaks into poetry in the *Historia* is
that on which, in traditional patristic style and convention, he
praises this virtue in the renowned Abbess Etheldreda.[65] In attestation of the abbess' many virtues—about which in particular
cases, as we shall see, Bede goes into some detail—he cites various
miracles and marvels, but that of the body's being preserved intact
after death and burial he attributes to the prerogative of virginity
alone.[66] Only prudence and wisdom and regular discipline enjoy
a place near to that of chastity in Bede's treatment of a great
abbess.

The personal marvels, such as prophecy and the benefit of supernatural presages and revelation, which Bede occasionally reports
of some abbesses, deepen, of course, the impression he creates of
their sanctity. When one abbess, in doubt about where to lay out
the community cemetery, fails to gain advice from her community
—each member of which, quite typical of a group of pious nuns,
hesitates to be the first to broach her personal opinion—a resplendent light descending from heaven indicates to the abbess the site
to be selected.[67] Another abbess prophecies how many of her community will fall victims to an epidemic and correctly includes
herself among the number.[68] A third, through revelation granted
to one of her monks, is informed of the lamentable state of her
subjects. She is told that a calamity is about to strike the monastery because of the sins of the community, but that she herself
will be spared the harrowing experience because of her innocence.
The divine vengeance, she is informed, will descend only after her
death.[69]

Marvels even with which an abbess is merely casually or more

[64] Cf. *ibid.*, III, viii, 142.
[65] Cf. *ibid.*, IV, xviii, 247-248.
[66] Cf. *ibid.*, IV, xvii, 243.
[67] Cf. *op. cit.*, IV, vii, 219-220.
[68] Cf. *ibid.*, IV, xvii, 244. Cf. also L. E. 54.   [69] Cf. *ibid.*, IV, xxiii, 264.

8

or less impersonally connected in the course of Bede's *Historia* also serve—unintentionally we can but believe in some instances, but none the less effectively in all—to enhance the impression of holiness. Such instances are all of a serious and supernatural character. All have to do with extraordinary phenomena about cemeteries or relics; with astounding cures. The simple dignity and reverence, accordingly, with which Venerable Bede relates them, reflect upon the character of the abbess who is associated however remotely with them in Bede's account. The personality already distinguished for virtue gains therefrom a quality of awe. About the consecrated spot set apart for the monastic cemetery the brightness of heavenly light and a fragrant perfume are wont to play during the lifetime of one abbess.[70] Among many other persons an abbess witnesses an extraordinary light reaching from the relics of a saint to the height of heaven. Impressed by the marvel and the account that the Queen of Mercia gives her of the salutary potency of even secondary relics of the saint, the abbess acquires some and by their means effects an impressive cure.[71] Another, in anguish at the fatal illness of her daughter, a young nun, prevails upon a holy bishop to bless the sick religious and is rewarded by her almost instantaneous recovery.[72]

But the marvels reported of the death and posthumous career of the abbess redound most to the glorification of her particular personality and to the reputation of love and esteem in which her community hold her.[73] In the first place, death itself possesses no horror for these women. It is looked upon as the victorious close of a virtuous life and the triumphal entry to their eternal home and queenly life, for each, as a religious, considers herself the spouse of the Celestial King,[74] a dignity which Venerable Bede in full accord with the patristic tradition [75] mentions as surpassing that of royal birth and earthly rule.[76] It is not surprising, conse-

[70] Cf. *ibid.*, IV, x, 224.

[71] Cf. *ibid.*, III, xi, 149-150.

[72] Cf. *op. cit.*, V, iii, 285-286.

[73] Cf. *ibid.*, III, viii, 143-144; *ibid.*, 144; IV, ix, 222-224; xvii, 244-246; xxi, 257-258.

[74] Cf. *ibid.*, III, viii, 142; xxiv, 179; IV, xvii, 245.

[75] Cf. p. 29 above.   [76] Cf. *op. cit.*, IV, xvii, 243; xix, 248; xxi, 252.

quently, that in narrating the death of the abbesses whose virtue he is most intent upon explaining, Bede should surround the report with every marvel associated with it in the affectionate and reverent tradition of each abbess' monastery.

Bede's description of the first nun of whom he writes in the *Historia* (one of the two monastic leaders who are probably abbesses, although Bede does not specify them as such [77]) is, insofar as it is an account preponderantly of the marvels attendant upon her death, typical [78] of his description of the death of abbesses specifically named. Although many wonderful works and miracles were attributed to this religious, a Kentian princess, Bede considers it sufficient to record in detail only her passage out of this world to the celestial kingdom. A group of white robed men have come to the monastery, and upon her asking them their mission, they reply that they seek the golden coin brought thither from Kent. She immediately visits the cells of the infirm and those noted for signal probity of life, commending herself to their prayers, for the errand of the strange visitants she considers as symbolic of her death. That same night (sic) as dawn is breaking, Bede writes poetically, she passes from the darkness of this world to supernal light. The brothers in another building at that time hear the sound of angels singing and the noise as it were of a multitude entering the monastery. Going out to investigate, they behold a great light streaming from heaven which guides the holy soul, freed from the bonds of the flesh, to the eternal joys of her heavenly country. On the same night, moreover, many other marvels are wrought in the monastery. These Bede mentions merely. He adds that her tomb being opened three days after her burial, an exquisite perfume as of balsam issues from its depths.[79] This religious is mentioned in the chronicles as late as the fifteenth century.[80] Another typical description of an abbess' last days—in some respects more typical than the foregoing—is

---

[77] Cf. p. 71 above.

[78] Cf. Delahaye (2) 196-198, 307.

[79] Cf. *op. cit.*, III, viii, 143-144.

[80] Cf. A-S. Chr., 639, 27; G. P. 323; HHH, 94; Gai. Lest. E. 1; 52; Fl. Hist. 1; 311; CM, 1; 280-281; H. P. 6; 52; NLA 2; *De Sancta Sexburga,* 357.

the account of the marvelous presage of another superior's approaching death, of an abbess again whose virtue had been manifested even during life by miracles.[81]   It is typical in the first place because the marvelous phenomenon represents the soul of the abbess a few days before her death being borne in the midst of brilliant light into the open heavens.[82]   It is typical in the second place because—although the remarkable vision is ostensibly to accrue to the glory of the abbess' sanctity—it is beheld by one of her devoted nuns—one of Venerable Bede's customary witnesses to the marvelous.[83]   Death, moreover, does not break the bonds of affection and dependence between the abbess and her nuns.   This fact is manifested by the touching confidence in the departed abbess' abiding care, evinced by one nun who prays to her.[84]   It is indicated also by the familiar and loving colloquy of a dying nun with her departed superior who appears at her death bed.[85]

Beyond the accounts of other abbesses, the careers of two in particular stand out as types in the pages of Bede and after him in the pages of many chroniclers down to the sixteenth century. Rarely does a later historiographer fail at least to mention them, despite the growing burden of repetitions from the past.

The first of these and the nun of whom Venerable Bede gives the most complete and interesting account [86] is, quite naturally, a lady of his own district, Northumbria.[87]   In Book III, chapter xxiv, he introduces her without previous explanation as the Abbess Hilda,[88] assuming her to be, as she undoubtedly was, a familiar figure to his readers.   In Book IV [89] he devotes two lengthy chapters to her biography and her patronage of the shepherd-poet Caedmon.   In the manner that becomes typical of the monastic chronicler in England, Bede makes the date of Abbess Hilda's death his starting point.   Then, in retrospect, after giving the age she attained; her noble birth; the circumstances of her becom-

---

[81] Cf. *op. cit.*, IV, vi, 219; *ibid.*, 219-220.
[82] Cf. *ibid.*, IV, ix, 221-222.
[83] Cf. p. 114 ff. below.
[84] Cf. *op. cit.*, IV, ix, 222-223.
[85] Cf. *ibid.*, 223-224.
[86] Cf. *ibid.*, III, xxiv, 149; xxv, 183; IV, xxi-xxii, 252-262.
[87] Cf. *ibid.*, IV, xxi, 252.   [88] Cf. *ibid.*, 179.   [89] Cf. *ibid.*, xxi-xxii, 252-262.

ing a Christian and in her thirty-third year a religious, Bede brings out the salient qualities of her character and the most notable of her deeds as abbess. His account of Hilda, as of all abbesses, is in truth a eulogy. His story of her is repeated in chronicle after chronicle with all his details down to the fifteenth century [90] and its salient features become the model, it would seem, for accounts of abbesses found in English chronicles down to the same century. As far as English literature is concerned Bede's account seems as prototype. The schema of the eulogy is as follows:

I. Date of Death

II. Life

    A. Genealogy

        1. Royal or noble birth

    B. Brief account of life in the world

    C. Abbatial career

        1. Virtues

            a. Wisdom

            b. Prudence

            c. Regular discipline

            d. Charity and peace

        2. Administration

            a. Material

                1. Erection of monasteries

            b. Professional

                i. Among religious

                ii. Among Externs

                    Kings

                    Ecclesiastics

                    Laymen

[90] The repetition is found in: O-E Mart. 206-208; Fl. Wig. Chr. C. 1; 36; Fl. Hist. 1; 336-337; CM, 1; 302; H. P. 6; 140-142; NLA 2; 29-33. Abbess Hilda is referred to but not so elaborately as in the H. E. in: An. Ass. 124; G. R. 1; 56; G. P. 198; Ger. Cant. G. R. 2; 336-337; Gai. Lest E. 1; 60; Ethelward's Chr. 13; L. E., 16, 23-24; Fl. Wig. Chr. C. 25; CM, 1; 393; P. L. Chr. 1; 81; SWC 19, 25. This list is not exhaustive.

III. Miracles
    A. During Life
        1. Presage of sanctity
        2. Phenomena at death
    B. Posthumous

That this is not a necessary schema is indicated by the traditional schema of Greek patristic eulogies.[91] The points of Hilda's character emphasized by Bede, are, moreover, plainly conventional. The points that one soon comes to look for, that one grows accustomed to in all Bede's accounts of abbesses, are there.[92]

Among her virtues, her innate wisdom.[93] is treated first. It is so fully developed even at the beginning of her abbatial career, when she has been but one year in religion, that, with her evident desire for the advancement of the service of God, it inclines Bishop Aidan of Lindisfarne and other learned religious to visit her often, in order to foster and improve it by their erudition.[94] From these Hilda acquires the science of religious life,[95] the principles of which she applies so practically when—as often falls to her lot as abbess—the reorganization or establishment of religious discipline in a monastery becomes her duty.[96]

Next to the regular life, charity, peace, and the virtues emphasized in monasteries are Abbess Hilda's chief concern,[97] her personal example of piety and kindliness being her subjects' most effectual stimulus thereto as well as the cause of their calling her by the affectionate term, Mother. Not only they, however, but everyone who knows the holy Abbess calls her Mother and feels the influence of her example, the very report of her virtue and zeal leading many, remote from the monastery, to amendment of life.[98]

Hilda's prudence also Bede singles out for remark. So great

---

[91] Cf. Hürth, 4, 8.

[92] Despite this fact, the remarkable individuality and charm of the holy and highly intelligent woman appear. Although Bede's account of Hilda is not untypical of his accounts of other abbesses, Abbess Hilda is nonetheless the paragon of the type.

[93] Cf. *op. cit.*, IV, xxi, 253.

[94] Cf. *ibid.*

[95] Cf. *ibid.*

[96] Cf. *ibid.*, 254.

[97] Cf. *op. cit.* Repeated verbatim, Fl. of Wor., 28.

[98] Cf. *ibid.*, 255.

and extensive is her repute for this virtue that not only persons of indifferent position, but princes and kings seek her out for advice.[99]

Among the activities of the Abbess Hilda Bede recounts her erection of the great monastery of Whitby [100] and the dependent monastery of Hackness.[101] To her prudent interest in the education of the monks in her various monasteries, notably Whitby— where she obliges those under her direction to devote great care to the study of Scripture and the exercise of works of justice [102]— Bede attributes the fact that many of her religious are raised to the priesthood and five even to the episcopacy.[103]

Her interest is not confined to the monks and nuns, however. Bede recounts in great detail her patronage of the lowly brother, Caedmon. When the Abbess recognizes his gift and has tested his inspiration—again with the assistance of learned men [104]—she advises the poet, who seems to have been a menial upon the monastic property,[105] to become a monk. When he has entered her community she cultivates his poetic gift by having him instructed thoroughly in sacred history, the exclusive subject of his song.[106]

The most remarkable activity of Abbess Hilda—one, indeed, of which Bede makes very little, so consonant is it with the official course of the abbess' life—is her participation, referred to in the *Vita Wilfridi,*[107] amidst kings, princes, bishops, priests, prominent monks, and other ecclesiastics in the Synod of Whitby, convened by King Oswy in 664 at the monastery over which Abbess Hilda presides.[108] Venerable Bede shows her there not as a passive spectator, but as one who with her followers constitutes a formidable factor within a party,[109] a point upon which Eddius and some subsequent writers comment.[110]

Sanctity as attested by miracles is, nevertheless, the note upon which Venerable Bede closes his laudatory account of the famous

[99] Cf. *ibid,* 254.
[100] Cf. *ibid.*
[101] Cf. *ibid.,* 257.
[102] Cf. *ibid.,* 254.
[103] Cf. *ibid.*
[104] Cf. *op. cit.,* xxii, 260.
[105] Cf. *ibid.,* 259.
[106] Cf. *ibid.,* 260-261.
[107] Cf. p. 69 above.
[108] Cf. *op. cit.,* III, xxv, 183; cf. also H. P. 237; NLA 2; 427.
[109] Cf. *op. cit.,* III, xxv, 183.
[110] Cf. Raine (2) 1; 171; cf. also G. P. 240.

abbess' career.[111] Her renown, he avers,. is the necessary fulfillment of a dream which her mother had had when Hilda was but
an infant.[112] Her mother dreamed that she was in possession of
a jewel so brilliant that its gleam brightened all Britain.[113] Hilda's
salutary influence, Bede infers, is no less restricted.[114] Her death
also has its attendant marvels,[115] witnessed by nuns who suffer
keenly at being deprived of the privilege of being present at the
abbess' deathbed. But a scene takes place here that for its exquisite
simplicity surpasses by far the greatest marvel recorded of the
famous abbess. After about seven long years of physical pain
and interior suffering, Abbess Hilda comes to her last day. Having
received the Holy Viaticum shortly before dawn and having summoned to her bedside the " handmaids of Christ," the nuns who
are about the monastery, she admonishes them to mutual service
and recommends them to live in evangelical peace with all. Sudden
joy then lights up her countenance as, in the midst of her exhortation, she beholds death at hand. Breaking off her words of spiritual
counsel to her religious, she passes, not to death, but from death
to life.[116] This scene also has its counterpart in similar accounts
of later abbesses.

The other abbess in the *Historia Ecclesiastica* whose career is
distinctive and the source of a tradition is Queen Etheldreda of
Northumbria.[117] Etheldreda also is a great abbess and found-
ress; [118] and in describing the administrative phase of her abbatial
career, Bede follows the schema used for Hilda, but in addition
he makes a great point of Etheldreda's personal sanctity, of her
virginity, of her virtues as a person as distinct from her virtues
as an abbess.[119] In fact, the commonplaces of her abbatial career
take second rank in his account. Married twice, Queen Etheldreda
finally obtains the consent of her second husband, King Ecgfrid,
to retire to a convent " to serve the true King ".[120] Having taken
the veil and spent a year in the monastery presided over by her
husband's aunt, the Abbess Ebba of Coldingham, Etheldreda

---

[111] Cf. *op. cit.*, IV, xxi, 255 ff.

[112] A hagiographical commonplace.

[113] Cf. *ibid.*, 255-256.

[114] Cf. *ibid.*, 256.

[115] Cf. *ibid.*, 257-258.

[116] Cf. *op. cit.*, 256.

[117] Cf. *ibid.*, IV, xvii-xviii, 243-248.

[118] Cf. *ibid.*, 244.

[119] Cf. *ibid.*, 244, 246.

[120] *Ibid.*, 243.

founds a magnificent monastery at Ely in her native province of East Anglia. There she becomes, as Bede expresses it, by works and the example of a heavenly life, the virgin-mother of many nuns. Her mortification—some of it peculiar to the time, but carefully repeated by many of her historians [121]—and prayer Bede lauds, and her humble burial in a wooden coffin he is careful to observe.[122]

Sixteen years after Etheldreda's death, her sister, the former Queen of Kent, who succeeded her as abbess, exhumes the body to re-inter it more suitably in the church.[123] At the transferal of the venerated remains, a ceremony at which many dignitaries are present, the body and the enveloping garments are found perfectly intact and an incision on the throat, made the day before the abbess' death, is neatly healed to a slender scar. Miracles and marvels immediately ensue, one of which is faithfully repeated, being the wonderful manner in which the marble coffin—for which the abbess had sent the brothers on a voyage and which they had remarkably found—perfectly adjusts itself to the body of the saint.[124]

Virginity among the personal virtues of this great queen and abbess is unmistakably the distinctive feature of her life as Venerable Bede recounts it. Bede's language and ideas on this subject reflect the traditional treatment of the same theme in patristic and contemporary religious didacticism. Allusions to *casta*,[125] to *sacrae virginis*,[126] to *sponsae Christi* [127] in the course of the historical account of Etheldreda's exhumation seem inevitable and suggest the literary convention. The influence of traditional patristic thought on virginity is patent, moreover, in the conventionalized ideas and expression in an anecdote recalled by the discovery of the cicatrice on the throat of the intact body. In reference to this, Bede relates a report that, when in her last illness, Etheldreda acknowledged that she bore at her throat the burden of the painful tumor—the trace of whose lancing is the present scar—both justly and joyfully;—justly, because in her youth she

---

[121] Cf. *op. cit.*, 244; cf. L. E., 50-51, verbatim; *Vita S. Etheldredae*, Horstmann (7) 289.

[122] Cf. IV, xvii, 244.

[123] Cf. *ibid.*

[124] Cf. *ibid.*, 244-246.

[125] Cf. *ibid.*, 246.

[126] Cf. *ibid.*, 245.

[127] Cf. *ibid.*

had borne about her neck the vain weight of pearls, and gladly, because now, instead of gold and jewels, she wears the ornaments of virtuous pain.[128]   Venerable Bede sees in Etheldreda, as he states, the woman of royal birth, the earthly queen, ennobled and more truly the queen because the spouse of Christ.[129]   He inserts in the *Historia,* furthermore, a series of elegiac verses, an earlier composition of his, wholly in the traditional didactic vein in praise of virginity.   The work recapitulates, it is true, the historical facts of the renowned abbess' career,[130] but beyond clothing all in the garb of conventional patristic phraseology, it contributes no new facts to the account.   In the poem Bede refers to the Blessed Virgin as the model and leader of virgins, the beginner of heavenly virginity.   She rejoices the celestial choir which gleams with the radiance of that virtue.   From her, virginity flowers on earth in the virgin martyrs, Agatha, Agnes, Cecelia, and the other virginal saints customarily mentioned in similar contexts.[131]   Among the heavenly virgins Bede places Etheldreda who glows also with the glory of virginity.   Daughter of a king, royal by birth, she is nobler through her Heavenly Father; the consort of a king, on earth a Queen, she is more truly regal as spouse of Christ.   She will reign in heaven.   The familiar text, *Audi filia* . . . on the beauty of the virgin is applied to her.   The paean of praise closes with the declaration that Etheldreda, having lived in the monastery as the consecrated bride of Christ, having been untouched by the corruption of the grave, now fills the earth with her glory.   The Bridegroom having come, she exults in heaven with the Spouse; she sings the new song of the virgins and forever will dwell with them in the company of the Lamb.[132]   The poem attaches to the traditional history of Etheldreda and very often in later years is quoted in whole or in part with other references to the holy abbess.   The point of particular interest here is that one of the earliest, and certainly the most influential, historiographical works is penetrated with the thought and phraseology of patristic didacticism on the subject of the nun.

---

[128] Cf. *op. cit.,* 246.   Cf. also p. 32 above and St. Ambrose, *De Virginibus,* I, 197 and 286.

[129] Cf. *op. cit.,* xvii, 247.   Cf. also p. 29 above.

[130] Cf. *ibid.,* xviii, 248.   [131] Cf. p. 34 above.   [132] Cf. *op. cit.,* 248.

The story of Etheldreda, like that of Hilda, is repeated many times in the subsequent literature of England,[133] being expanded and elaborated with conventional details in Latin and Middle English *vitae* composed in the twelfth century and after.[134] There are accounts of many other renowned abbesses or queen-abbesses in the later literature of England.[135] Insofar as the administrative phase of their abbatial careers, both without and within the monastery is concerned, these accounts follow faithfully the schema used by Bede for Hilda. Many of them, in addition, follow his treatment of Etheldreda in their emphasis upon personal sanctity.[136] Bede's account of Etheldreda, therefore, is another notable literary type which was accepted by subsequent literature.

The schema of his treatment is the following:

    I. Genealogy

        A. Royal ancestry

        B. Royal marriages

[133] Cf. for a more or less complete repetition: A.-S. Chr. (An. 670, 679) 35, 39; *Martyrology* (Bede, PL 94) 954; O-E Mart. 102; Historical Fragment " (*Leechdoms*, Cockaygne 3) 430; Aelfric's *Natale Sancte Aeðeldryðe Virginis*, Skeat (2) 1; 432-440; Chr. of Fl. Wor. 23, 27, 33; Fl. of Wig. 1; 30, 31, 36, 44; Raine (2) 1; 185-186; Gai. Lest. E. 57; L. E. 16-85; Abbr. Chr. 1; 114, 116, 117; Fl. Hist. 1; 335-336; CM, 1; 299, 301-302; H. P. 6; 140; *Vita S. Etheldredae*, Horstmann (7) 282-307; NLA 1; 304, 424-427, 427-429; SWC. 20-22, 70-75. Etheldreda is mentioned briefly in many other similar works throughout the centuries: An. Ass. 123-124; *Vita Wilfridi*, Fridegoda, Raine (2) 1; 127; *Vita Oswaldi*, anon. *ibid.*, 427, 453; G. P. 323, 324; HHH, 63; Joc. B. Chr. 99, 100; NLA 2; 433.

[134] Cf. L. E. 1; 5-92, 2; 268-269, 290, 293-294. *Vita S. Etheldredae*, Horstmann (7) 282-307, NLA 1; 424-429.

[135] Cf. the following works:—Ethelberga of Barking in H. E. IV, vi, 219; vii, 219-220; ix, 221-224; x, 224-225; O-E. Mart. 186; Fl. Wig. Chr. C. 1; 26, 32. Cf. Fl. Wor. 20, 183-184; 187; G. P. 2, 143; H. P. 6; 124; NLA 1; 393; 312-315; 303-305; 306-307; Elfleda in H. E. IV, xxiv, 267-268.

[136] Cf. the following works:—Cyneburgh and Cyneswyth in A.-S. Chr. 117; G. R. 1; 35, 78; Fl. Hist. 1; 357; H. P. 5; xii, 442; vi, 681; Cf. Note 241, p. 97; Cf. NLA, 1; 420-421; 1; 379-380; L. E. 25, 52-53, 63-68, 76; NLA 2; 356; SWC 75-79; NLA 2; 424; SWC passim; L. E. 76-77; NLA 1; 406; A.-S. Chr. 43; Gai. Lest. E. 1; 67-68; Fl. Wig. Chr. C. 1; 49; Fl. Hist. 1; 369; NLA 1; 244-247. Cf. p. 97 below, note 248.

II. Virtues

    A. Virginity

        1. In married life

        2. In monastic life—Hymn

    B. Monastic virtues

        1. Austerities

        2. Regularity

III. Marvels

    A. During life

    B. After death

Abbess Elfleda, Hilda's successor, receives in her abbatial capacity but passing reference in the *Historia*.[137] The very little which is recorded of her as abbess, moreover, conforms to similar instances in Bede's account of Abbess Hilda. Elfleda, nevertheless, is an historical personage whose earlier life is too frequently repeated from the pages of the *Historia* to allow of her not being at least adverted to as abbess here.

Bede is the first and most influential of the chroniclers in the process of the development of the nun-type in the literature of England. The writers who follow will repeat for the most part the essentials of his treatment, although in many instances they treat of seventh-century nuns who are not even mentioned by Bede. In the pages which follow their works will be referred to and in some instances cited, first, to show their agreement with—in fact, their dependence upon—Bede; secondly, to show what their accounts add to the traditional figure of the nun. Anyone familiar with the medieval chronicles understands how much of the material therein is mere repetition plus the additions of continuators. It is, moreover, a commonplace that the chroniclers who follow Bede in time follow him for the most part in materials; that they merely take over *verbatim* what he wrote and compress it and add thereto materials that after his time become a part of historiography.

[137] Cf. *op. cit.*, III, xxiv, 179; IV, xxiv, 267-268. Cf. also G. R. 1; 56; G. P. 254; HHH, 97.

2. From the Eighth to the Tenth Century

A late contemporary of Bede and one who, as far as the records show, does not reflect the treatment of nuns in the *Historia Ecclesiastica,* although he includes some of Bede's facts, is Boniface. In the collected correspondence, which includes letters [138] not belonging strictly to the correspondence of Boniface, twenty-two letters [139] throw light upon the contemporary abbess of England. Boniface has in common with Bede the following points—the abbess of royal family or related to a bishop; [140] the abbess presiding over monks [141] and apparently shown more deference than male superiors; [142] the abbess profiting of the counsel and friendship of bishops; [143] being visited by the king; [144] the abbess concerned with the education of her subjects,[145] and reporting marvels occurring in the monastery.[146] Boniface's correspondence, moreover, implies the same qualities, the same details as seen in Bede. The letters of Lul,[147] his companion and successor, included among his own, specify, in fact, the royal abbess as more noble through her religious position,[148] as the promoter of religious discipline in the monastery,[149] as distinguished for wisdom [150] and solicitous about the care of guests attacked by illness.[151]

The letters, however, bring out the following abbatial qualities and vicissitudes not mentioned by Bede; an abbess is shown suffering from discord among her subjects, male and female,[152] troubled by kings, queens, and other secular rulers,[153] who, instead of being friends and patrons, as in Bede, are hostile [154] to the abbess. For

[138] Cf. BRG 3; ep. 2, 8, 46, 98, and the letters of Lul, Boniface's companion and successor: ep. 41, 75, 95, 97, 113.

[139] Cf. ep. 2, 8, 10, 14, 16, 23, 32, 41, 46, 70, 72, 73, 75, 86, 88, 91, 93, 95, 97, 98, 103, 113.

[140] Cf. ep. 23, p. 83.

[141] Cf. ep. 10, p. 53.

[142] Cf. ep. 98, p. 247.

[143] Cf. ep. 10, p. 64; ep. 14, pp. 69-70; ep. 72, p. 212; ep. 73, p. 213.

[144] Cf. ep. 103, p. 254.

[145] Cf. ep. 93, pp. 241-2.

[146] Cf. ep. 10, pp. 54-61 and ep. 16, p. 75.

[147] Cf. footnote, p. 138, above.

[148] Cf. ep. 95, p. 242.

[149] Cf. *ibid.*

[150] Cf. *ibid.*

[151] Cf. ep. 95, p. 243.

[152] Cf. ep. 14, pp. 66-67.

[153] Cf. *ibid.*, p. 68.

[154] Cf. *ibid.*

these reasons as well as because of the impoverished [155] state of the monastic property and her personal griefs [156] she is eager to depart from Britain to seek peace and repose at Rome.[157]   Pilgrimages of nuns to the holy city, as we learn from this letter [158] and another [159] in the collection, being looked at askance at the time, the abbess asks Boniface's advice whether or not to go to Rome.[160]   His reply, while not conclusive, throws light upon legislation on the subject, it evidently not being prohibitive of pilgrimages undertaken by nuns in quest of peace of soul or moved to pious veneration of the sacred places, particularly of the tombs of Sts. Peter and Paul.[161]   Native abbesses who have settled in Rome [132] are noted as extending generous hospitality to pilgrims [163] and guests and welcoming there bishops [164] and priests.[165]   The abbess is also shown here as making splendid gifts to Boniface and his companion.   The archbishops ask or give thanks for copies of the Scriptures,[166] and the Passions of the Martyrs,[167] for vestments,[198] money,[169] and clothing.[170]   One abbess, for the edification of the pagan converts, undertakes at Boniface's request,[171] to transcribe the Epistles of Saint Peter in gold.[172]   The abbess appears also as a literary student.   She is conscious of her literary style,[173] begging Boniface to correct it; [174] she exercises her skill in verse, considering it a graceful accomplishment.[175]   Verses are sent her as tributes of gratitude for her care of a guest who was nursed dur-

[155] Cf. *ibid.*
[156] Cf. *ibid.*
[157] Cf. *ibid.*, pp. 69-70.
[158] Cf. *op. cit.*, p. 70.
[159] Cf. ep. 70, p. 208. Cf. p. 102 below.
[160] Cf. ep. 88, p. 236.
[161] Cf. ep. 8, pp. 49-50; ep. 88, p. 236.
[162] Cf. ep. 8, pp. 49-50; ep. 95, p. 243; ep. 103, p. 254.
[163] Cf. ep. 8, pp. 49-50 and note to footnote p. 21; ep. 88, p. 237.
[164] Cf. ep. 103, p. 254.
[165] Cf. ep. 95, p. 243.
[166] Cf. *ibid.*, p. 75, ep. 32, p. 98; ep. 88, p. 237, cf. ep. 16, p. 75.
[167] Cf. *ibid.*, p. 75.
[168] Cf. ep. 32, p. 99; ep. 16, p. 75.   [172] Cf. *ibid.*
[169] Cf. ep. 16, p. 75.   [173] Cf. ep. 14, p. 70.
[170] Cf. ep. 88, p. 237.   [174] Cf. ep. 23, p. 84.
[171] Cf. ep. 32, p. 99.   [175] Cf. *ibid.*

ing a long illness at her monastery [176] and are at the same time submitted to her kindly but capable criticism.[177]   The abbess is both a student of metric under Boniface [178] and a teacher [179] of the art to another.   Accounts of deaths, furthermore, are devoid of attendant marvels in this correspondence; they take the form of simple requests [180] for prayers for the soul of the departed religious.   Most of the above-mentioned features are found in several of the letters in the correspondence of Boniface.

Boniface's contribution to our knowledge of the Anglo-Saxon abbess consists in his emphasis upon the difficulties and unpleasantness of the position of abbess under certain circumstances; in the diligence of the abbess in literary pursuits; in her presenting ecclesiastics with rich and serviceable gifts; in the question of pilgrimages for nuns.   These details, not found in Bede, are a supplement of and not contradictory to Bede's account.   Writing in a different literary form and for a different purpose, but at practically the same time and to the same place, Boniface reinforces what Bede had to tell.

Three nuns—two of whom are mentioned as abbesses [181] and the third [182] probably an abbess—are described in the *Vita S. Guthlaci* of the time [183] of Saint Boniface.   In the Latin version [184] by Felix of Croyland and the two Anglo-Saxon versions,[185] the treatment of these three women follows a schema [186] that is a compound

---

[176] Cf. ep. 95, 243-244.

[177] Cf. *ibid.*, 244.

[178] Cf. ep. 23, p. 84.

[179] Cf. *ibid.*

[180] Cf. ep. 16, p. 75; ep. 46, p. 126; cf. ep. 113, p. 279.

[181] " Abbatissa . . . Oelfryd," " Edburgh Abbatissa."   Cf. L. E. 25-26; NLA, 2; 7; AA. SS. Boll. Apr. 2; 40, 47.

[182] " Pega."   Cf. NLA, 2; 8; AA. SS. Boll., *ibid.*, 47.

[183] Original not after 749.

[184] Cf. AA. SS. Boll., *ibid.*, 37-49.

[185] Ed. Gollancz, *The Exeter Book*, 104-188; Goodwin, *The Anglo-Saxon Version of the Life of St. Guthlac.*

[186]   I. Genealogy.

      A. Royal or distinguished origin (FC, 48, 49; Ex. B. 176).

  II. Abbatial activity.

      A. Presiding over monks (FC 47).

      B. Gifts to holy ecclesiastics (FC 47).

of Bede's schema with details found in Boniface. There is, moreover, a charming story about the death and burial of an anchorite
brother of one of these religious that is repeated *in toto* as late
as the fifteenth century.[187]

The corpus of Alcuin's works,[188] conforming almost exactly to
the tradition of Bede and his successors,[189] adds very little to the
Anglo-Saxon abbess as presented by Venerable Bede and by Saint
Boniface. The *De Pontificibus et Sanctis Ecclesiae Eboracensis
Carmen*[190] merely repeats in great condensation three pertinent
passages from the *Historia Ecclesiastica:* that of the abbess and
accompanying nun hastening at night to the relief of a guest,
possessed by the devil;[191] some of the verses by Bede in praise of
Etheldreda's virginity and the preservation of her body from the
corruption of the grave;[192] and an allusion to the cure of the
nun-daughter of another abbess.[193] Except in the first instance,
where the abbess is designated as such,[194] Alcuin makes no reference to these persons as religious women. The nine[195] letters
to English religious women in the extensive correspondence add
but a contemporary and circumstantial detail or two.[196]

Of the historical literature of the reign of Alfred the Great, the

        C. Concerned with burial and glorification of holy persons (FC
            48; Ex. B. 188; Goodwin, 93).
  III. Miracles.
      A. Foreseeing events by aid of ecclesiastic's prophecy (FC 47).
      B. Perceiving supernatural indications of sanctity, etc. (FC 48;
          Goodwin, 88-90, 92, 96-98).

[187] Cf. Fl. Wig. Chr. C. 1; 44-45; NLA 2; 8-10.

[188] Ed. BRG 6.

[189] Cf. p. 55 above, for Alcuin's picture of ideal nun.

[190] Cf. BRG 6; 81-131.

[191] Cf. *ibid.*, lines 396-426, pp. 93-94 with H. E. III, xi, 149-150.

[192] Cf. *ibid.*, lines 750-785, pp. 104-105 with H. E. IV, xvii-xviii, 243-248.

[193] Cf. *ibid.*, lines 1120-1132, p. 115 with H. E. V, iii, 285-286.

[194] Cf. *op. cit.*, line 396, p. 93; line 407, p. 94.

[195] Of the three hundred and six letters, twenty-two are addressed to
nuns, and one is from a nun. Eight of these letters are directed to abbesses
of England. One of them is addressed to an English nun. I have not
been able to identify the abbess addressed in epistles 225 and 280.

[196] Cf. *Elimosinae*, 276, 293, 732, 858. Cf. contemporary references, *ibid.*,
294, 737.

life of Alfred by Asser refers to the King's daughter as a nun.[197]
The *Annales Asserii* record the King's having a monastery erected
in which his daughter Ethelgiva is made abbess over a community of many religious of noble birth. The wealth of this monastery, endowed richly by Alfred, becomes a tradition, mentioned
ordinarily in the subsequent chronicle records of the monastic life
of Ethelgiva.[198]

3. From the Eleventh to the Sixteenth Century

Although after Alfred and during the supremacy of the Danish
kings there was not the prolific production of historical materials
that came later with the Conquest, and although the historical references to nuns in the later chronicles display a growing terseness
in keeping with the diminishing importance of the nun in the
external life of England and the growing burden of repeating early
chronicles, the abbess of literary historical materials continues
throughout these centuries very much in the original tradition.
Historical *vitae* in conjunction with excerpts from chronicles both
fill in lacunae of the eighth, ninth, and tenth centuries and repeat
and expand earlier references as well as add current facts in such
a way as to carry the tradition essentially unchanged from Anglo-
Saxon England to the later fifteenth century. A number of tenth
and eleventh century *vitae*—redactions, for the most part, of earlier
lives—and also the eleventh, twelfth, thirteenth, and fourteenth
century chronicles contain merely repetitious and annotative references to abbesses. They add nothing, consequently, of significant
import to the historical tradition. They merely serve to propagate the materials of earlier records.

While these *vitae* and chronicles, as well as ecclesiastical letters
and episcopal registers, dating respectively from the eleventh and
the thirteenth century on, add nothing important to the historical
tradition of the abbess, they carry the literary historical type from
Venerable Bede to modern literature. The nature of the elaboration in *vita* and chronicle, the quality of the additional details

[197] Cf. *op. cit.*, Stevenson, 58; Cf. also Chr. Rog. Hov. 1; 41.
[198] Cf. *op. cit.*, Giles (5) 173. Cf. the following for later references:
Fl. Wig. Chr. 1, 88, 104; 563; S. D. Hist. H. 88, 90-91; G. R. 1; 131;
G. P. 186; Chr. Rog. Hov. 1; 49; Fl. Hist. 1; 446; C. M. 1; 426.

9

reveal that the biographer or annalist of these abbesses is strongly influenced by literary religious didacticism. The language as well as the ideas are formed more closely, as time goes on, upon the pattern of traditional didacticism. As a result it becomes increasingly clear that the nun-figure of historiography is the concrete, as the didactic nun-figure is the abstract, representation of patristic monastic idealogy. The historical abbess becomes such in a limited degree at this time, when her pre-abbatial career and the historical facts of her active career share the page with a record of her virtues detailed in a stereotyped manner. It was the common medieval practice to adapt individual lives to a general biographical schema.

During the last decade of the eleventh and the first decade of the twelfth century Saint Anselm, Archbishop of Canterbury, composed letters [199] to abbesses which are written in the epistolary tone [200] of Boniface and Alcuin. In fact only one letter [201] to an abbess in his extant correspondence is not wholly in this mode. Many chronicles and *vitae* [202] from the early twelfth to the sixteenth century refer to Wulftrude and her daughter, Editha, who presided, the daughter before the mother, over the monastery at Wilton in the late tenth and early eleventh centuries. The burden of the chronicle records about them, however, consists in their relation to Edgar, King of Wessex. He had withdrawn Wulftrude as a young girl from the monastery at Wilton. But upon the birth of their child, Editha, Wulftrude returns with her to the monastery. Both become religious, and at the death of Editha, whom King Edgar had placed over three great monasteries, her mother Wulftrude succeeds her in office. Reference to the latter as abbess

[199] Cf. PL 158, cols. 1159-1208; 159, cols. 9-272.

[200] St. Anselm addresses the abbesses as " Mother "; *ibid.*, ep. 30, 62; 125, 161; 128, 270; 129, 270-272. He stimulates them and their nuns to fervor; ep. 125, 161, 162; 128, 129, 269-270; 129, 270-272, and he begs their prayers: ep. 70, 108; 30, 60; 125, 161; 128, 270.

[201] Cf. *op. cit.*, 159; ep. 10, 207.

[202] Cf. Fl. Wor. Chr. 1; 140; Stubbs, *Vita S. D. Eadmero*, 209-210; *ibid.*, *Vita S. D. Osberno*, 111-112; Vita S. E. G. 622-626; G. R. 1; 179-180; G. P. 188-191; Chr. Rog. Hov. 1; 62; Vita S. D. Wm. Malmesbury, 310-312; *Abbr. Chr.*, 1; 151; Fl. Hist. 1; 509; Horstmann (9) 23-24, 36-62 ff.; NLA 1: 284-285; NLA 1; 314.

is scant, only one brief account emphasizing her abbatial career.[203] Editha, on the contrary, appears in many records as the typical royal abbess. An eleventh-century *vita* [204] presents her as Bede presented the abbess in the eighth. She is, like Hilda, a mother [205] to her religious communities; an intimate friend of renowned ecclesiastics.[206] Marvels announce and attend her death,[207] and after it she appears to a nun of the monastery.[208] Other marvels follow. Geoffrey of Monmouth, in the next century, recounts the exhumation of her body and the attendant marvels.[209] Two fifteenth-century works—the earlier, a long Middle-English verse treatment of her life; [210] the latter, a Latin *vita*,[211], based upon a thirteenth-century work [212]—bring out the abbatial career of Editha in even a more completely typical fashion, reminiscent both of Bede and of traditional didacticism. The former explains that the young nun, upon the advice of prominent ecclesiastics, is raised to the position of abbess on account of her wisdom [213] and other suitable qualities.[214] She prefers her monastic life and abbatial office to that of the royal court and dignity of Queen of England.[215] She prefers to serve God and preserve her virginity, evaluating both this service and the virtue above all earthly joy and honor.[216] Her death is remarkably foretold [217] and the sisters are presented as in deep grief at her loss.[218]

In addition to these time-honored details, this work includes two features associated at this period with the abbess-tradition and borrowed obviously from religious didacticism. Advanced to the dignity of abbess, the religious demurs, preferring to remain in an humble position and to serve her sisters rather than to rule them.[219] Her death, moreover, is announced by the ecclesiastic Saint Dunstan, her venerated friend and advisor, in phraseology replete with figures of patristic didacticism,[220] which by this time

---

[203] Cf. Horstmann (9) 62.
[204] Cf. Vita S. E. G., 624-625.
[205] Cf. *op. cit.*, 624.
[206] Cf. *ibid.*
[207] Cf. *ibid.*, 624, 625.
[208] Cf. *ibid.*, 624.
[209] Cf. G. P. 189.
[210] Cf. Horstmann (9).
[211] Cf. NLA 1; 311-315.

[212] Cf. *ibid.*, ix.
[213] Cf. Horstmann (9) 36.
[214] Cf. *ibid.*
[215] Cf. *ibid.*, 39.
[216] Cf. *ibid.*, 40.
[217] Cf. *ibid.*, 45.
[218] Cf. *ibid.*, 47.
[219] Cf. *op. cit.*, 36.
[220] Cf. *ibid.*, 45.

have become part and parcel of the vernacular. A familiar Reformation complaint, moreover, is anticipated here. Abbess Editha prefers abbatial rule to that of the throne of England, and makes the choice, the author is careful to observe, for the sake of her interior spiritual life and " not for the abbeys." [221]

The Latin *vita* also reiterates familiar details associated since the early seventh century with the abbess type. Abbess Editha here learns in a dream of the approaching death of her brother the King; [222] she foretells other future events; [223] she erects a church; [224] and when she herself is about to die one of her community beholds marvels; [225] and after her death she appears to her mother, who is a religious, of the same community.

A group of writings on seventh-century abbesses begins to appear not earlier than the eleventh century and are found in elaborate detail in the fifteenth century. Despite their elaborateness, they remain faithful to the manner of Bede, however.

Mildreda and Milburga were two of these seventh-century abbesses. The story of Mildreda [226] begins with her royal genealogy; [227] she is appointed abbess by Bishop Theodore; [228] she stimulates her community to fervor by the force of her good example.[229] Marvels occur during her lifetime and at her death.[230] Summoning the community about her death bed, she exhorts them to maintain charity and peace [231] and to live in humble obedience.[232] Her remains are later translated and miracles wrought at her intercession.[233] With this abbess throughout the records

---

[221] Cf. *ibid.*, 40.

[222] Cf. *op. cit.*, 312.

[223] Cf. *ibid.*, 313.

[224] Cf. *ibid.*, 312.

[225] Cf. *ibid.*, 313.

[226] Cf. Mildreda in: *Saxon Leechdoms* 422, 424, 430; Cf. references to the *Vita* by Goscelin in MS. Vespas, B. xx., Harl. 105, Harl. 3908 Rawl. C. 440, in NLA 2; 193, note 1. S. D. Hist. R. 12-13; G. R. 1; 78; G. P. 306; L. E. 52; Ger. Cant. G. R. 2; 30; Abbr. Chr. 1; 115; CM, 1; 299; Fl. Hist. 1; 333 NLA 2; *De Sancta Mildreda* 193-198; NLA 1; *De Sancta Edburga*, 308, 309; NLA 2; *De Sancta Milburga* 188.

[227] Cf. NLA 2; 193.

[228] Cf. *ibid.*, 195.

[229] Cf. *ibid.*

[230] Cf. *ibid.*

[231] Cf. *ibid.*

[232] Cf. *ibid.*

[233] Cf. *ibid.*, 196-197.

and *vitae* from the eleventh to the fifteenth century [234] her sister abbess, Milburga, is mentioned. Milburga herself is presented in a fifteenth century *vita* [235] very much as is Mildreda here. Her royal ancestry is traced,[236] her erection of the monastery of Wenlock, over which she becomes abbess is stated;[237] her command of the regular life is recounted,[238] and in the resume of the words she addresses her community from her death bed are the statements that she has loved them as her own flesh and blood and has governed them and been solicitous for them as a mother would her children.[239] Miracles, moreover, follow upon her death.[240]

Traditional details alone make up the account of two other Anglo-Saxon royal abbesses, whose names are also familiar in historical records from the eleventh to the fifteenth century.[241] Their royal birth,[242] their despising the riches and pleasures of the world,[243] their becoming the abbess of many nuns,[244] and the translation of their bodies are, each in turn, remarked.[245] These points the accounts of the abbesses have in common. The first, Cyneberg, like Etheldreda of the *Historia Ecclesiastica,* is a queen who, after a holy life with her husband, obtains his consent to relinquish the court and the world in order to become, for the love of Christ, a nun.[246] Of the second, Cyneswith, her sister, the *vita* remarks her solicitude for the monastic virtues of charity and peace.[247]

Richer in traditional details and treated more fully and frequently from Anglo-Saxon times to the fifteenth century [248] is the

---

[234] Cf. works cited in footnote 226, p. 96 above.

[235] Cf. NLA 2; 188-192.

[236] Cf. *ibid.*, 188.

[237] Cf. *ibid.*, 190.

[238] Cf. *op. cit.*

[239] Cf. *ibid.*, 192.

[240] Cf. *ibid.*, 191.

[241] Cf. Cyneburg in:—A.-S. Chr. 117; G. R. 1; 78, 267; G. P. 306; Fl. Hist. 1; 357; H. P. 5; 442; 6; 128-130; 146; NLA 2; 130-132, and Cyneswitha in:—A.-S. Chr. 117; Fl. Hist. 1; 357; H. P. 5; 442; 6; 128-130; NLA 2; 130-131.

[242] Cf. NLA 2; 130.

[243] Cf. *ibid.*

[244] Cf. *ibid.*

[245] Cf. *ibid.*, 131.

[246] Cf. *ibid.*, 130.

[247] Cf. *ibid.*

[248] Cf. the Fragments attached to the third volume of *Saxon Leechdoms*, 430; Fl. Wig. Chr. 1; 186-187; SWG xix-xxvi; G. R. 1; 78; G. P. 308-309; 323; L. E. 25, 48, 51-52; 62-63; 77-78; 80-82; Fl. Hist. 1; 32-33; CM, 1; 298; H. P. 6; 126-128; 176-178; NLA 1; 405-406; NLA 2; 422-424.

life of Werburga, another abbess of seventh-century England. To the recital of her royal family;[249] her being appointed abbess on account of her sanctity[250] and prudence;[251] her governing according to the rule[252] and with perfect discipline;[253] her carefully providing for all[254] and setting all a good example;[255] her Hilda-like renown throughout the land for holiness and royal prestige;[256] her largess in alms[257] as recommended to abbesses by Alcuin;[258] her monastic and personal virtues[259] reminiscent of those practiced by Etheldreda;[260] her foreknowledge of the day of her own death;[261] and her arrangement for her own burial;[262] the marvels performed during her life;[263] the joy with which she meets death;[264] subsequent miracles,[265] the preservation of her body from the grave,[266] and its solemn translation[267]—to the recital of these traditional historiographical details are added details equally traditional, borrowed from the didactic genre. Thus, as in the *vitae*,[268] such didactic commonplaces as the following are elaborated—that she tried to avoid election to the office of abbess;[269] that she is otherwise very humble;[270] that, while her body dwells upon the earth, her mind

[249] Cf. Vita S. W. G. xix; G. R. 1; 78, 267; G. P. 308; L. E. 25, 51; NLA 2; 422, 423.

[250] Cf. Fl. Wig. Chr. 186-187; Fl. Hist. 332; CM, 1; 298.

[251] Cf. Vita S. W. G. xxii.

[252] Cf. Fl. Wig. Chr. 186-187; Fl. Hist. 332; C. M. 1; 298.

[253] Cf. Vita S. W. G. xxii.

[254] Cf. Fl. Wig. Chr. 186-187.

[255] Cf. Vita S. W. G. xxii; NLA 2; 423.

[256] Cf. Vita S. W. G. xix; NLA 2; 422.

[257] Cf. Vita S. W. G. xxii.

[258] Cf. p. 24, above.

[259] Cf. Vita S. W. G. xxii; NLA 2; 423.

[260] Cf. p. 85, above.

[261] Cf. NLA 2; 423.

[262] Cf. *ibid.*

[263] Cf. Fl. Wig. Chr. Vita S. W. G. xxii-xxiv; G. P. 309; L. E. 52; NLA 2; 423.

[264] Cf. Fl. Wig. Chr. 186-187; Vita S. W. G. xxiv; Fl. Hist. 332; CM, 1; 298.

[265] Cf. Vita S. W. G. xxv; G. P. 309; NLA 2; 424.

[266] Cf. Fl. Wig. Chr. 186-187; Vita S. W. G. xxv; NLA 2; 424.

[267] Cf. L. E. 77.

[268] Cf. p. 93, above.

[269] Cf. Vita S. W. G. xxii, L. E. 62-63; NLA 2; 123.

[270] Cf. Vita S. W. G. xxiii.

is in heaven; [271] that when her body is disinterred and found intact, the beauty of her white face and rosy cheeks [272] is remarked.

Conventional and traditional details persist to the exclusion of other items in many other *vitae* and chronicle records during these centuries. Of one abbess these intermittent materials [273] repeat her royal birth; her queenly dignity; her separating by mutual consent from the King to found a monastery; and her dwelling there as abbess over many nuns, her own daughter among them. [274] Of another [275] queen abbess, mentioned in the *Historia Ecclesiastica* [276] and later historical literature, reference is made to her despising the pomp of court for the monastic life; [277] to her love of regular discipline; [278] her exhumation and more honorable burial of her predecessor, the saintly Etheldreda; [279] her careful instruction of all in the doctrine of true religion; [280] her humble service to all; [281] her holy death; [282] and her preservation from decay. [283] Practically the same details are given of another queen abbess [284] of the seventh century whose life is retold with more or less completeness until the sixteenth.

Fifteenth-century *vitae* of abbesses who are mentioned in the *Historia Ecclesiastica* [285] or in chronicles [286] later than Bede, add, with two exceptions, [287] nothing new to the abbess type. Despite elaboration or condensation, the typical manner persists. And so

---

[271] Cf. Vita S. W. G. xxii.

[272] Cf. Vita S. W. G. xxv.

[273] Cf. Domneva in: S. D. Hist. R. 12; NLA 2; 188-190.

[274] Cf. *ibid.*

[275] Cf. Sexburga in: L. E. 63-65; 66-68; 76; NLA 2; 355-356. Cf. footnote 80, p. 79, above.

[276] Cf. p. 131, below.

[277] Cf. L. E. 52; NLA 2; 356.

[278] Cf. L. E. 63, 76.

[279] Cf. L. E. 64, 64-68.

[280] Cf. L. E. 76.

[281] Cf. NLA 2; 356.

[282] Cf. L. E. 76; NLA 2; 256.

[283] Cf. NLA 2; *ibid.*

[284] Cf. L. E. 77; S. W. C. 20, 80-81.

[285] Cf. NLA 1; *De Sancta Ebba*, 303-308; Cf. *ibid.*, *De Sancto Erkenwaldo*, 392-3.

[286] Cf. H. P. 6; 318; NLA 2; 207; *ibid.*, 2; *De Sancto Guthlaco*, 7; *ibid.*, 1; *De Sancto Edburga*, 309; *ibid.*, 1; *De Sancto Cuthberga*, 244-246; *ibid.*, 2; *De Sancta Wlfhilde*, 508-510. Cf. also Fl. Wig. Chr. 1; 140; V. S. D. Eadmero, Stubbs, 209; G. R. 1; 180; G. P. 143; Fl. Hist. 1; 509; Vita S. E. G. 623; G. P. 143; NLA 1; 311.

[287] Cf. p. 100, below.

familiar do the outstanding facts of an abbess' life become that
even the mere citations of her name in a terse annal suffices to
suggest to the reader of this material her entire history.

4. Exceptions to The Type

Specific exceptions to the traditional abbess type in the historiographical literature of England from Bede to the sixteenth century are remarkably few. One is the sorry episode—whether fact
or fiction—repeated in the chronicles from the twelfth to the fifteenth century [288] of the atrociously wicked and banished Anglo-
Saxon queen, Eadburga. Charlemagne, at whose court she takes
refuge, disgusted with her levity, appoints her, nevertheless, abbess
of a wealthy continental monastery. Her evil life here, however,
necessitates her expulsion, and she is said to have passed her days
thereafter in beggary upon the continent. Another is the record
in a contemporaneous [289] portion of *The Chronicle of the Reigns
of Henry II and Richard I* of the deposition, in 1177, of the infamous abbess of Almsbury and the disbanding of her community
upon episcopal visitation at the instance of the king.[290] The notorious community, the chronicle also records, is replaced by religious
from another monastery.[291] Another variant of the type is found
in the course of a fifteenth-century account [292] of a typical abbess
of the seventh century. An evil abbess appears here who might
well be the prototype of the vicious abbess in the Elizabethan play,
The Death of Robert, Earl of Huntingdon,[293] so exact a parallel

[288] Cf. the following: *Fl. Wig. Chr. C.* 1; 76-77; *S. D. Hist. R.* 66-68;
G. R. 2; 118; *Chr. Rog. Hov.* 1; 18-19; *Fl. Hist.* 1; 407-408; *Chronicon
de Mailros*, 140-141; C. M. 368-369; H. P. 6; 276.

[289] Cf. *op. cit.*, 1; pref. xliv.

[290] Cf. *op. cit.*, 1; 135-136.

[291] Cf. *ibid.*, 165. The incident is recorded tersely in *Chr. Rog. Hov.* 1;
in *The Chronicle of the Reigns of Stephen, Henry II, and Richard I*, of
Gervase of Canterbury 1; 261. *The Chronicle of the Reigns of Henry II
and Richard I* also mentions the excommunication in 1192 of a prioress
and those of her community who refuse to submit to Geoffrey of York's
attaching their nunnery to that of Godstow. Cf. *op. cit.*, 2; 240.

[292] Cf. NLA 2; 193-194.

[293] Cf. Hazlitt, *Dodsley's Old Plays* (15 vols. London, 1874-1876) vol. 8,
Act. iv, sc. 2; Act. v, sc. 1, pp. 290-297; 305-309, 311. Cf. also the religious

is her rôle to that of the abbess in that drama. Our seventh-century abbess, presiding over the monastery of Chelles, is presented as a wicked woman who tries to force a young girl, a prospective nun studying in her convent, to marry one of her relatives. When the maid persists in her refusal, the abbess seeks to destroy her, and the girl escapes her murderous schemes only by a miracle and her treacherous hands by stealth. The life of Saint Modwenna, finally, an abbess in a few respects resembling the typical Anglo-Saxon abbess, is, as recounted by Capgrave [294] in the fifteenth century, so replete with elements of Irish legendary lore that it cannot be considered proper material for this study.

There are, of course, references here and there in the chronicles that neither contribute to nor detract from the type. They are records [295] such as that repeated in at least two chronicles [296] about the heroic conduct of a ninth-century Abbess Ebba and her community who, aware of an approaching attack by the Danes upon

who fatally " bloods " Robin Hood (Gutch, *A Lytell Geste of Robin Hode,* 2; 314-315.

[294] Cf. NLA 2; 198-212.

[295] Cf. the annals; Gai, Lest. E. 1; 172-173; Ann, Wint. 2; 13; G. R. 1; 179, 184; G. P. 175, 188; Ger. Cant. G. R. 2; 52; Fl. Hist. 1; 517; CM, 1; 470; Horstmann (9) 45; R. G. Chr. 1; 291; NLA 1; 530, recounting the striking penance of the glamorous Alfreda at Wherwell Abbey for the murder of her stepson, King Edmund of England. This material is used in the modern works: *Dead Man's Plack* (New York, 1920) by W. H. Hudson and " The King's Henchman " by Edna St. Vincent Millay. Cf. also the seventeenth-century drama, *King Edgar and Alfreda,* by Edward Ravenscroft, cited by Brinkley, 115-116. Cf. also the case of a repudiated queen consigned to a monastery recorded in: G. R. 1; 243; Fl. Wig. Chr. C. 1; 207; S. D. Hist. R. 168; Chr. W. H. 1; 5; Fl. Hist. 1; 571; CM, 1; 521; P. L. Chr. 1; 60. Modern interest centers also about the problem whether or not Maud, or Matilda, as the chroniclers designated the Anglo-Saxon princess, was a professed nun or merely a resident of the monastery over which her aunt was abbess, and whether, as recorded for the year 1100, the princess emerged willingly or unwillingly from the convent to become the queen of Henry Beauclerc. For this incident, cf. Ann. Wint. 40 (Matilda not yet professed) ; Eadmer, *Vita Anselmi,* 56-57 (Matilda free) ; G. R. 2; 470-471 (Matilda not a nun) ; CM, 2; 121 (Matilda a nun and unwilling to quit the convent). Cf. also the modern story, *The Lady of the English,* by Edith Barrington, *Good Housekeeping,* 9 (1930), 32-34.

[296] Cf. Fl. Hist. 432; C. M. 1; 391-392.

the monastery, deliberately mutilate their countenances, preferring, thus repulsive, to be consigned to the flames that consume the monastery than to fall into the hands of the pagan horde. The historical event is the outstanding fact of an annal of this kind, and although the character of the abbess concerned is susceptible of elaborate treatment, historiography left the incident and the character undeveloped. It remained free of the traditional treatment.

5. Instances of Monastic Abuses

(a) Eighth to Twelfth Century

Throughout the entire period, however, there are contemporary records of monastic abuses, which until the twelfth century do not, it is true, present an abbess as a specific exception to the type, but which necessarily implicate her, as a member of a community, the moral or disciplinary state of which is irregular or completely lax. Among such general references from as early as the *Historia Ecclesiastica* [297] itself are accounts of more or less demoralized monastic congregations. Boniface [298] and Alcuin [299] write of monastic evils occasioned by the trespassing of the cloister by royal and distinguished persons of the world. Walter Map in *De Nugis Curialium* [300] paints in lurid hue the utter ruin of an eleventh-century community—abbess and nuns—by Godwin and his wanton company. Chronicles record only less dastardly conduct of his son.[301] From Bede on, also, into the thirteenth century at least, are records adverting to and condemning nun's vanity in dress.[302] From Boniface's letter to the Archbishop of Canterbury on the moral risk incurred by religious women on the road to Rome [303] follows repeated general legislation, outside monastic rules, against public

[297] Cf. *op. cit.*, IV, xviii, p. 265.

[298] Cf. BRG, 3; ep. 59, p. 170.

[299] Cf. *ibid.*, 6; ep. 22, p. 181.

[300] Cf. *op. cit.*, 210.

[301] Cf. S. D. Chr. An. 1049, 164.

[302] Cf. H. E. IV, xviii, 265; cf. Boniface, BRG 3; ep. 70, 209. Cf. Hefele 3; 561-566; Cf. *Reg. Epist. Jno. Peckham*, 3; 849, c. 1284; *Register of Henry of Newark* (vol. 2 of *Register of Jno. Le Romeyn*), 224, c. 1298 (?). Cf. Hefele 5; 399, 437; 797; 925-926. Cf. also p. 54, above.

[303] Cf. ep. 70, 208; Cf. Hefele, 3; 561-566.

pilgrimages undertaken by nuns.[304] Unnecessary journeying, visiting, and needless wanderings outside monastic precincts are frowned upon consistently throughout the entire period by religious and ecclesiastical authorities.[305] Such references point to the reversal, in many instances, of conditions in which the typical abbess appears, and suggest an abbess diametrically opposed to the type.

(b) Twelfth to Sixteenth Century

The official correspondence of churchmen and the registers and injunctions of episcopal visitation of monasteries, extant from the twelfth and the thirteenth century respectively, also witness to abbatial abuses. From about 1159 to 1164, the letters of John of Salisbury [306] to abbesses and, in the next century, the correspondence about religious women, particularly letters between the great friends and reformers Robert Grosseteste [307] and Adam of Marisco,[308] come to grips with ugly and hard reality. Traditional phraseology is torn aside and bare facts of monastic abuses are exposed and expressed tersely and unadornedly. Episcopal registers [309] of visitations of monasteries contemporary with these churchmen and continuing into the sixteenth century inevitably reflect the abuses at which they too strike. These registers of their nature are at grips with hard reality too and equally terse and unadorned in expressing it. They report definite cases of monastic laxity on the part of the abbess, and are reinforced in

[304] Cf. *ibid.*, and St. Gregory, PL 77, ep. 9, cols. 675-676; Hefele 6; 221.

[305] Cf. the constitution " Periculoso ", C. un de statu regul., 16 pp. 555-560 in *Liber Sextus Decretalium Bonifacii Papae VIII.*

[306] Cf. Giles (4). Cf. p. 104, below.

[307] Cf. Luard, ep. 107, 108, 130, 317-321, 439-443. Cf. *ibid.*, 69.

[308] Cf. Brewer (1), 1; ep. 29, 122; 21, 130-131; 108, 239-240; 239, 403-404, and 23, 108.

[309] Cf. among others Visitation to Swyne Priory, Jan. 13, 1267-1268, *Register of Walter Giffard*, 146-148; March 15, 248-249; *Archbishop Wickwane's Register*, March 1279-1280, 92, 312; *Register of Jno. Le Romeyn*, 1; Sept., Dec. 1290; 213-214, 216; *Reg. Epist. Jno. Peckham*, 2; 650-653, 654-655; 658-661; 661-665; 704-3; 805-806; 846-848; 849; 851-852; 916-917; 924; 928. Cf. *The English Register of Godstow Nunnery*, Pt. 3, lxxxi-lxxxvii, 15th century, etc.

the sixteenth century by letters [310] of governmental functionaries who, in justification of the suppression of monasteries, cite instances of flagrant turpitude.   There is, for example, in the twelfth century the Abbess of Almsbury whom John of Salisbury reproves for having, as unbecoming a woman and a religious, taken up arms against a lawful incumbent of an ecclesiastical preferment and deprived him of his property, and who persists contumaciously in refusing to restore it, although incurring thereby severe ecclesiastical penalties. [311]   Another abbess, also repeatedly warned and to no effect, is threatened with excommunication unless she amend her defective conduct and within so many days remove from the church and monastery an official whose presence and mode of life there give occasion of notorious scandal.[312] Abbesses of relatively similar conduct are recorded in the letters of Archbishop Peckham [313] and of Adam of Marisco, [314] while the letters of Grosseteste [315] both imply and specify the evil conduct— moral and administrative, and ranging in separate cases from minor faults to flagrant defects—of many abbesses of later medieval England.[316]

The very antithesis of the tradition is found in the abbess who, repeatedly threatened with ecclesiastical penalties, remains disobedient and returns to her delinquencies; [317] in her who, *propter culpas suas* [318] is removed from office; in the prioress incapable of ruling the community and of maintaining discipline; in the

[310] Cf. Wright (4) passim.   After all due allowance is made for the self-interest of the investigators, a measure of truth must be conceded to their charges.

[311] Cf. Giles, (4) I; ep. 72, pp. 95-96, ep. 74, p. 98.

[312] Cf. *ibid.*, ep. 130, pp. 180-181.

[313] Cf. *op cit.*, 2; 658-659; 3; 928.

[314] Cf. Brewer (1) 1; ep. 23, p. 108.

[315] Cf. Luard, lxix. Cf. also ep. 107 and 108, 317-321, for examples of disordered religious and ecclesiastical conditions in the thirteenth century.

[316] Cf. Visitation of Swyne in *Register of Walter Giffard*, 146-148; 248-249; *Reg. Epist. Jno. Peckham*, 2; 651, 653, 2; 851, 928; *Reg. of Visitation of Godstow* in the fifteenth century by William, Bishop of Lincoln, 3; lxxxii; cf. Jessopp, *Visit. Dioc. of Norwich* (1492), 17.

[317] Cf. *ibid.*

[318] Cf. Luard, lxix.

superior incompetent to administer the community property [319] and who must, therefore, be enjoined to consult in administrative affairs prudent nuns of the community; [320] in the abbess who lives in abundance while the community is in want; [321] in her who neglects to care for the sick and to provide necessities for her subjects; [322] in her who mingles with the world, allows the nuns to do the same,[323] and allows the world to intrude within the cloister; [324] in the head of a monastery who, instead of profiting by the advice and guidance of ecclesiastics, withstands it; [325] in her who must be cautioned to avoid vanity and extravagance in dress and to observe conventual regulations in this respect; [326] and in her who, in order to quell defamation, must be warned to prevent seculars—among whom, in the thirteenth as in the fifteenth century injunctions, are included the students of Oxford— from frequenting the monastery.[327] Historiographical literature, nevertheless, does not reflect them.

Even these strictly official documents testify in part to the presence of the literary tradition. The introduction and conclusion of such records are frequently couched in the language of traditional patristic didacticism. In them the monastic ideal is often held up against the conditions actually discovered by the visitors. And in correcting the defects of a given abbess, they frequently recall the virtues and abbatial qualities so often and

---

[319] Cf. *Register of Walter Giffard* (To Swine Priory) Jan. 13, 1267-1268, 147. Cf. also *Reg. Epist. Jno. Peckham*, 3; 805-806 (To Uske Nunnery). Cf. *Visit. Dioc. of Norwich* (1520), 185-186; 190.

[320] Cf. *ibid.*, 3; 846 (To Godstow).

[321] Cf. *ibid.*, 2; 651 (To Wherwell).

[322] Cf. *Register of Walter Giffard*, 147 (To Swyne). Cf. also *Visit. Dioc. of Norwich* (1532), 290-292.

[323] Cf. *Reg. Epist. Jno. Peckham*, 2; 664 (To Romsey); *ibid.*, 3; 847 (To Godstow).

[324] Cf. *Register of Walter Giffard*, 148; *Reg. Epist. Jno. Peckham*, 2; 652-653; 662-663 (To Romsey); *ibid.*, 3, 848 (To Godstow).

[325] Cf. *Reg. Epist. Jno. Peckham*, 2; 707 (To Catesby).

[326] Cf. *op. cit.*, 3; 849 (To Godstow); also *Register of Henry of Newark* (vol. 2 of *Register of Jno. Le Romeyn*), 224 (To Swyne).

[327] Cf. *Reg. Epist. Jno. Peckham*, 3; 851 (To Godstow); 924 (To Sheppey); *Visitation of Godstow by William, Bishop of Lincoln*, lxxxiii; *Register of Henry of Newark*, 223.

so faithfully repeated in the traditional historical literature.   One example of this fashion is the flowery, metaphorical passage prefacing the injunction (c. 1284) of John Peckham, Archbishop of Canterbury, to Romsey Abbey.   He draws an analogy between the consecrated nuns in the abbey and the *in horto lilii* among whom the Spouse finds His delight; he refers to the "lily of virginity," "a heavenly ornament," "the adornment of angels." [328] In addressing Godstow Abbey at about the same date, the Archbishop alludes to *pudicitia virginum* as *ecclesiae ornamentum,* as "angelic," an "especial treasure," as attracting the particular predilection of the King of Glory. [329]   To the minds of the Abbess of Wherwell and the Abbess of Romsey he recalls the fact that they are to be as mothers [330] to their community.   To the latter he suggests prudence [331] and that she be a model of virtue, fasting, watching, and prayer to her nuns; [332] to the former, whom he alludes to as one of Christ's spouses, [333] he recommends kindness and care of all, if she desires the heavenly reward. [334]

6. Summary

Historiographers of England from the seventh to the sixteenth century impose, with only a few variations that are insignificant, the same compound of qualities upon the abbess of whom they treat.   A large number of the references to abbesses found are merely "continuations" of Bede (sometimes of Eddius), faithful incorporations of Bede's text on a given abbess.   These "continuations" undoubtedly had their part—and a great one—in impressing the description typical of Bede on the consciousness of later generations.   But they are far more significant as examples of a marked habit of medieval historiography than of our

[328] Cf. *op. cit.,* 2; 661-662.   Such traditional symbols of sublime truths, familiar to every religious, are presented by ecclesiastical authority in order to recall to the mind of the nuns the lofty character of their vocation. Such injunctions, moreover, are often couched in a decidedly paternal and conciliatory tone—a circumstance not noted, as far as I have been able to observe, in studies of these medieval registers.

[329] Cf. *ibid.,* 3; 846.   [332] Cf. *ibid.,* 658.

[330] Cf. *op. cit.,* 2; 650-651.   [333] Cf. *ibid.,* 650-651.

[331] Cf. *ibid.,* 662.   [334] Cf. *ibid.*   Cf. also Alcuin p. 24 above.

chief interest here. The fact significant for us is that, outside the "continuation" passages, the historical writers of later generations follow so faithfully and implicitly the portrait of the abbess painted by Bede.

That portrait is one of a royal abbess of striking and pleasing personality; the capable administrator and executive of the complex activity of a medieval double monastery; the able woman, participating, in virtue of her abbatial position, in ecclesiastical matters of national import and wielding therein the formidable power with which her abbatial office invests her and the personal prestige of a member of a royal family; the ideal monastic superior, endowed with the gift to control and promote the material, educational, and spiritual phases of the religious life of monks and nuns within the monastery; the woman, enlightened and counselled by eminent ecclesiastics and herself sought out for advice by members of all ranks of society, a woman known for her virtue and wisdom and loved both within and without the monastery for her maternal qualities. But, above all, the portrait is that of the saintly religious whose holiness is attested in life and in death by marvels.

All the abbesses in the *Historia Ecclesiastica* conform to this picture, although all of the details found in one portrait are not always found in another. In fact, Bede so far emphasizes virginity and personal virtue in the case of one abbess that he is really following a distinct schema in his account of her, although she is on the whole a typical abbess of the *Historia Ecclesiastica*. Both schemata, now differentiated, now blended, are faithfully repeated and followed throughout the eight succeeding centuries of historiography.

In Bede and Eddius we can believe that we have a portrait taken from life. But when we consider the records revealing monastic conditions which imply an abbess not the ideal whom Bede presents, when we recall the specific evidence of episcopal records which report instances of abbesses who are the antithesis of Bede's abbess, when we recollect that the historiographical accounts were written in most instances by Churchmen and in many instances by monastic churchmen too, who must have been cognizant of abuses—when we consider these facts and then remember that in the historiography of England from Bede to the sixteenth century only so few striking deviations from Bede's type occur, we are forced to conclude that a powerful literary tradition is at work in historiographical literature from the time of Bede.

Historiographical records yield only four really outstanding exceptions to the type, so far as I know; the notorious Eadburga of the early ninth century; the infamous abbess of Almsbury in the twelfth century; the vicious seventh-century abbess of Chelles, and the legendary traits of Abbess Modwenna. Of a wholly individual character are the annals repeating the magnificent though gruesome deed of Abbess Ebba in the ninth century to save herself and her community from the Danish marauders. Untypical also—and negligible as well, were it not for the interpretation modern literature has put upon the identical or similar episodes—are the annals recording Alfreda's penitential retirement to Wherwell Abbey in the tenth century; an abbess of the next century being given custody of a dishonored queen, and at the beginning of the twelfth century, the Saxon Princess Maud's quitting the abbey where her aunt is abbess to become England's queen. The majority of these exceptions are obviously due to circumstances so special that the traditional manner of treatment was not employed: the annals, in fact, were not developed at all.

Bede's schema, his method of treatment, is followed faithfully by many historiographers until the sixteenth century at least. In the eleventh century, however, a new manner of treatment can be discerned, which persists parallel to Bede's treatment from that time on. It consists chiefly in the embellishment of facts essentially no different from Bede's facts with the time-worn, flowery, decorative commonplaces of patristic literature. It also frequently includes an elaborate preface to the abbatial career consisting of the abbess' edifying life before she became abbess. In short the abbess of English historiography from the end of the seventh to the sixteenth century (and beyond) is the abbess of Anglo-Saxon England as presented first in extant literature by Venerable Bede and repeated sometimes without variation, sometimes with patristic elaborations by subsequent writers.

Many of the chroniclers after the twelfth century, unlike some of the few chroniclers of preceding ages, are merely continuators.

Whether exhausted by the sheer effort of continuating, as one chronicler confesses, or out of loyalty to pre-Norman England and corresponding hostility to the Plantagenets, they record nothing of their own times; many write continuations and also treat of their own times: some treat of their own times only. Yet, with the exception of the author of *The Chronicle of the Reigns of Henry II and Richard I,* who makes contemporaneous references to the disreputable abbess and community at Almsbury in the late twelfth century, neither of the latter treats in any detail [335] of the abbess or of the nun of their own times. The pre-Norman abbess is still presented in great detail. Contemporary abbesses are found only in a brief and infrequent record.

It is not, however, to be inferred from the barrenness of chronicles on the subject of contemporary abbesses that specialized records, such as the episcopal registers and injunctions following upon monastic visitation, are the exclusive witness to abbesses of later medieval England. There are, or course, throughout this period worthy abbesses, abbesses even strikingly reminiscent of the great Anglo-Saxon superiors written of by Venerable Bede. Documents composed even in the heat of the Reformation testify to this fact.[336] The circumstance, moreover, that the irregularities were so severely reprehended in official documents must not be lost sight of in assessing monastic conditions of the times.

Bede, finally, as no others writer of his time was an historian.[337] He had a regard for, some sense of, sources.[338] Others repeat him.

[335] Cf. p. 100 above for annnotation of condensed references to this convent in continuators.

[336] Cf. Wright (4) 229-231. Cf. *Visit. Dioc. of Norwich,* 1492-1532, passim.

[337] "A primary and original authority which stands alone": quoted from Gehle (*Disputatio . . . de Bedae . . . vita et scriptis,* Lugd. Batau, 1838, 79) by Plummer, H. E. 1; note 3, p. xlii. Cf. also Stubbs. pref. to G. R. I; p. ix. Cf. Manitius (4) 1; 81-82; CMH 3; 511.

[338] Cf. H. E. 1; pp. xxiii-xxiv. Cf. note 3, *ibid.,* p. xxiii. The abbesses mentioned by Gregory of Tours in his *Historia Francorum* (v. g. IV, 26; VI, 29; IX, 40 and 42) and celebrated by Fortunatus in his verse (v. g. VIII, no. 5; XI, no. 2-26) suggest superficially a possibly common source with Bede for the abbess. But the resemblances are only superficial and inevitable. The abbesses of Gregory and Fortunatus were formed upon the

With Bede or Bede's immediate sources, therefore, the abbess is original. She is an indigenous product of Anglo-Saxon England and, presumably, usually the embodiment of Bede's list of abbatical characteristics. She is not a mere personification of patristic theory nor a continental importation. The conditions in which she lives and the demands made upon her by her abbatial position undoubtedly make her so. Nevertheless, there is no reason for supposing, in spite of the consistent and constant formative force of a religious rule and the stability of the principles of the religious life, and in spite of the fact that some non-literary historical records testify to the presence of abbesses in later England quite comparable to those in the *Historia Ecclesiastica;* —there is, in spite of these circumstances, no reason for supposing that the abbess of England always presented the qualities detailed by Bede. The fact that, with one exception, historiographers, apart from blind continuators, write of the abbess in the manner of Bede even centuries after him and in actual conditions which afford both admirable contemporary abbesses and also those who deny the ideal, is the result of the imposition of a literary tradition. Historiographers, generally, were neither keen psychologists nor innovators. They looked to the past both for matter and manner. They sought there a guiding traditional manner of treatment and a model sanctioned by the authority of precedent. And the didactic urge was never entirely absent.

The abbess of the literary historiographical records of medieval England is, as a result of this habit, the saintly Anglo-Saxon abbess of the *Historia Ecclesiastica.* In the eighth century an authentic historical fact, she becomes, through the force of tradition, a type. Through the force of the tradition, again, persisting and progressing, through similar and dissimilar actual conditions, that type is carried from the eighth century to the sixteenth, from history, through historiography, to English literature.

rule of Caesarius of Arles. Bede's abbesses followed undoubtedly some Celtic rule until the Benedictine rule became dominant in Britain. This fact alone would make for important differences.

III. *The Simple Nun*

1. In the *Historia Ecclesiastica*

The nine simple nuns in the *Historia Ecclesiastica* suggest the ideal consecrated virgin expounded in the didactic writings of patristic Latin and of medieval England. Seven of them are in attendance upon the Mother Abbess and the other two also are introduced by Bede incidentally. In conformity with their subordinate rôle a full picture of none of the nine is given, but enough details are present in each instance to show the unity of inspiration with the didactic writers. Accounts of nuns in historiographical materials are naturally rare. The rôle of a simple nun is at all times an other-worldly, self-effacing rôle, removed from the world of affairs treated in historiography. It is only some very special circumstance, some accident, something not peculiar to the life of a nun which will bring her to the pages of history. After Bede no nuns are found in the historiography of England until the eleventh century and from that time only a few.

Two of the nine nuns of the *Historia Ecclesiastica* have to do with miraculous cures. The first of these appears as the companion of an abbess who has been summoned at night to the bedside of a guest who is, as Bede expresses it, *a diabolo arreptus*. She remains modestly in the background, emerging only at the order of the abbess to procure from the monastery of the church a relic to be applied, in the failure of all remedies, to the suffering visitor. At the approach of the nun, returning with the reliquary, the guest, as he states later, finds instant relief.[339] Another nun is herself the subject of an instantaneous cure. She is suffering severely and is in imminent danger of death from an infected arm when John of Beverley, Bishop of York, with another ecclesiastic, visits the Abbess, Hereberg of Watton. Quoenburg, as the young nun is called, is the abbess' own daughter as well as a member of her community. Blessed by the bishop at the instance of the abbess, the nun, of whose life all but the abbess, urged by maternal affection and the hope to have her daughter succeed her in the abbatial office,

---

[339] Cf. *op. cit.*, III, xi, 149-150. This episode is repeated in the fifteenth century. Cf. NLA 2; 266.

had despaired, is cured. Gaily she declares and proves her recovery to the ecclesiastic whom she has called to her presence about an hour after the episcopal blessing.[340] Quoenburg, alone of the nine nuns of Bede, has a distant personality. The stereotyped meekness and other-worldly simplicity so outstanding in the other portraits are in her case subordinated to a native sprightliness of disposition rarely noticed in accounts of nuns.

The remaining instances of simple nuns in the *Historia Ecclesiastica* are in connection with records of holy deaths, five of them occurring at the same monastery of Barking and within a comparatively short time of one another. Death is robbed of horror and gruesomeness in the accounts of the simple nun as in those of the typical saintly abbess. It is looked upon as the entrance to eternal life, and is, therefore, usually depicted as majestic and luminous with supernatural glory. Less majestic than sweetly appealing, however, is the first of these accounts, the most simply told and the only one of its kind in Bede, devoid of visions or of other supernatural marvels. A little boy, as it seems, not over three years of age, being reared among the nuns at Barking, is stricken fatally with the plague then raging. At his last breath, the child calls out the name, " Eadgyd, Eadgyd, Eadgyd ". The nun of that name, not present at the time, falls a victim to the plague that very day and the same day follows the child who had called her to the celestial kingdom.[341]

In the same monastery another nun, dying of the same disease, requests those watching about her bed throughout the night to extinguish the light. When they do not comply, it being about midnight, she tells them that she is aware of the fact that they think her delirious, but that, in very truth, she sees the whole house filled with a light so brilliant that, in comparison, their taper is dark. As they make no move to obey her, she concedes, but declares that their light is not hers, that her light will come to her at the beginning of dawn. At that time she will enter into eternal light, she informs them, as she has learned from the vision of a holy man who had

---

[340] Cf. *op. cit.*, V, iii, 285-286. This episode is repeated in later works. Cf. O. E. Mart. 78; Alcuin, *Poema de Pontificibus et Sanctis Ecc. Eb.*, lines 1120-1132, BRG 6; 115; Vita S. J. E. E., Raine (2) 247-249 (11c).

[341] Cf. *op. cit.*, IV, viii, 220-221.

died that year. The truth of her words is proved by her death at daybreak.[342]

At the death of the abbess of the same monastery, a nun, Torctgyd, who has dwelt there many years, serving God humbly and sincerely and assisting the abbess in the routine of monastic government by maintaining regular discipline among the young, beholds a remarkable vision. For nine years this holy religious had been perfected and purified by sickness, her faults of ignorance or negligence being eradicated by daily pain. Early one morning, as dawn is breaking, she sees as it were a human body, more brilliant than the sun, wrapt in a sheet, borne on high from the house where the religious live. The glorious body is raised higher and higher upon the gleaming golden ropes until it disappears in the heavens. The nun does not doubt but that some one of the community whose good deeds, like the golden cords, would carry her to heaven, would soon die. The abbess' death fulfills the portent.[343]

Three years later, Torctgyd, now paralyzed in limb and tongue, is dying. Suddenly she opens her eyes, and, gazing towards heaven, begins to speak as if welcoming a visitor. She pauses for a reply. Again she speaks as if in response to a statement made by the unseen visitant. She is not, she declares, so pleased with this decision. After a second pause, the venerable nun says, " If it cannot be to-day, I beg that it will not be long ", and then finally, " If it is definitely fixed and cannot be changed, then I pray that it may not be delayed longer than tomorrow night ". The attendants ask her with whom she is speaking. She tells them that she has been conversing with her dear Mother (the abbess, who had died three years before) and that she had come to announce the hour of her death. As the holy nun had requested, she " cast off the chains of infirmity and entered into eternal joy at the close of the next night ".[344] Recounted by Venerable Bede, obviously to publish the virtues of the abbess, the instance helps, nonetheless, to depict the lineaments of the simple nun—docile, obedient, affectionate, naïvely

---

[342] Cf. *op. cit.*, 221. Repeated in close detail in 15c. NLA 1; 421.

[343] Cf. *op. cit.*, IV, ix, 221-222. Repeated practically verbatim in the 15c. NLA 1; 421.

[344] Cf. *op. cit.*, 223-224. Repeated in a condensed but complete form in the 15th century. NLA 1; 421-422.

unruffled at the supernatural privilege enjoyed, supremely confident in the departed abbess even at the hour of her own death.

Another aged and paralyzed nun, " of noble birth and ", as Bede avers in conformity with conventional patristic idealogy on this subject, "nobler in her love of the future life ",[345] is carried to the bier of this same abbess and there, with her head bowed, speaks to her in prayer as a child would plead with its mother, begging the abbess to obtain her release from her pains. The prayer of this faithful and venerable nun, as the *Historia Ecclesiastica* records, is promptly heard. Twelve days after, she exchanges earthly affliction for an eternal reward.[346] The simplicity of the aged nun's action; the utterly childlike reliance upon the saintly abbess' aid; the mutual affection of abbess and nun which the familiar prayer bespeaks, as well as the glow of personal holiness the incident reflects upon herself, are all indicative of the typical simple nun.

At the death of Abbess Hilda of Whitby, one of her nuns, Begu by name, beholds a vision quite similar to that seen by Torctgyd before the death of the abbess of Barking. Begu, a religious, having served God for over thirty years, awakes one night at the monastery of Hackness, a branch of Whitby monastery, as if summoned by the bell rung to assemble the community for prayer at the death of a member of the order. A flood of light pours through the roof, and she sees the soul of Abbess Hilda being conducted by angels through the light to heaven. Frightened and in tears, she hastens to Frigyd, the nun who represented the abbess at Hackness, and with heavy sighs announces the death of their beloved abbess. The community, having been aroused and having prayed until morning for Abbess Hilda's soul, learns from messengers that she had died at Whitby at the moment that Begu had witnessed the heavenly vision.[347] Again at Whitby, at the moment of Abbess Hilda's death, another nun, who loved her intensely but at the time was in another part of the monastery, also sees her soul ascend to heaven in the company of angels.[348]

Every nun mentioned in the *Historia Ecclesiastica* is employed as a witness to the marvelous, usually to the marvelous attendant

[345] Cf. S. Ambrose, *De Virginibus*, I, 206.
[346] Cf. *op. cit., ibid.*, 222-223.
[347] Cf. *op. cit.*, IV, xxi, 257-258.   [348] Cf. *ibid.*, 258.

upon the death of a holy person. The most outstanding of such marvels in each instance are physical manifestations, of which a brilliant light [349] is one feature, announcing the departure of the soul from the body. These singular facts recall the treatment of simple nuns under like circumstances by Saint Gregory the Great in the fourth book of his *Liber Dialogorum*,[350] which Bede or his sources could have known. In the first twenty-seven chapters [351] of that book Saint Gregory is much concerned to expound by examples the immortality of the soul and the joys of heaven. He declares, among much else, that the soul, though spiritual, can be seen by very holy persons at the moment of its departure from the body.[352] In proof of this statement Gregory devotes the next four chapters [353] of his work to recounting visions observed at the hour of death and recalls the thesis in many passages, along with accounts of similar visions.[354] The vision of a soul being conducted, as recorded in the *Historia Ecclesiastica,* by angels through a brilliantly lighted way from earth until lost from human sight in the heavens, is a common phenomenon in the *Liber Dialogorum*.[355] The simple nun of Gregory's accounts is depicted in greater detail than in the corresponding accounts of Bede, but with the exception of the nun Quoenburg, Bede's nuns, even those most faintly outlined, recall in the details given the fuller accounts of Saint Gregory. Thus, the dying nun calling out in the middle of the night to her sisters to extinguish their pale light in the midst of the heavenly brilliance surrounding [356] her and filling the entire house has a parallel in the deathbed scene of a nun in *Liber Dialogorum* IV, xv: *Cumque noctis medio lectulo jacentis assisterent, subito coelitus, lux emissa omne illius cellulae spatium implevit.*[357] The apparition of a venerable old man in the midst of the light, who discloses to the nun in the *Historia Ecclesiastica* the hour of her death, is a close parallel also to another deathbed scene in *Liber*

---

[349] " Saint Gregory's favorite symbol to which he returns again and again in describing contemplation is Light. He conceives of God as the boundless or unencompassed light."—Butler (2) 110.

[350] PL 77, 317-430.

[351] Cf. *ibid.*, 317-365.

[352] Cf. *ibid.*, VII, 332.

[353] Cf. *ibid.*, viii-xi, 332-337.

[354] Cf. *ibid.*, xii-xvii, 337-349 particularly.

[355] Cf. *ibid.*, vii-xxvii, 317-365 passim.

[356] Cf. H. E. IV, viii, 221.

[357] Cf. *op. cit.*, 345.

Dialogorum IV. In the latter, Saint Peter appears to the dying nun. He stands between two candelabra burning at her bedside and invites this holy nun to heaven.[358] The prolonged physical suffering with which some of the nuns in the *Historia Ecclesiastica* are visited is considered, as in the *Liber Dialogorum IV,* a final purification and perfecting of the soul after a very holy life and the preparation for the glorious reward of heaven, a brief foretaste of which these religious are granted at their last hour.[359] In the sole instance, moreover, in which Venerable Bede in the *Historia Ecclesiastica* enters at all into detail about the virtues characterizing the life of the simple nun,[360] he enumerates virtues which correspond with those recounted of the simple nun in the *Liber Dialogorum,*[361] emphasis in both cases being placed upon such monastic virtues as obedience, humility, and sincerity in the service of God to the exclusion of many other possible points.

We are not interested in proving here Bede's indebtedness to Saint Gregory, although the details used by Bede are of such a character as to make plausible that assumption. The pertinent point here is that insofar as it suits his purpose, Bede, or his source, is drawing upon sources not peculiar to England. He is following a convention in his treatment of simple nuns (with the one exception noted above); something the materials now available allow us to assume scarcely at all in the case of his abbesses. The nun in Bede (again with the exception of Quoenburg) is Saint Gregory's nun—*ancilla Dei, virgo sacrata, sanctimonialis*—abbreviated to make way for the ampler portrait of the abbess. But she fits perfectly into the type found in Saint Gregory, found in the more elaborate portraits of didactic literature, and in the ampler accounts of later English historiographers. The very words, *virgo, Deo dicata,* with which she is always designated in the Latin of the period create the impression of holiness, of a person consecrated and set apart from the commonplace as well as from the profane aspects of ordinary worldliness. The restricted and singular uses to which Bede puts the simple nun, the incidents he chooses, the

[358] Cf. *op. cit.,* xiii.

[359] Cf. H. E. IV, ix (two instances), pp. 223, 223-224 with *Liber Dialogorum* IV, xiii, and xv.

[360] Cf. *op. cit* (Torctgyd) IV, ix, 222.   [361] Cf. *op. cit.,* XIII, xv.

details he gives, bring into strong relief this divorce from the things of earth and the childlike guilelessness, simplicity, and other-worldly sweetness frequently found in consecrated women. This character she preserves throughout historiographical literature and with it, as we shall see, she enters romantic literature in the six-teenth century with the richness of detail which the romantic imagination adds.

2. Pre-abbatial Monastic Careers of Anglo-Saxon Abbesses

With few exceptions each of the portraits of simple nuns found in historiographical writers after Bede appears because the nun in question was, in the first place, of royal birth; secondly, became an abbess; and thirdly, became a saint. The simple nun, therefore, with these same few exceptions, again fills in the abbatial picture; only, in these later-told instances it is the picture of her own abba-tial self rather than of some other abbess.

Each of the abbesses whose pre-abbatial career is treated by historiographers subsequent to Bede flourished—one excepted—in the seventh century. Bede, in fact, mentions many of these reli-gious as abbesses, and one, Etheldreda, he treats in great detail. The later accounts of them as nuns are removed by many centuries, therefore, from the times in which they lived. These later authors are harking back to the good old Anglo-Saxon times before the Conquest and before the growth of French abbeys in England. That enormous and disproportionate emphasis is given to those times will be discerned by anyone who will take the trouble to read these books. That the pre-abbatial career is being elaborated for the sake of those good old times is also evident. The accounts are much longer than even the abbatial accounts of pre-Conquest litera-ture, but these new dimensions are swollen by materials borrowed wholesale from the traditional didactic genre.

a. Editha and Her Mother

The foregoing facts are all borne out in the various accounts of Editha, the daughter of King Edgar, whose life as a typical royal abbess has been considered. Editha was from infancy confided to her mother, Wulftrude, to be reared by her at the great monastery of Wilton. Soon, as one chronicle after another records,[362] she becomes a nun and thus passes her life in consecrated virginity. Her entire history, as suggested more or less extensively in the chronicles and detailed in two Latin *vitae*—one of the late eleventh century, the other of the fifteenth—and in a lengthy Middle English verse account of the fifteenth century, is radiant with holiness and spirituality, modest retirement, simplicity of character, guilelessness, and utter other-worldliness. Her obedience is complete, and so meek is she that miracles attest this virtue. In the earlier Latin *vita* [363] she is represented as passing her girlhood in a monastery under the guardianship of her mother, a religious. As becomes a princess, Editha is dressed in rich and royal robes, but in conformity with the patristic ideal virgin, she considers them as naught and prefers study and the adornment of virtue to gold and jewels.[364] She chooses—as again patristic didactic convention dominates both thought and expression in the *vita*—the part of Mary, loving retirement rather than the publicity of external activity. She lives frugally and even as a young girl wears harsh garments of hair cloth beneath her glowing robes. Rebuked on one occasion by an ecclesiastic, deceived undoubtedly by the richness of her dress, she bespeaks the holiness of her heart in the reply— strikingly suggestive of Saint Agnes' immortal avowal—*Habeo Dominum meum, qui non tam vestem quam mentem attendit.*[365] William of Malmesbury repeats this incident in the *Gesta Pontificum,*[366] varying, however, the holy maid's reply.

In the foregoing items the commonplaces of didactic literature have obviously impressed themselves on the historiographical genre. From now on these commonplaces are appealed to in increasing abundance. They are the one resource open to the later writers, who, in lieu of new materials wherewith to embellish Anglo-Saxon tales for Anglo-Norman minds and to make the heroines fit into a preconceived mold, ring the changes on patristic commonplaces.

In the Middle English verse treatment, Editha becomes all the more definitely and completely the typical simple nun-figure as modeled upon traditional didactic thought. The " sacryd maden's "

---

[362] Cf. *Fl. Wig.* 1; 140; G. R. 1; 180; G. P. 188; Fl. Hist. 1; 509.

[363] *Vita S. E. G.* 623-624.   [365] *Op. cit.*, 623-624.

[364] Cf. p. 32, above.   [366] Cf. *op. cit.*, 189.

birth and holy life are foretold to her father in a symbolic dream. In this dream a glowing lamp which

"... ȝefth gret lyȝt
To euery creature abouȝt hit dwellynge ",

signifies his future daughter, who shall

... ȝeue to euerry weyȝt
Gret ensampull of gode leuyng.[367]

The radiant spirituality of the nun who has grown to angelic girlhood under her mother's care in the monastery amply fulfils the portent. So virtuous is the life she leads and so replete is she with God's grace that simply to be in her presence is to share in her supernal joy.[368] Many long to catch a glimpse of the " semely face "[369] of this modest, black-robed nun,[370] who comes from prayer as

Gladsome as þaw he had come ouȝt of paradys.[371]

She is loved by men and women for her sweet amiability and lowliness, and even the birds and beasts come readily to her call, wild animals feeding gently at her hand and feathered creatures fluttering peacefully there to rest. Doves, of all birds, are her special predilection. These she loves most tenderly and caresses most frequently,

By-cause þey ben legenyed to þe holy gost.[372]

" Fulle clere " is " here voys ... in syngynge "[373] to the accompaniment of the harp which " welle he couthe ".[374] She is learned;[375] skilled in the arts of painting, sculpture,[376] and clever at gold and silk embroidery. The last accomplishment she exercises in decorating ecclesiastical vestments, adorning them with " golde fulle redde " and " mony a ryalle ston ". But of " worldlyche clothus of pryde ", she takes " no hede ".[377] When she herself had appeared in such regal and costly robes, she wore—as is faithfully

[367] Horstmann (9) 22.
[368] Cf. *op. cit.*, 25.
[369] *Ibid.*
[370] Cf. *ibid.*, 27.
[371] *Ibid.*, 24.
[372] Cf. *ibid.*, 26.
[373] *Ibid.*
[374] *Ibid.*, 27.
[375] Cf. *ibid.*, 26.
[376] Cf. *ibid.*, 27.
[377] Cf. *op. cit.*, 26-27.

recorded in account after account of this holy maid—penitential clothes beneath.[378]   Despite her royal birth and many accomplishments, she is modestly retired and humble.

> For he couetede neuer in no wyse
> To be worshepud for here hey3e lynage,
> But euer to be meke in lowe seruyse,
> For all to mekenes was here currage.[379]

She refers to

> ". . . here mateynesse & masse
> & vpon hure boke to rede and spelle,
> Nen to be duchas, quene or cowntasse.[380]

Her prayers said, she occupies herself serving her sisters as Mary or Martha served Christ,[381] and bears herself lovingly and lowly towards all creatures, never injuring anyone in word or deed.[382]   A great part of the night she spends in prayer and penance. At early morning she hastens to prayer, seeking first the " kyndam of heuene " and the " heuene kynge " in Whom is all her trust.[383] Miracles proclaim her holiness,[384] and the king and prominent churchmen find her at the age of fifteen " so wyse, gentylle & so fre "[385] that they make her abbess.

The fifteenth-century Latin *vita,* although of much less pretentious proportion than the Middle-English verse work, is no less conventional in detail.   It emphasizes the same virtuous qualities of the young nun in the same symbolic fashion created by patristic didacticism.   It remarks her careful education;[386] her being adorned with learning and virtue rather than with gold and jewels;[387] her contempt for earthly things;[388] her penitential garb disguised under beautiful robes;[389] the miracles,[390] and her humble demurral before advancing to the dignity of abbess.[391]

The mother of Editha is also represented throughout these materials,[392] though with much less detail than is her daughter, as a

---

[378] Cf. *ibid.,* 27-28.

[379] *Ibid.,* 24.

[380] *Ibid.,* 36.

[381] Cf. *ibid.,* 24.

[382] Cf. *ibid.*

[383] Cf. *ibid.*

[384] Cf. *ibid.,* 29.

[385] *Ibid.,* 36.

[386] Cf. NLA 1; 311.

[387] Cf. *ibid.*

[388] Cf. *ibid.*

[389] Cf. *ibid.,* 311-312.

[390] Cf. *ibid.,* 312.

[391] Cf. *ibid.*

[392] Cf. Fl. of Wig. Chr. 1; 140; Vita S. D. Eadmero, Stubbs, 209-210; Vita S. D. Osberno, *ibid.,* 111-112; Vita S. E. G. 623, 625; G. R. 1; 180; G. P. 190-191; Fl. Hist. 1; 509; Horstmann (9) 23-24; 36; 37; 62.

typical simple nun before becoming abbess. The records differ on the question whether she was a religious as a school girl at the monastery when King Edgar forcibly withdrew her from the convent. But all agree that upon her return she became a nun. Some works offer sufficient characterization to permit our picturing her as a typical simple nun. William of Malmesbury records the holiness of her religious life.[393] The Middle English verse life of Saint Editha recounts her noble family;[394] her perfection in religion,[395] and her elevation to the post of abbess.[396]

b. Other Anglo-Saxon Abbesses

In the twelfth century the *Liber Eliensis* repeats and enlarges in the typical fashion upon the records of some abbesses and queens mentioned in the *Historia Ecclesiastica*. Of the pre-abbatial religious life of Queen Sexburg,[397] who succeeded Etheldreda as abbess of Ely,[398] this work notes that, having renounced all, she subjects herself to severe discipline at Ely. She lives as a simple nun wholly obedient to the abbess.[399] Her greatest desire is to subject herself to another and, although she has reared a family and has shared a throne, she becomes, nonetheless, a docile religious,[400] humbly subordinating herself to her own sister, Abbess Etheldreda, whom she begs to train her in regular discipline. As might be expected in a history of Ely, the pre-abbatial life of Etheldreda is greatly expanded. It is formed, however, upon the schema and material offered in the *Historia Ecclesiastica;* often, indeed, repeating the *Historia* verbatim. It elaborates the material, however, and includes details of the remarkable nun's life as a simple religious. These are cited in the typical fashion. As a girl, the *Liber Eliensis* recounts, Etheldreda had been studious and enamoured of holy virginity.[401] Having entered the monastery of Coldingham, she is, like the ideal of patristic and later monastic literature, humble both in garb and in manner;[402] she delights, as Aldhelm's embodiment

---

[393] Cf. G. P. 191.
[394] Cf. *op. cit.*, 23.
[395] Cf. *ibid.*, 24.
[396] Cf. *ibid.*, 62.
[397] Cf. H. E. III, viii, 142.

[398] Cf. *ibid.*, IV, xvii, 244-246.
[399] Cf. *op. cit.*, 52.
[400] Cf. *ibid.*, 53.
[401] Cf. *ibid.*, 17.
[402] Cf. *ibid.*, 36-37.

of the consecrated virgin, in seclusion, and like her, longs for the quiet of contemplation, which, as Mary, she chooses for her "part" in preference to the activity of Martha.[403] She is, again like the ideal, exceedingly obedient to the monastic rule,[404] and, even more typical of patristic idealogy, she rejoices in having despised all earthly pomp for the love of Christ.[405] She soon surpasses her companions in virtue, and the renown of her sanctity spreads throughout the land.[406] Pursued by her husband, the King, who had consented to her relinquishing the throne and married life, she takes flight to Ely. Marvels attend her passage and protect her from peril.[407] At Ely, she establishes her own monastery and in time is elevated to the position of abbess.[408] A fifteenth-century life of Etheldreda in Middle English verse,[409] while developing many of the traditional facts of her monastic life, does not add anything to the simple nun-figure.[410]

In some fifteenth-century *vitae,* moreover, John Capgrave both develops according to the traditional plan of the simple nun the monastic life of some religious mentioned in the *Historia Ecclesiastica* solely as abbesses [411] and elaborates in this manner that of religious not treated exclusively as such in preceding works.[412] Capgrave's treatment of the great Anglo-Saxon missionary nun, Walburga, abbess of Heidenheim and contemporary of Saint Boniface, is not at all in the typical manner.[413] Walburga's career belongs to Germany.

3. Nuns Who Were Not Abbesses

Capgrave also recounts according to the same device the *vitae* of nuns who are not so familiar, although they are not, indeed, complete strangers to the earlier historiographical tradition,[414] and in

---

[403] Cf. *ibid.,* 37.
[404] Cf. *ibid.*
[405] Cf. *op. cit.*
[406] Cf. *ibid.*
[407] Cf. *ibid.,* 37-39.
[408] Cf. *ibid.,* 48.
[409] Cf. Horstmann (7) 282-307.
[410] Cf. *ibid.,* 288-300.

[411] Cf. NLA 1; 303 with Eddius, *Vita Wilfridi,* Raine (2) 55-56, and H. E. IV, xxii, 243; xxiii, 264-265. Cf. NLA 1; 292-293 with H. E. IV, vi-vii, 219-220; ix-x, 221-225.

[412] Cf. NLA 1; 46 with L. E. 49, 76-77. Cf. NLA 1; 308-309; 2; 190-191.

[413] Cf. NLA 2; 404-406.

[414] Cf. *op. cit.,* 1; 457-460; 2; 207-208, 232-234, 506-508.

two instances he describes a group of nuns.[415] With a single exception,[416] one after the other of the individual *vitae,* however, emphasizes, among few differentiating episodes, the original time-honored characteristic qualities of the traditional simple nun.[417]

4. Pre-Monastic Careers

Scanty and scattered references, however, here and there throughout the chronicles [418] suggest more or less fully the simple nun type. A story recounted among twelfth century historiographical records [419] of Edburga, the daughter of Edward, King of England (985), while not of a nun, is in conformity with the simple nun tradition. When a mere child, Edburga forecasts her future life in the religious habit, her great humility and devotion, the marvels occurring during her life and after her death, by choosing freely from among many rich gifts and jewels, a sacred chalice and the Gospels.

Certain fifteenth-century *vitae* of early Anglo-Saxon abbesses, recorded tersely in chronicles and other historiographical works of earlier periods, often expand the life to include characteristics which, although attributed even to the pre-monastic career of the religious, are, notwithstanding, typical of those commonly identified with the simple nun tradition. Thus one seventh-century abbess, referred to briefly in the *Anglo-Saxon Chronicle* [420] and later annals,[421] is depicted in a fifteenth-century *vita* as being, before her entrance into religion, a mirror of sanctity, one given to ardent prayer and pious tears, generous with alms, and associated with marvels.[422] Another contemporary, i. e. seventh-century,

[415] Cf. *ibid.,* 2; 200. Cf. Munro, J. J., 67-68, 82-86.

[416] Cf. note 413.

[417] A quasi-historical work written in the twelfth century by Gaimar refers to the deserted young wife of the hero as retiring to Croyland and there taking the veil. Cf. Duffy, " Gesta Herewardi ", *Lestorie des Engles* 2; 397-398.

[418] Cf. Chr. Mon. de Ab. 1; 19; H. P. 6; 318; P. L. Chr. 2; 243.

[419] Cf. G. P. 2; 174-175; G. R. 1; 137.

[420] Cf. *ibid.,* 117.

[421] Cf. G. R. 1; 78; Fl. Hist. 1; 357; H. P. 5; 442.

[422] Cf. NLA 2; 130.

abbess mentioned in an early undated historical fragment in Anglo-Saxon,[423] is described in a fifteenth-century account as having been from infancy devoted to the service of God; detached from the pomp of the world; eager for heaven; zealous in religion, and desirous of the regular life and habit of a nun.[424] When her father proposes that she marry, she proclaims, in words again suggestive of those of Saint Agnes, frequently repeated in religious didactic literature, [425] that she has chosen Christ as her Spouse.[426] The story of Abbess Mildred's [427] pre-abbatical career is also expanded in this manner in the fifteenth-century account of her life. The royal maid is sent in secular dress, although she is a prospective nun of her mother's monastery, to the monastery at Chelle in France to pursue sacred studies. She soon surpasses the other virgins with whom she lives in humility and other virtues. Urged to marry by a scheming abbess,[428] the young woman rebukes her and reminds her of her intention to live a consecrated life. Saved miraculously from the flames into which the abbess casts her, the maid manages, by including a message of distress in a psalter which she has transcribed and sent to her mother, to gain assistance and make her escape. On her return to Britain and after miracles which attest her virtue, she is immediately appointed abbess of a community of nuns.[429]

5. Records of Monastic Abuses

Extant records of episcopal visitation of many English monasteries from the thirteenth century on, preceded for a century or more by occasional references of a similar nature in the correspondence of ecclesiastical authorities,[430] disclose instances both

---

[423] Cf. *Saxon Leechdoms* 3; 422.

[424] Cf. NLA 1; 297.

[425] Cf. p. 34, above.

[426] Cf. *op. cit.*, 298.

[427] Cf. reference to this abbess in: S. D. G. R. 13; *Saxon Leechdoms* 3; 422; G. R. 1; 78; G. P. 306; L. E. 52; Abbr. Chr. 1; 115; CM, 1; 299; Fl. Hist. 1; 333.

[428] Cf. p. 101, above.   [429] Cf. NLA 2; 193-195.

[430] Cf. ep. 127 of St. Anselm, PL 159, 163-164; cf. also Luard, ep. 107, 108, 130 of Grosseteste, 317-321, 439-442.

of venial delinquencies and serious irregularities which point, just as in the case of the abbess, to the existence of nuns who were the direct antithesis of the ideal religious and of the nun of historiographical literature. The general historical and historiographical references, moreover, quoted in the study of the abbess,[431] dating from the beginning of the Anglo-Saxon period until the appearance of such particularized documents as visitation registers and injunctions, and recording instances of monastic laxity and abuses, apply, it goes without remarking, to the nun as well. As the number of nuns, moreover, so far exceeded that of abbesses, these references apply obviously even more extensively to simple religious than they do to their superiors. In the case of the monastery of Coldingham, mentioned by Venerable Bede in the *Historia Ecclesiastica*,[432] it was the community, not the abbess, which was at fault. The allusions [433] of Boniface and of Alcuin to monastic demoralization, not imputed personally to any particular religious, point ostensibly to the community rather than to abbesses, whose name and whose conduct were at that time always in the public eye. In most of the later general [434] accusations, furthermore, discrimination even between monks and nuns and, after the beginning of the thirteenth century, between monks and nuns and friars,[435] is not ordinarily made.

But some evidences of monastic abuses attach specifically to the simple nun, contemporary with the historiographical records quoted. There is, for instance, among the letters of Anselm, one in which he gently, even affectionately, advises a nun, to refrain from intercourse with seculars and from too great intimacy with her relatives.[436] The irregular intercourse of nuns in varied degrees and ways with the world within and without the cloister becomes

---

[431] Cf. p. 102, above.

[432] Cf. p. 74, above. But cf. the general reference in Visit. Dioc. of Norwich (15-16 cent.) 138-140; 142-144.

[433] Cf. p. 102, above.

[434] The reference in *The Chronicle of the Reigns of Henry II and Richard I* to the lax community of Almsbury in 1177, of course, implicates the nuns as well as the abbess. Cf. *op. cit.* 1; 135-136.

[435] Cf. Howlett 2; xxx.

[436] Cf. ep. 127; PL 159, cols. 163-164.

11

the subject of manifold, repeated, and increasingly serious admonitions and corrections in visitation records, as the abuse itself generates greater abuses and, in frequent instances, weighty offenses.[437]   Examples of evil [438] and of deceived [439] nuns are cited; of nuns who have left the monastery even many times; [440] of nuns deprived of the veil; [441] of nuns sent to other monasteries for penance; [442] of insubordinate and conspiring nuns, nuns who have raised the standard of rebellion no less than three times within a convent; [443] and of nuns removed from one convent to another on account of their rebellious spirit.[444]   One nun is reported as *detractrix mendax, impatiens, odibilis concentui et rebellis*.[445]   There are general recommendations to the nuns of different monasteries that the community in each case as a whole revere [446] the superior, regard her as a mother, and cease murmuring.[447]   Indications of violation of the spirit and of the vow of poverty are present in these records.[448]   They betray, likewise, the presence of a spirit of extravagance, of worldliness, and of (perhaps unconscious) levity,

---

[437] Cf. Hefele 5; 926; 6; 221.   Cf. *Register of Walter Giffard* to Swyne Priory, 1267-1268, 148; *Reg. Epist. Jno. Peckham* 2; to Wherwell, 1284, 652-653; *ibid.*, To Romsey Abbey, 662-663, 664; *ibid.*, 3; to Uske Nunnery, 806; *ibid.*, to Godstow Abbey, 847-848, 849; *ibid.*, 851; *ibid.*, to the Convent of Sheppey, 1286, 924; *ibid.*, to Romsey, 928; *Register of Henry of Newark*, Visitation of Swyne, 1298(?) 2; 223; *Eng. Reg. of Godstow Nunnery*, 1451, lxxxiii.

[438] Cf. *Visit. of Godstow Nunnery* (15 cent.) lxxxii; cf. also import of *Reg. Epist. Jno. Peckham* (13 cent.) 3; 851.   Cf. *Visit. Dioc. of Norwich* (15 or 16 cent.) 109.

[439] Cf. *Reg. Epist. Jno. Peckham* 3; ep. 657, 916-917; Wright (4) 47-48.

[440] Cf. *Archbishop Wickwane's Register*, 92.   Cf. also *Register of Thom. Corbridge, . . . Archbishop of York*; 101-103, 144.   Cf. reference in ep. 21 of Prioress of Rowney to Henry IV (1400), Hingeston, *Royal and Hist. Letters during the Reign of Henry IV*, 48.

[441] Cf. *Register of Jno. Le Romeyn*, 216.

[442] Cf. *Archbishop Wickwane's Register*, 312.

[443] Cf. *Register of Walter Giffard*, 147.

[444] Cf. *Register of Jno. Le Romeyn* I; 213-214.

[445] *Register of Walter Giffard* (to Swyne Priory, 1267-8) 187.

[446] Cf. *Reg. Epist. Jno. Peckham*, 2; 660.

[447] Cf. *ibid.*, 665.

[448] Cf. *Register of Henry of Newark*, 223; cf. *Register of Jno. Le Romeyn*, I; 35.

which, despite the fundamental seriousness of the monastic abuses they indicate, are in their peculiar manifestation as cited, amusingly preposterous to the modern reader. Nuns are, in this connection, warned to eschew tight sleeves, deep collars, jeweled and ornate belts [449] and silk veils. Legislation prohibits their daring to fasten their veil with silver or golden tiring pins or to wear rings other than the one symbolizing their religious profession,[450] while one espiscopal recommendation enjoins that the nuns keep no monkeys in the convent, and (recalling Chaucer's "smal houndes" in connection with Madame Eglentyne) that the dogs be not numerous.[451]

General records, of course, as well as the specific indictments of particular nuns in the episcopal registers, represent, it is obvious, but a one-sided view of contemporary conventual life and of the religious life in a particular monastery.[452] The peculiar subject-matter of such registers and injunctions is that which is discovered amiss during an episcopal visitation; the good discovered is not recorded. These records, show nevertheless—again as in the case of the abbess—that while historiographers continued to present the simple nun as depicted in the foregoing pages, contemporary monastic life continued to present examples of nuns who were the total negation of the ideal nun of historiographical literature. Although we do not know to what extent the public shared the information of contemporary records, particularly that of episcopal visitation records, we do know that medieval historiographers as a class were men acquainted with the internal life of English monasteries and that those who wrote extensively of the simple nun were themselves exclusively—as far as the anonymity of some works allows us to generalize—religious or churchmen, ecclesiastics either living in or intimately connected with the monastic life of the period in which they lived.

---

[449] Cf. *Register of Henry of Newark,* 224; *Reg. Epist. Jno. Peckham,* 3; 849. At the Synod of Westminster in 1199 black nuns (Benedictines) were forbidden to wear colored mantels. Cf. Hefele 5; 797.

[450] Cf. *Reg. Epist. Jno. Peckham, ibid.* Cf. Synod at Oxford in 1222, Hefele 5; 925-926.

[451] Cf. *Reg. Epist. Jno. Peckham,* 2; 660. Cf. also *Visit. Dioc. of Norwich* (1520), 191.   [452] Cf. Bateson (1) 35; Liveing 94; Howlett 2, xxxi.

6. Summary

The simple nun appears as a distinctive type in the historical literature of England first in the *Historia Ecclesiastica* of Venerable Bede. The nine simple nuns depicted therein are, in their ancillary and wholly religious character, perfect embodiments, insofar as their outlines are drawn, of the ideal monastic virgin of patristic and contemporary religious didacticism. Subordinate to Bede's primary interests in the *Historia,* they, nevertheless, derive from the unchanging milieu in which he invariably presents them, a definite impress of palpable holiness, of the monastic virtues and qualities of reticence, obedience, childlike simplicity, and perfect regularity. All of them pleasing and wholly edifying in a general, uniform way, one alone among them is given a personal individual touch. To this extent her portrait constitutes an exception.

The character of these nuns in the *Historia* and particularly their constant association with the supernatural as well as the particular nature of the supernatural found in their lives strongly suggest analogous figures and subjects in the fourth book of Saint Gregory's *Liber Dialogorum.* The association is so close that Bede, although writing from such indigenous sources as he records in the preface [453] to the *Historia,* may justly be considered here to be under the direct or indirect influence of Gregory the Great.

After Bede, examples of the simple nun in the historiography of England are few, as one would expect from the cloistered life of religious. The accounts predominantly found are the pre-abbatical lives of Anglo-Saxon women known in history because royal and saintly abbesses. Most of these, moreover—in fact all but two, Editha and her mother, who lived during the tenth century—are abbesses of seventh-century England, called back to the recollection of later times, it may not rashly be suspected, by Anglo-Saxon sympathizers, protesting against the Norman dominance of the contemporary English church and the justified Norman contempt of Anglo-Saxon ecclesiastics who lived just before the Conquest. Apart from an isolated and barren chronicle record, which may be contemporary, none of the extant historiographical works in which

[453] Cf. H. E. praef. 6-8.

the simple nun appears as a distinctive personage after Bede was written before the late eleventh century, and most of these were written in the twelfth and in the fifteenth. They consist of the two *vitae* of St. Editha—one in Latin prose and the other in Middle English verse—and of many *vitae* (all in Latin but one) expanded to include details of the simple religious life of abbesses mentioned in the *Historia Ecclesiastica* or of others contemporary with those mentioned there. Some of the *vitae* written in the fifteenth century are of nuns who were not abbesses, but these nuns also are of pre-Conquest England. All these accounts of simple nuns reveal in more or less complete detail, in proportion to the extent of the *vita,* the traits of the simple nun who is found in the *Historia Ecclesiastica*. In addition they reveal the pronounced effect of patristic didactic literature. Details of personal virtue and monastic perfection of these abbesses' pre-abbatical life, perhaps never recorded, or, if recorded, lost in the distant perspective stretching from the eleventh or the fifteenth century to the seventh, are supplied by borrowings from didactic thought and applied in their conventional form to the story of the abbess' simple religious life. The same is true of the few accounts of nuns who did not become abbesses. All of these *vitae,* moreover,—the *vitae* of Saint Editha, the *vitae* of Anglo-Saxon abbesses, the *vitae* of Anglo-Saxon nuns, written from after the mid-eleventh century to the fifteenth—are couched in the language of religious didactic literature. Put to this use, the seemingly fragmentary, esoteric, and sterile items of didacticism manifest their literary significance and religious connotation. The essential facts of monastic perfection as revealed in the simple nun of the *Historia Ecclesiastica* remain. The way those items are represented in the later *vitae,* however, is in the conventionalized phraseology of patristic didactic thought. Historiography offers but very few and insignificant exceptions. Outstanding are the record of the dispersed community of Almsbury; the melodramatic story of Mildred's experiences at Chelles, and the distinctive career of the great Anglo-Saxon missionary nun, Saint Walburga. Despite changing times and despite the attestation of contemporary life and its examples (if few and rare, nonetheless striking) of nuns who were the direct opposite of the ideal, historiography continues in its typical way, turning out the same simple-nun character and turning back to Anglo-Saxon sources for the model.

IV. *Saint Werburge of Chester*

When Henry Bradshaw in the early sixteenth century put his antiquarian interest to the service of his piety and " with trem- blynge penne and hand ful of drede" Englished " the noble his- torye of saynt Werburge ",[454] he brought both the historiographical nun and the historiographical abbess types out of the realms of chronicle and hagiography into literature. The materials compris- ing this chapter find their proper close in this work in which both the simple nun and the abbess of historical tradition are presented together, essentially unchanged, yet entering into a new genre, that of artistic literature. It is a fitting close, moreover, because in it the English origins of the new type meet modern literature.

The *Life of Saint Werburge* is written in rhyme royal with an eight line stanza here and there. The first book is composed of five hundred and three of these stanzas, the second, of two hun- dred and forty, with fifty-nine additional stanzas appended. The whole is a legendary epic in the style of the Lydgate legend.[455] It has decidedly literary qualities and more than an infrequent touch of poetic grace. It is, nonetheless, but an expansion of the schema according to which Venerable Bede and many of his followers presented the Anglo-Saxon abbess in the *Historia Ecclesiastica* and later historical material respectively, and of the simple nun as depicted in the *Historia* and elaborated with didactic details in *vitae* following later. Although Saint Werburge is not one of the religious treated by Bede, she is a contemporary and relative of many of them and, as they, appears constantly in the traditional manner in historical and chronicle material from late Anglo-Saxon times until the fifteenth century.[456] The very expansion of the six-

---

[454] Horstmann (13).   [455] Cf. *op. cit.*, ix.

[456] Cf. *Saxon Leechdoms*, 3; 430; Fl. Wig. Chr. 1; 32; Vita S. W. G. xix-xxvi; G. R. 1; 78, 267; G. P. 309, 323; L. E. 25, 48, 51-52, 62-63, 77-78; Fl. Hist. 1; 332-33; CM 1; 298-299; H. P. 6; 126-128, 176-178; NLA 1; 406; NLA 2; *De Sancta Werburga*, 422-424.

teenth-century *Life* consists largely, in fact, in the inclusion of historical material about seventh-century abbesses borrowed from Bede and from later historiographers. Beginning, according to the traditional pattern, with the royal genealogy of Werburge, Bradshaw mentions many of Bede's typical abbesses [457] and those of later works.[458] In the course of the narrative of Werburge's life, moreover, he breaks off to develop—again according to the customary schema—the history of two [459] of the abbesses of the *Historia Ecclesiastica,* and that of one [460] contemporary abbess not treated there but treated in later works.[461] The names and a few familiar facts of the life of other abbesses of the *Historia Ecclesiastica* occur inevitably in connection with the development of these inserted *vitae.*[462] He adheres indeed to the schema followed by Bede in relating the *vita* of these abbesses, but, heir as he is to a convention long accumulating, he includes in two of them details of their pre-abbatical career in the fashion of writers later than Bede. The details, notwithstanding, are still those faithfully associated with the description of the simple nun from Bede to the fifteenth century. Of Abbess Sexburga,[463] Bradshaw states the royal genealogy; [464] her relinquishing the world and the honors of the court for the monastic life; [465] her erection of a monastery; [466] her being made abbess,[467] and, as abbess, her many virtues; [468] her gift of prophecy,[469] her exhumation of the body of her saintly predecessor, and her reburying it with greater honor.[470] These points are plainly the time-honored ones of the literary historical abbess tradition. Of Etheldreda (called Audry here), he repeats, according to

---

[457] Cf. Earcongota, *op. cit.,* 23; Ethelburga, 20; Hilda, 19, 25; Sexburga, 20; Audry (i. e. Etheldreda of the H. E.) 20, 22; Elfleda, 25.

[458] Cf. *ibid.,* Enswyde, 22; Keneburge, 24; Keneswyde, 24; Domneue, 24.

[459] Cf. *ibid.,* Sexburga 75-79; Audry, 70-75.

[460] Cf. *op. cit.,* Ermenylde, 80-84.

[461] Cf. note 478, p. 132, below.

[462] Cf. *ibid.,* Hereswith, 70; Ebba, 70, 71. Cf. also references to Erkengode and Ethelberga, 77, with H. E. III, viii, 142-144.

[463] Cf. H. E. IV, xvii, 244-246. [467] Cf. *ibid.,* 78, 79.

[464] Cf. *op. cit.,* 75. [468] Cf. *ibid.,* 78-79.

[465] Cf. *ibid.,* 78. [469] Cf. *ibid.,* 79.

[466] Cf. *ibid.* [470] Cf. *ibid.*

Bede's pattern: [471] her royal ancestry and her several marriages; [472] her perpetual virginity; [473] her abandoning the world with her husband's consent to enter the monastery of his aunt, Abbess Ebba of Coldingham; [474] her foundation of a monastery at Ely, and her becoming abbess there; [475] her holy death,[476] and the preservation of her body from decay and its honorable reinterment by her abbess successor.[477]   Of Ermenylde, the queen-mother of Werburge, who, as historical works throughout this period have recorded,[478] also became a nun at the death of the King, he recounts again traditional incidents: her giving up the world and its pomp, which, in her heart she has never loved, to enter the monastery; [479] her succeeding to the position of abess; [480] her edifying fulfilment of the duties of that office; [481] her holy death, and the subsequent miracles.[482]   But he also represents these two abbesses' pre-abbatial life in terms suggestive of the traditional simple nun.   Audry was a maiden:

> Encreasynge in vertue and constaunt sobrynes;
> Worldely pleasures, dysportes, and wantonnes,
> Lyghtnes of language and all presumpcyon
> In this sayd vyrgyn had no domynacyon.
> Sad and demure she was in countenaunce,
> Nothynge enclyned vnto fragylyte;
> Benynge and pacyent without perturbaunce,
> Meke, curteys, gentyll, full of humylyte;
> Pryde, statelenes, and sensualyte
> Were not in her founde . . .
> She was so meke, and full of pacyence,
> That people desyred to come to her presence.
> She was beauteous, fayre and amyable,

---

[471] Cf. pp. 87-88, above.

[472] Cf. *op. cit.,* 70-71.

[473] Cf. *ibid.,* 73.

[474] Cf. *ibid.*

[475] Cf. *ibid.,* 73-74.

[476] Cf. *ibid.,* 74-75.

[477] Cf. *ibid.,* 79.

[478] Cf. *Saxon Leechdoms,* 3; 430; Vita S. W. G. xxi; G. R. 1; 78, 267; G. P. 323; L. E. 77; Fl. Hist. 1; 332; H. P. 6; 126; NLA 1; *De Sancta Ermenilda,* 406.

[479] Cf. *op. cit.,* 80.

[480] Cf. *ibid.,* 82.

[481] Cf. *ibid.*

[482] Cf. *ibid.,* 82-84.

Pleasaunte to beholde in gyftes of nature,
Her countenaunce comly, swete, louely, and stable;
More lyke an angell . . .
Than a fragyll maydė. . . .[483]

Ermenylde, as Bradshaw states of her pre-abbatial career,

Refusynge this worlde pleasures, possessyon,
Instauntly requyred with perfyte humylyte
To be a moynes accepte in relygon.[484]

She was

. . . obedyent
To her mother Sexburge . . .
Also to her doughter, the spouses of Ihesu.
It passeth mannes reason playnly to expresse
Her vertuous lyfe and ghostly conuersacyon,
In prayer, penaunce, and proued mekenesse,
In perfyte obedyence and synguler deuocyon,
In vygyls, abstynence, and in hye perfeccyon.[485]

But it is in Bradshaw's presentation of the life of Werburge herself that the material of historical tradition is brought to the verge of modern literature. His facts as well as the ordering of those facts are conventional and traditional, but a quality of his literary expression of them removes both the simple nun and the abbess, as he presents them in successive phases of Werburge's career from the dull records of chronicle, hagiographical, and historical materials into an artistic milieu. The age-old characteristics of the simple-nun type are, it may be well to repeat once more, the salient qualities of his portrayal of Werburge as a simple nun. The schema followed with rare exception from seventh-century historical accounts of the abbess type to those of the fifteenth century is clearly discernible in the outline of Bradshaw's presentation of Werburge as an abbess. As a simple nun Werburge is radiantly spiritual; [486] she is humble,[487] modestly retired; [488] docilely obedient,[489] sweetly submissive to her superior,[490] and utterly unworldly

---

[483] *Op. cit.*, 70-71.
[484] *Op. cit.*, 80.
[485] *Ibid.*, 80-81.
[486] Cf. *op. cit.*, 67 and passim.

[487] Cf. *ibid.*, 69.
[488] Cf. *ibid.*, 68.
[489] Cf. *ibid.*, 67.
[490] Cf. *ibid.*, 81.

and simple.[491] As an abbess of royal lineage, Werburge is renowned
for wisdom; [492] she has been raised to the position on account of
her virtue and great perfection,[493] the renown of which spreads
throughout the land and draws many, even kings, to seek her
counsel and to follow her advice.[494] Despite the retirement and
humble modesty of her life as a simple religious, like the typical
abbess, when placed in a position of responsibility, she rules wisely
and well; governs and administers both the material as well as the
spiritual affairs of the monastery so ably that the institution
flourishes under her rule.[495] She erects new monasteries,[496] and
invests endowments.[497] She is, however, no less intent upon the
internal administration. She herself sets the example of perfect
regularity and of virtue; [498] she cares for her subjects as a mother
cares for her children.[499] Her personal virtues are great; [500]
miracles are common during her life; [501] her death, which she foretells,[502] is a glorious, triumphal departure from exile,[503] and
miracles follow upon it.[504] Her body is found intact [505] and strikingly beautiful.[506]

All these points are the traditional ones and denote simply the
persistence of the tradition and the fidelity of the medieval author
to established norms. The adherence of a sixteenth-century author
to such conventional methods of representing the nun is in itself
noteworthy, but for that matter, a seventeenth-century [507] work
may be cited which still adheres to the same content and style.
Bradshaw's work is significant on account of the way in which he
expresses these familiar facts. He makes of their treatment literature, and makes of the nun a literary figure. Werburge as a
simple nun, as a young girl desirous of renouncing the world to

[491] Cf. *ibid.*, 60, 68.

[492] Cf. *ibid.*, 92.

[493] Cf. *ibid.*, 85.

[494] Cf. *ibid.*, 85, 87, 91.

[495] Cf. *ibid.*, 93.

[496] Cf. *ibid.*, 86.

[497] Cf. *ibid.*

[498] Cf. *ibid.*, 93.

[499] Cf. *ibid.*, 94-95.

[500] Cf. *ibid.*, 93-94.

[501] Cf. *op. cit.*, 95-104.

[502] Cf. *ibid.*, 104.

[503] Cf. *ibid.*, 104-107, 112.

[504] Cf. *ibid.*, 122 ff.

[505] Cf. *ibid.*, 122.

[506] Cf. *ibid.*

[507] Cf. Horstmann, ed. *The Lives of Women Saints of Our Contrie of England*, EETS 86.

enter the convent, is here put in a somewhat sentimental, romantic, or it may be, a merely human, light. The attitude of the author remains that of the earlier historians. He venerates monasticism and understands the principles of religious life; he is unmistakably modern in casting a romantic glamour over the departure of a young girl from the world into religion. In the eleventh century [508] the tendency on the part of an author to remark the beauty of one who became a nun is perceptible. In the fifteenth century [509] the emphasis upon her natural gifts and lofty worldly position is pronounced. But it is still regarded as nothing remarkable that one so endowed should enter a convent. Regardless of her gifts she was to be congratulated for taking the veil. Bradshaw in the sixteenth century still regards such a girl as privileged by admission to a convent, but he dwells upon the pathos of such a step quite in the modern manner.

He describes Werburge as

> . . . replete with gyftes naturall:
> Her vysage moost pleasaunt, fayre and amyable,
> Her goodly eyes clerer than the crystall,
> Her countenaunce comly, swete and commendable;
> Her herte lyberall, her gesture fauourable.

Then adds that she, nonetheless,

> . . . lytell consyderynge these gyftes transytory,
> Set her felycyte in chryst perpetually.[510]

Strongly suggestive of Milton's pensive nun, " sober, stedfast, and demure ", Werburge is

> Sadde [511] and demure of her countenaunce,
> Stable in gesture proued in euery place.[512]

Offers of marriage, of which she has many, " abasshe " her " sore ". She rejects such proposals and begs her father to permit her to become a nun. In the king's reply to his daughter both the new,

[508] Cf. *Vita S. W. G.* xix, xxi.
[509] Cf. NLA 2; 423. Cf. p. 130, above.
[510] *Op. cit.*, 35.
[511] " steadfast ", " serious ", " grave ". Cf. Jones 102, 107.
[512] *Op. cit.*, 33.

human point of view is clearly defined and an element of pathos, not included before in this material, is in evidence.

> ' O my dere doughter,' (he responds)
> ' My pleasure, solace, and hope of my gladnesse,
> Moost dere byloued and my synguler swete derlynge,
> I well consyder your vertue and sadnesse,
> Your instaunt request and humble gentylnesse,
> And of your desyre inwardly I am gladde;
> But yet your mocyon makes my herte full sadde.
> All my ioye and conforte now restet in the,
>
> . . . .
>
> Thou arte the trusty treasure to thy mother and me,
>
> . . . .
>
> Wherfore, swete derlynge, as for my heyre alone
> I wolde the mary and a quene the make,
> If thou wyll consent and my counseyll take.
>
> . . . .
>
> Swete louely creature ryght ioyfull wolde I be
> To kysse a chylde of thyne hauynge thy lykenesse,
> And se the also coronate as a myghty pryncesse! . . .[513]

The author clearly reflects the full development of a point of view toward the simple nun and her vocation found neither in the historiographical nor in the religious didactic literature of Anglo-Saxon and post-Conquest England. Natural considerations out-do the supernatural. Bradshaw depends for his efforts not on the didactic commonplaces, which even in their most extravagant form are in the supernatural world exclusively, but upon thoroughly secular emphasis, such as regret that a beautiful girl should take the veil; that she should give pain by her course to so many suitors; in short, ringing the conventional romantic commonplaces now rather than the didactic.

The magnificence of the feast set by the king at Werburge's entrance to the convent, the digressions to describe the splendor of the decorations and the sumptuousness of the banquet[514] are all novel. So is the description of Werburge's formal renunciation of her right to her inheritance,[515] and the poetic contrast between her royal garments and the humble, simple habit donned as a nun.

---

[513] *Op. cit.*, 54-55, 56.

[514] Cf. *op. cit.*, 60-66.   [515] Cf. *ibid.*, 60.

The holiness attributed to all traditional simple nuns is recorded of Werburge in the flowery stanza:

> So Werburge professed to her rule full ryght,
> A redolent floure all vertue to augment,
> As Lucyfer shynyge, a clere lampe of lyght;
> For whome her spouse, god sone omnypotent,
> Shewed many miracles to euery pacyent,
> A sygne her loue was supernaturall,
> Closed in our lorde by grace supernall.[516]

The practical aspect of an abbess' life necessarily leaves little room for sentimentalizing. Bradshaw's lengthy narrative of the abbatial career of Werburge, though related in a poetic vein, has not the striking contrast to earlier materials that his presentation of Werburge as a simple nun has. The scene at Abbess Werburge's death-bed, however, is feelingly and poetically told. She calls the sisters together, and addresses them in these words:

> . . . 'dere byloued systers in our sauyour,
> O spyrytuall chyldren, my derlynges moost dere,
> Whiche have refused all worldly honour
> To serue our lorde with herte and mynde clere,
> Suffer no synne in your soule to apere,
>
> . . . .
>
> And trust ye well, your true obedyence,
> Your chast lyuynge and wylfull pouerte,
>
> . . . .
>
> That ye haue obserued her vnder me,
> Shalbe recompensed a thousande-folde, trule.
>
> . . . .
>
> As for my dethe . . .
> I drede nothynge . . .
> I knowe for certayne who departeth well here
> Is newe-borne agayne to Ioye and felycyte.[517]

Upon her death, Bradshaw philosophizes in the following suggestive fashion:

> The swete byrde, closed in a cage a longe season,
> Gladly entendeth to fly at lyberte;
> The prysoner fetered and cast in depe dongeon

---

[516] *Ibid.*, 69.   [517] *Op. cit.*, 106.

Euer supposes to be rydde frome captyuyte:
The soule of mankynde . . .
Naturally desyreth . . .
To be delyuered from bodyly pryson.[518]

Then he states that

She toke her leue and kyssed them ycheon.
Alas, what herte myght shewe the lamentacyon,
The wepynge, waylynge and wofull heuynes
At the departure of theyr swete maystres? [519]

At the later exhumation of her body, her " louely countenaunce so comly to beholde ", " her swete face ", is found

. . . more white than the lile
Mixt with rose colour. . . .[520]

The rest of the work is devoted to the many miracles performed at Saint Werburge's intercession and to the vicissitudes of her relics at the hands of the inimical Danes and of those of her religious posterity who strove for possession of her venerated remains.

V. *Summary*

The literary figures of the abbess and of the simple nun, which continue essentially the same in the historiography of England from the eighth to the sixteenth century, are those depicted first in greatest detail by Venerable Bede upon the pages of the *Historia Ecclesiastica.* The abbess is a lady of rank, a personage of Anglo-Saxon history. She is an enterprising, authoritative, considerable figure both in the monastic and the political life of Anglo-Saxon England. Her sanctity and her statemanship are considered equally a matter of historical record. The simple nun here is the complement of the abbess rather than an independent historical personage. She does not seem to be recorded upon Bede's pages for her own sake. In this she is radically different from the abbess. She has, nevertheless, a distinctive religious character. She is the personification of monastic perfection. She is holy, humble, retiring, obedient, and unworldly. The spirituality of her character is enhanced, moreover, by association with instances of the marvelous

[518] *Ibid.,* 107.   [519] *Ibid.,* 111.   [520] *Op. cit.,* 122.

and the supernatural. She resembles the consecrated virgin similarly associated with marvels in the *Liber Dialogorum*. The abbess and the simple nun, presented by Venerable Bede each in her proper sphere, is a perfect religious. Each retains this character throughout the historiography of England for eight centuries. The exceptions in historiography, during this time, are so few that they have no effect upon the type.

The materials display an evolution of the abbess and of the nun figure within the compass of these eight centuries but no divergence from the type. From the eighth century until the post-Conquest decades of the eleventh century the abbess and the nun-figure remain as presented in Bede. In the late eleventh century the influence of religious didacticism is perceptible upon Bede's abbess and simple nun. The abbatical life of the former is inflated with patristic details and adorned with patristic conventions. Her *vita* is extended, moreover, to encompass her pre-abbatial monastic life. This addition is formed upon the model of the ideal consecrated virgin of patristic treatises on virginity and monasticism. The life of the simple nun is brought into even more complete conformity than heretofore with this patristic ideal. Here perhaps most clearly the connotative power of patristic didactic phraseology and conventional expression about the nun is revealed. The application of the didactic commonplaces to the nun-figure of historiography throws both traditions into bold relief. At this time also an infinitesimal suggestion of later romantic treatment of the nun can be discovered in one presentation of her. The fifteenth century witnesses the development of the romantic element in this genre and with it a new and human point of view. The nun-figure even at this date, however, is still the same fundamentally and in essential features. The abbess remains the historical personage of the *Historia Ecclesiastica;* the simple nun, despite elaborations, is unchanged. Both, thus retaining their original character, pass from historiography into modern literature.

Historiography, of course, in that day, as almost down to our own, was at its best only a branch of literature and frequently enough through much of the Middle Ages it was literature only by a wide extension of the term. How thoroughly it could be a branch of literature is evident in its treatment of the nun, in its rigid adherence to a pattern through many changing centuries even outside the repetitious parts of continuators, even when describing nuns whom the writer could have known easily.   There is, from the thirteenth century on, testimony of the episcopal visitations to monastic conditions the very contrary of the traditional nun-ideal.   While we have no right to state that the cases cited in these episcopal records are typical of nunneries, while the existence of such records constitutes a contemporary protest against lapses from an ideal still accepted without compromise, such cases would be numerous enough and wide-spread enough to condition at least slightly the statements of nuns by a modern historiographer, situated as was his medieval forerunner.   Such a modern, no more than his medieval predecessor, would have access to episcopal records of his time in all probability, but if he were a member of a religious community, as were many of the English medieval historiographers, the oral traditions of the community would have made him generally familiar with cases whose details were locked up in archives.   And if he were to write on the nun, he would not impose upon her without change the traditional and only the traditional characteristics, cast in the traditional and only the traditional language.   I do not say that he would wallow in such cases, if they exist, or even touch upon them as being typical—as a trained historian he would do neither—but his account would be tempered by his knowledge and not be dominated by tradition.   We should no more apply twentieth century standards of historiography to medieval historians or chroniclers than twentieth century standards to medieval writers in any other genre, but since historiography was the most responsive of medieval genres to the influence of facts, the domination of it by tradition is eloquent of that tradition's power.

CHAPTER IV

The Nun in Arthurian Romance [1]

I. *Introduction*

The extant Arthurian literature of medieval England dates only from the period [2] 1135 to 1147, during which Geoffrey of Monmouth wrote his *Historia Regum Britanniae*—the universally recognized starting point of extant Arthurian romance. Geoffrey, of course, did not create [3] these materials. They reach back to sources, unfortunately for the purpose of my study, not at present available. Although by means of regressive argumentation, decided and contrary opinions [4] are held by modern scholars on the

[1] This chapter includes, of course, those chronicles that contain Arthurian materials. It does not consider references to nuns in non-Arthurian romances, because such references are incidental and without significance.

[2] But cf. Loomis (3) 423.

[3] On the problem of Geoffrey of Monmouth's sources cf. Griscom, 99-113; Faral 1; 1 and 11.

[4] On the problem of Arthurian origins scholarship has been divided for almost a century. The literature of the controversy is extensive, reaching back continuously to at least 1839 (the earliest date on the subject which I have noted). Gaston Paris, pursuing the thought of Paulin Paris's work, *Les romans de la table ronde*, 1, Paris, 1868, 4, became quite prolific on the question v. g. in *Romania*, 10 (1881), 465-496; *ibid.*, 12 (1883), 459-534; in his *La poésie du moyen âge*, 2, Paris, 1895, 45-74; in his *La littérature française au moyen âge*, Paris, 1905, 94-111. In the *La histoire littéraire de la France*, 30, Paris, 1888, 1-270, he gave particular development to what came to be called the "Insular Theory", i. e. that the sources of the Arthurian legend are to be sought in the main in the Celtic folklore of the island of Britain. Eighteen years after the appearance of Gaston Paris' first monograph on the subject, Wendelin Foerster published in his *Christian von Troyes*, 4, Halle, 1899, *Einl.* XCIX-CLXXIX, a survey and criticism of Gaston Paris' theory, readvancing and expounding what has become known as the "Continental Theory", i. e. that the sources of the Arthurian tradition are to be found in Amorica, whence they came to the knowledge of Chrétien de Troyes. Arthurian scholarship divides in allegiance to one or the other of these two theories. Despite the growing number of American scholars who enter the field, it is perhaps a not

place of origin, the character, and chronological development of these vanished materials, nothing positive is really known of this period of hypothetical beginnings. It is, therefore, impossible to study the nun type in the Arthurian tradition before the time of Geoffrey of Monmouth. But from his day down to the unsympathetic days of Roger Ascham we can follow the materials with some security.[5]

II. *Perceval's Sister*

If it were not for one possibility I could ignore the period of hypothetical origins altogether. This is the possibility that Perceval's sister, about whose figure in some of the sources now available there hovers the suggestion of a nun, may some day be proven by materials yet to be discovered from what is now the period of hypothetical origins to have been really presented as a nun.

It is for Arthurian scholars to determine whether the authors of the earliest extant materials in which the character appears created the character or simply took it over from an earlier version.[6] Could it be shown that an earlier source exists and that in it Perceval's sister is a nun, then the religious suggestions clinging to the character in some of our materials could be interpreted in the light of this original. But versions earlier than what until very recently [7] has been considered without question Wauchier's continuation of *Perceval le Gallois* by Chrétien de Troyes not being extant, the character can be studied solely upon its face value in extant works.

unwarranted assumption that old world chauvinism still constitutes an unconscious principle of division.

[5] But cf. Loomis (3) 424.

[6] Brugger maintains that the character is a creation of Wauchier's and that all other Perceval versions in which the character is found go back directly or indirectly to Wauchier. He also contests the view that the character was regarded " von Anfange an " as an exalted and saintly being. Cf. " Neue Arbeiten über den sog. Didot-Perceval " *Zs. f. fr. Spr. u L.,* 36 (1910), 62 and 65. Miss Weston holds that the character is taken from an earlier Perceval-Grail form and that Wauchier lacked the ability to create the figure. Cf. Weston (2) 1; 68; 2; 170-172.

[7] Evidence which Maurice Wilmotte offers in *Le poème du gral et ses auteurs,* convinces him " that, except for certain interpolations by later scribes, Chrétien himself is responsible for the poem up to the point where Manessier and Gerbert took it up ". The question of authorship is, therefore, opened anew. Cf. Parry, *Speculum,* 7 (1932), 164.

The extant Arthurian works in which Perceval's sister appears are the " Wauchier " continuation of *Perceval le Gallois* [7a] by Chrétien de Troyes; Gerbert's [8] addition to the latter; *Perlevaus*; [9] the Didot [10] and the Modena [11] *Perceval*; *La Queste del Saint Graal*,[12] and—the only English work of the group—Sir Thomas Malory's *Le Morte Darthur*.[13]   In some [14] of these materials Perceval's sister plays a very minor and insignificant part; in others [15] her rôle is larger and of great importance.   But in only four of them—the Gerbert addition, *Perlevaus, La Queste del Saint Graal*, and *Le Morte Darthur*—are there features of her story which some Arthurian critics interpret as indications that she was a nun. And it must be admitted, even by those who cannot follow these scholars in their interpretation of these features, that one version of her story (that found in *La Queste del Saint Graal* and in *La Morte Darthur*) assigns to Perceval's sister qualities suggestive of the traditional nun-figure.

The points in question in these four works are few and very insignificant, just as the four works themselves, while not insignificant, are few among the vast Arthurian accumulations.   The points, however, must be taken into consideration, since the interpretation of them by Arthurian scholars brings them to bear upon the nun-tradition.

In the Gerbert addition there is a *Chastel as Puceles* where

> *Les dames gardent chasteez*
> *Et puceles virginitez.*[16]

Perceval leaves his sister here while he undertakes the quest of the grail.   Two critics [17] refer to the castle as a " nunnery ", and one [18]

[7a] Cf. Potvin 4; 188-209.

[8] Cf. Williams 1; 4 and 88-100.   [11] Cf. Weston (2) 2; 37-44.

[9] Cf. Potvin 1; 41-346.   [12] Cf. Pauphilet (2) 198-276.

[10] Cf. Hucher 1; 445-472.   [13] Cf. Sommer (1) 1; 689-706.

[14] In the " Wauchier " continuation she plays a simple and charming domestic part.   She plays the same part with a few minor variations in Gerbert's addition.   Her rôle is minor also in the Didot and in the Modena *Perceval*.

[15] *Perlevaus, La Queste* . . . , and *Le Morte Darthur*.

[16] *Op. cit.*, 1; lines 3197-3198, p. 99.

[17] Weston (2) 2; 178; Loomis (2) 273.

[18] Cf. Weston, *ibid.*, 1; 68.

of them seems to consider it significant for the question that in this same work Perceval's sister is called *une sainte chose*.[19]   This critic designates her subsequently as a "maiden of devout and consecrated life "[20] and one " vowed to the religious life ".[21]

Dandrenor, as Perceval's sister is called in *Perlevaus*—the only place where she is given a proper name—is abducted by an hostile knight whose practice it is to marry, then behead, the maidens whom he carries off. For Dandrenor to meet this fate seems a desecration particularly heinous, because experiences of a supernatural and sacred nature related of her in earlier portions [22] of the lengthy tale have invested her person with an air of holiness. Perceval, however, rescues his sister before the marriage. When he then plans her future, proposing to arrange a noble and befitting alliance for her, Dandrenor declares, *Certes, biaux frère . . . je ne seroi jà mariée se à Deu non.*[23] Her subsequent life at "Kamaalot" and later at the castle of the Fisher King are described in this work as respectively a *bone vie et seinte* [24] and a *seinte vie et religieuse.*[25] One critic interprets the statement made by Dandrenor to her brother as a declaration that she " will live as a nun all her days ".[26] This opinion is strengthened by the contention of another Arthurian scholar [27] that *Perlevaus* is based upon an earlier non-extant Perceval poem, the author of which created the character of Perceval's sister, the supposed poem being the source not only of *Perlevaus,* which retains the larger share of original features, but also of the *Queste,* in which the religious character of Perceval's sister is paramount.

The combination of chivalrous romance and religious didactic allegory, of which *La Queste del Saint Graal* and Malory's *Le Morte Darthur* are compounded, make of Perceval's sister in these

[19] *Op. cit.*, line 2847, p. 88.
[20] Weston, *ibid.*, 2; 173.
[21] *Ibid.*, 1; 121.
[22] Cf. *op. cit.*, 171-177.
[23] *Op. cit.*, 251-307.
[24] *Ibid.*, 308.
[25] *Ibid.*, 346.
[26] Loomis (2). This same scholar holds that Perceval's sister represents " a flower maiden, identical with Floree and ultimately going back to Blothnot ".—*Ibid.*, 282.   [27] Cf. Weston (2) 2; 172-173.

two works not only a romantic but also a highly and sacredly symbolic figure. The impression created by the character here is undoubtedly responsible for the popular idea, perpetuated by Tennyson,[28] that the character represents a nun. Apart, however, from the lofty sanctity of the character in particular and from the religious tone of the two works in general, two circumstances about the maid in the familiar story of her summoning [29] Galahad and girding [30] him for the "highest adventure knight has ever known " [31] directly suggest the nun. One of these is the prerogative of voluntary perpetual virginity [32] with which the holy maid is endowed and upon which there is so much insistence [33] as the condition in virtue of which she can perform her remarkable deeds. The other is the fact that the belt with which she girds the mystic sword upon Galahad for the "high emprise " has been made at the sacrifice of her hair [34]—a note highly suggestive of the nun in Arthurian romance.

These few detached and scattered allusions from the extant Perceval materials are the only ones by which those who consider Perceval's sister a nun support their opinion. A careful review of the materials reveals that these are the only ones upon which they could base their views. Not one of the items in itself nor all of them combined is conclusive. From these materials it cannot be proven that the character represents a nun. The circumstance, as related in Gerbert's addition to *Perceval le Gallois*, that Perceval's sister was left at the *Chastel as Puceles* does not by any means suffice to make of her a nun. Whether she was to remain there only until her brother's return or permanently, the text does not explain. After the fashion of many an Arthurian romance, the Gerbert addition leaves the episode unresolved. It does not return to Perceval's sister. The monastery of medieval England, moreover, was frequently [35] the prolonged residence of royal and noble

[28] Cf. *The Holy Grail*, line 67 ff. Cf. Brinkley, 1.
[29] Cf. Pauphilet (2) 198; Sommer, 1; 690.
[30] Cf. Pauphilet (2) 228; Sommer, 1; 692-694.
[31] Cf. Pauphilet (2) 198; Sommer, 1; 694.
[32] Cf. Pauphilet (2) 206; Sommer, *ibid.*
[33] Cf. Pauphilet (2) *ibid.*, 239, 247, 249; Sommer, 1; 239.
[34] Cf. Pauphilet (2) 227.
[35] Cf. pp. 101 and 117, above.

maidens, as it was an ordinary hostelry or hospital for transient guests. Dandrenor's life at " Kamaalot " and at the Castle of the Fisher King, as related in *Perlevaus,* can only be made to mean that she lived a single and pious life until the end of her days. It does not make of her a nun. And the same must be said of the treatment of her in *La Queste del Saint Graal* and in *Le Morte Darthur.* She may be a symbol of a nun—her perpetual virginity and the trivial but representative episode of the sacrifice of her hair [36] indicate this much—but with certainty she can be designated no more than a picturesque, exalted, sacred figure—if one wills, " a ray of purest light serene blended of sacrifice and holy desire ".[37] Sacrifice and holy desire may make her nun-like to some, but she is not thereby a nun. In short, nowhere in the extant Arthurian remains is it legitimate for us to assert that Perceval's sister is represented as a nun, however much she suggests and perhaps even symbolizes in some passages the traditional nun-figure. This fact becomes unmistakable when she is compared with other characters in Arthurian materials who are nuns definitely and realistically.

Despite the uncertain witness of these materials as to the monastic character of Perceval's sister, the Gerbert addition contains details of pertinence to this study. Everything in the Gerbert addition related of the *Chastel as Puceles* justifies the interpretation of it as a nunnery, and a nunnery, too, whose members are presented with and only with the traditional characteristics. The summons of Perceval and his sister at the castle entry is answered by a *dame*

---

[36] Perceval's sister giving her hair is an incident with which the romantic imagination plays. The fact that young women give up their hair on assuming the religious habit is a point carefully noted, but no more than noted, in other Arthurian romances. But here the circumstance of the maid's devoting her hair to the making of Galahad's girdle is elaborated and dwelt upon all the more impressively to distinguish the holy maid from the ordinary woman. The light of holocaust and sacrifice in which the incident is depicted, the unmistakable play for human appeal in the emphasis upon the surpassing beauty of this maiden's hair in comparison with that of other women are touches typical of Arthurian romance. It is a phase of the presentation of the nun which, it must be admitted, could be wholly justified by a similar, though not identical, attitude in patristic disquisitions on the characteristics of the ideal consecrated virgin. It is a point utterly alien, however, to the early pre-Romantic literature of England on the nun.   [37] Scudder, 298.

. . . *d'eage* and *molt sage,* accompanied by *une pucele . . . joine,* both *vestues de deus chainses blans.*[38] The elder, whose name Perceval learns later is *dame sainte Ysabiaus*[39] and who gives every evidence throughout the story of being the superior of the establishment, makes all the preliminary enquiries and then admits the travelers to the castle. The younger seems to be but a companion. Within the castle portal they come upon

> *Mainte gente dame velee*
> *. . . et mainte pucele,*

each wearing

> *Un blanc voile desor son chief.*[40]

And conducted to the interior of the castle, they enter a hall

> . . . . . . *plaine*
> *De puceles blanches et simples:*
> *Asfublé orent blanches guimples,*
> *S'orent vestu camelos noirs.*[41]

Perceval and his sister are royally entertained at table, served by two *puceles.* The wounds Perceval has received in combat on the course of their journey are dressed, and *dame sainte Ysabiaus,* who proves to be a relative of their mother, with the wisdom of experience and of years and the prudence associated with the office she seems to hold, advises Perceval during their conversation after supper to leave his sister with her, while he pursues the quest. Both are extended hospitality, Perceval for the night and his sister indefinitely.[42] The identity of these details with the typical nunnery of the didactic and historical materials is quite obvious. Only the official names of conventual organization are lacking.

III. *Royal Wives Who Retire to the Convent*

The materials of Chapter III have made us familiar with the widowed queen or other royal woman in distress who withdraws to a convent to become a religious. References to such retirements are frequent in Arthurian romance. Of four royal and bereaved women who renounce the world elaborate reports are given. The

---

[38] *Op. cit.,* I; lines 3029-3034, p. 94.
[39] *Ibid.,* line 3243, p. 100.   [41] *Ibid.,* lines 3136-3139, p. 97.
[40] *Ibid.,* lines 3116-3121, p. 96.   [42] Cf. *ibid.,* lines 3155-3208, pp. 98-99.

stories of two of these women are told in the *Enfances* of Lancelot, whose widowed mother and aunt become nuns. They are repeated briefly in the fifteenth-century prose *Merlin*. An anonymous third royal lady is celebrated in the *Le Livre de Lancelot del Lac*. The fourth is the anything but anonymous Guinevere, whose retirement is the theme of many terse treatments in chronicle after chronicle and the occasion of elaborations in many romances. While these four women are romantic heroines rather than typical nuns as they are presented in these episodes, still the abbesses and the nuns of the communities which they respectively enter are religious typical of the literary tradition. The first three of them are presented here and Guinevere in section V.

Queen Elaine,[43] wife of King Ban of Benoic and young mother of the infant Lancelot, is despoiled of realm and husband. While she is mourning her double loss beside the neighboring lake, the Lady of the Lake seizes her child and disappears with it beneath the waters. She pours out her grief to an abbess who happens, with some nuns and attendants, to be passing by the scene of the unfortunate queen's disasters. Calling herself the " Queen of Great Sorrows ", Elaine begs the abbess *pour dieu* to accept her as a nun, for now she has no other desire. The abbess (with a wisdom and prudence that seem strange amid all the unreality of the piece, but that recall the typical abbess of historiography) suggests that Elaine dwell at the abbey but retain her present royal state. The queen, however, insists. The abbess then accepts her as a nun, cuts her hair, and vests her in the religious habit. Every morning thereafter the queen-religious, attended by three nuns, two chaplains, and three " converses ", having heard mass in the abbey-church, which with her remaining treasure she had had erected on the spot of her husband's death and in which edifice his body was buried, moves to the edge of the water into which the Lady of the Lake had disappeared with Lancelot, her infant son. Here she recites the psalter. A black friar coming upon her one day in the midst of her tears and devotions on the shore of the lake, consoles her, gives her news of her son, and advises her henceforth to weep in her cell over her sins. She invites him to the abbey to meet the nuns among whom is

[43] Cf. Sommer 5; 13-44, 106-107.

another queen who also has adopted the religious life.[44] This is Evaine, sister of Queen Elaine and widow of King Bohors of Gannes, the brother of King Ban.

The two former queens, to both of whom the friar brings consolation, live piously at the royal monastery. They watch, fast, weep, and meditate day and night. Though devout, Evaine languishes and soon becomes wan and frail. She therefore begins to follow the regulation for sleeping and rising laid down for the sick of the community. Pining for the sight of her children before she dies, she is granted this consolation in a dream. She then dies happy, and is buried as a queen.[45] Elaine, on the contrary—and here we have but a catalogue of religious observances in contrast with the mitigated regime followed by Evaine—rises at night for matins; wears hair-cloth; walks barefoot; abstains from meat; eats only in the refectory; sleeps in the dormitory; observes silence in the cloister; speaks only with the permission of the abbess. Dividing her life thus between vigil, prayer, and fast, she becomes, as the author puts it, despite the austerity of her practices, even more robust and beautiful.[46]

Under quite different circumstances the noble widow in the third episode becomes a nun. At vesper time a lady and Guerrehes, the man who has slain her husband, stop in their flight at a *blanche abbaye de nonains* to seek hospitality for the night. They are received and entertained. The next morning before mass the lady confides her sorry story to the abbess. The abbess tells her that she would counsel her in her plight, if she would renounce the world, don the religious habit, and remain with them. The lady assents at once, assumes the religious garb, and, led by the hand of the abbess, enters the church, where she takes part in the chanting of the divine praises. The abbess then seeks out Guerrehes, who since Mass has sought his companion preparatory to resuming their flight. The abbess informs him of the lady's decision and shows her to him among the nuns. The newly invested nun gives thanks to God and Guerrehes leaves. The nuns receive her kindly and hear from her lips the account of her noble extraction. The episode

---

[44] Cf. *op. cit.*, 19, 41-44, 106-107. Cf. the brief reference to these queen-religious in Merlin III, 416.

[45] Cf. *ibid.*, 107.   [46] Cf. *op. cit.*, 106.

closes with the statement that she leads a very holy life among them.[47] Here again, as in the account of Queen Elaine's entrance into religion, the historical type of abbess, capable, efficient, and in command of the situation, is impressed anew upon the materials. And the nuns, though not singled out individually and presented solely in community, create the effect of the typical simple nun. The readiness and geniality with which they receive the new member into their midst bespeaks the spirit of simplicity, guilelessness, and utter confidence in the judgment of the abbess characteristic of the traditional type.

IV. *The Knighting of Galahad*

But a few telling strokes suffice to suggest the same typical personage in the royal abbess to whose care the boy Galahad is committed. The child, the son of Lancelot and another Elaine, the daughter of King Pelles, is conducted by two knights to a convent of nuns near Camelot where King Pelles' sister is abbess.[48] Galahad is educated there until his fifteenth [49] or eighteenth year. The *La Queste del Saint Graal* (in which Perceval's sister plays so striking a part in connection with Galahad's later life) opens with the summons of Lancelot, on the eve of Pentecost, to this abbey of nuns. Arrived there, he finds his two cousins, Bohors and Lionel, awaiting him. As they are speaking together, three nuns enter the room; one of them, the highest in rank, conducting an handsome youth by the hand into Lancelot's presence and weeping tenderly the while.

" Sire ", she says, addressing Lancelot, " I bring you our ward, our whole joy, our comfort, and our hope, that you may make him a knight, for from no man better than from you can he, according to our knowledge, receive the order of chivalry."

Impressed with the noble bearing of the youth, Lancelot replies that whenever they wish he will gladly elevate the boy to knighthood.

" Sire ", the same nun responds, " we desire it to be done tonight or tomorrow."

Lancelot has Galahad spend the night in vigil in the church, and the next morning at the hour of prime dubs him knight. He then

---

[47] Cf. *op. cit.*, 32-33. Cf. *ibid.*, 415.
[48] Cf. *op. cit.*, 407-408.   [49] Lot (1) 61.

invites Galahad to return with him to Arthur's court, but meets
with a refusal from the youth. Lancelot then resorts to the abbess.

"Lady, suffer our new knight to come with me to the court of
my Lord, the King, for he will advance more rapidly there than he
will if he remain here among you".

"Sire", she answers, "he shall not go now, but as soon as we
deem it opportune, we shall send him thither".[50]

In *Le Morte Darthur* Malory varies a few details of this scene.
He specifies, for instance, that it is into the abbess' chamber that
Lancelot is introduced on his arrival at the abbey and that there he
meets his cousins, Sir Bors and Sir Lionel. Instead of three nuns,
twelve, all weeping,[51] conduct Galahad, "passing fayre" and, as
must behoove a youth brought up by nuns, "demure as a dove",
into Lancelot's presence. The request that he be knighted is
proffered by all, and when Lancelot, before acceding to their wish,
inquires whether the desire "cometh . . . of himself", they all
respond, "Yea".[52] As in the *Queste,* Galahad refuses to accompany Lancelot to Arthur's court, but the abbess' authoritative
decision upon Lancelot's appeal from Galahad to her is not given.[53]
Nevertheless, the few details here and the incomplete though significant lines in the delineation of the abbess' character in the earlier
version are sufficient to show that the character is formed upon the
model of the royal abbess of historical literature. Again, in both
versions, the nuns, by their tenderness, the evidence of their unity
of sentiment, are, in the few details afforded us, quite typical.
Their choral response, however, lacks the air of spontaneity that a
unanimous reply of an interrogated group of nuns might have.
The ceremonious unison may be a prelude to the solemn rite of the
reception of knighthood. But here it rather bespeaks the studied
art of Malory.

V. *Guinevere*

Paramount, however, among the nuns of Arthurian romance, as
she is peerless among its ladies, its lovers, and its queens, is the
"pearl of beauty", Guinevere. This most romantic of romantic

---

[50] Cf. *op. cit.,* 6; 3-4.

[51] Cf. the underlying theme of the modern drama *Canción de Cuna* by
Gregorio Martinez Sierra (*The Cradle Song,* translation by J. G. Underhill, N. Y., 1929). [52] Cf. *op. cit.,* 1; 612-613. [53] Cf. *ibid.,* 613.

forms, *bele . . . cortoise et gente,* is the most renowned nun-figure
not only in Arthurian but in all the literature of medieval England.

In the chronicles—the *Brut* [54] of Wace, the *Brut* of Layamon,[55]
Robert of Gloucester's Chronicle,[56] *Robert of Brunne's* [57] *Chronicle,*
the *Chronica Majora* of Matthew Paris,[58] and a work entitled
Arthur,[59] following the *Historia Regum Britanniae* [60]—Guinevere
is put down severely and with unmitigated condemnation as
Arthur's guilty queen who, despairing of her accomplice Modred's
success in battle against her husband, takes flight to a monastery
at Caerleon, where she becomes a nun and lives in deep seclusion
the remainder of her days. Layamon even adds to the obloquy of
the traditional pseudo-historical details by casting an ugly suspicion
upon the manner of her death. He avers:

> nuste hit mon to soðe,
> whaðer heo weore on deðe
> (and so ȝeo hinne ende)
> þa heo seolf weore
> isunken in þe watere.[61]

In chivalrous romance, nevertheless, where the laws of courtly
love reign and the canons of stern morality are, therefore, out of
place, Guinevere, as the paragon of *amour courtois,* is ever " the
noblest of queens and best of women ".[62] Even when she is condemned as a faithless wife, the charm of romance clings to her and
wins for her ready sympathy. And the convent serves only to
accentuate her romantic appeal. Although she is represented as a
member of the historical community at Almsbury and although she
now judges her former conduct according to the principles of
religion and monastic perfection, her attitude, her sentimentality,
as well as the description of her appearance in the presence of
Lancelot,[63] and of her corpse at repose in the cloister, conform

---

[54] Cf. *op. cit.,* 227-228. Cf. also the same in prose in *The Brut,* Brie,
89-90.

[55] Cf. *op. cit.,* 3; 9; *ibid.,* 10-12; *ibid.,* 122-38.

[56] Cf. *op. cit.,* 1; 220-222.

[57] Cf. *op. cit.,* 2; 493.   [60] Cf. *op. cit.,* 496.

[58] Cf. *op. cit.,* 1; 241.   [61] *Op. cit.,* 138.

[59] Cf. *op. cit.,* 19.   [62] Weston (1) 107.

[63] The name occurs first in extant Arthurian literature in the romance,
Eric (cf. 1, 1691 ff.), of Chrétien de Troyes, and Lancelot's appearance as

perfectly to the dictates and conventions of the literature of chivalry.

Guinevere maintains this character as a nun in each of the many versions of Arthur's death from *La Mort le Roi Artus* to Malory's *Le Morte Darthur,* with one exception. This is the alliterative *Morte Arthure,*[64] belonging to the late fourteenth or early fifteenth century.[65] It is based upon the chronicles. It alone, accordingly, continues the pseudo-historical tradition, making Mordred Guinevere's illicit lover and covering her retirement to Caerleon with ignominy. After detailing Guinevere's marriage with Mordred, the disruption of the realm, and the imminent approach of King Arthur, it records of Guinevere:

> Than cho ʒermys and ʒee at ʒorke in hir chambire,
> Gronys fulle grysely with gretand teres,
> Passes owte of the palesse with alle hir pryce maydenys,
> Towarde Chestyre in a charre thay chese hir the wayes,
> Dighte hir ewyne for to dye with dule at hir herte;
> Scho kayres to Karelyone, and kawghte hir a vaile,
> Askes thare the habite in the honoure of Criste,
> And alle for falsede, and frawde, and fere of hir louerde! [66]

All the others follow the romance tradition. In *La Mort le Roi Artus* [67] of the Vulgate Version, we are told the familiar tale of the havoc of war precipitated upon Arthur's kingdom by the exposure of the guilty love of Lancelot and the Queen and by the rebellion of Mordred. One morning at daybreak, before the issue of the great battle of the West is decided, Guinevere arouses two of her damsels and, on palfreys laden with treasure, they depart. She goes to an ancient abbey of nuns founded by her ancestors. She states her determination to remain and begs the abbess to receive her. The abbess—and nowhere is the wisdom and prudence of the traditional abbess more graphically illustrated than in this abbess' decision—replies that she cannot accept her as a nun while Arthur lives and that she fears, moreover, that the rule is too severe for Guinevere to observe. Guinevere states that she must, then, go elsewhere and that, should evil befall her, it will be the fault of

the lover of Guinevere appears first in the same poet's next romance, *Le Chevalier de la Charette.* Cf. Weston (1) 4, 5.

[64] Brock.

[65] Cf. *ibid.,* Introd. 7.

[66] *Op. cit.,* 115.

[67] Sommer, *op. cit.,* 6; 203 ff.

the abbess. The latter, thereupon, learns the details of the situation and permits Guinevere to await at the abbey the outcome of the battle. If Mordred prove the victor, Guinevere may take the veil; if Arthur, the abbess will herself make peace between Guinevere and the King, and the Queen will have to return to her husband. Guinevere agrees to this arrangement and remains. When she learns of Arthur's death, she cuts her hair, receives the religious habit, and assumes the life of a nun. On Lancelot's return from exile, he visits Guinevere and implores her to accompany him to France. On her refusal to relinquish the religious life, he also resolves to abandon the world. Years later he hears of her death, and, chastened by penance, he also dies a holy death.[68]

In English the subject is treated first in *Le Morte Arthur*,[69] a work of the late fourteenth century,[70] comprising four hundred and ninety-seven eight-line stanzas. As might be expected in a composition so prolix, details are added and the romance element is greatly heightened. The entrance of Guinevere—called Gaynor in this version—into the convent at Almsbury is described as in the preceding work, the incident of the abbess' demurring, however, being omitted. As a nun Guinevere is said to have

> . . . . . . lyved An holy lyffe,
> In prayers for to wepe And wake;
> neuyr After she cowde be blythe;
> There weryd she clothys whyte And blake.[71]

Lancelot, coming to the assistance of King Arthur, learns of the step taken by Guinevere. After he gains control of the realm — King Arthur having been slain — Lancelot hastens westward in search of the abbey wherein the Queen is now a nun. Coming

> . . . . . . throw A cloyster clere —
> All-moste for wepynge he was mad —
> he see A lady bryght of lere,
> In nonnys clothyng was she clad.
> Thryse she swownyd swyftely there,
> So stronge paynes she was in stad
> That many A man [nonne?] than nyghed hyr nere,
> And to hyr chambyr was she ladde.[72]

---

[68] Cf. *op. cit.*, 353-355, 383-389.
[69] Bruce.
[70] Cf. *ibid.*, xxv.
[71] *Ibid.*, 448, p. 108.
[72] *Op. cit.*, st. 455, p. 110.

Guinevere — for she, of course, it is, although the poet does not state the fact — having recovered her calm, summons Lancelot, the abbess, and the community into her presence. She declares before them all that, realizing, on the sight of Lancelot, how their love had brought war to the realm and death to her lord, the King, and to " many a doughty knyght ", she had " for sorowe . . . dyed nere ". Overwhelmed with the burden of her guilt, she cries out that she will abide here where God has placed her for her " sowle's hele " until — to use her own words —

> . . . . . . God send me som grace,
> Throw mercy of hys woundys wyde
> That I may do so in thys place
> my synnys to A-mende thys ilke tyde,
> After to have A syght of hys face
> At domys day on hys Ryght syde.[73]

Then addressing Lancelot, she says,

> There-fore, syr lancelot du lake,
> For my love now I the pray,
> my company thow Aye for-sake
> And to thy kyngdome thow take thy way;
> And kepe thy Reme from werre and wrake,
> And take A wyffe. . . . . . .
> And love wele than thy worldys make,
> God yiff yow Ioye to-gedyr, I pray! . . .
> But I be[se]che the in All thynge
> That newyr in thy lyffe After thysse
> Ne come to me for no sokerynge,
> Nor send me sond, but dwelle in blysse;
> I pray to god euyr lastynge
> To Graunte me grace to mend my mysse.[74]

Lancelot refuses to follow her advice and avows that he will share her destiny, will enter some religious house, and pray ever especially for her. He will do penance, will ultimately become a hermit.[75] Then, in parting,

> " madame ", . . . sayd launcelot de lake,
> " kysse me, And I shall wende as-tyte ".
> " nay ", sayd the quene, " that wyll I not;

---

[73] *Ibid.*, st. 459, p. 111.   [75] Cf. *ibid.*, st. 462-466, pp. 112-113.
[74] *Op. cit.*, st. 460-461, pp. 111-112.

> launcelot, thynke on that no more ; . . .
> lett vs thynk on hym that vs hathe bought
> And we shall please god ther-fore.[76]

With this they part, " wryngyng ther handis and lowde they yelle ",
until both swoon and must needs be carried from the scene.

Lancelot, true to his word, becomes a hermit, even a priest. His
death is heralded by a vision granted a holy bishop in which he
beholds Lancelot ascend to heaven with " Angellis XXX thousand
and sevyn ".[77]

Returning from the burial of Lancelot, a group of knights pass
Almsbury.

> Dede they faunde Gaynour the quene,
> With Roddys feyre and Rede as chery ;
> And forthe they bare hyr theym by-twene,
> And beryed hyr with masses full merry
> By syr Arthur. . . .[78]

Many of these details are repeated in the twenty-first book of
Malory's *Le Morte Darthur*.[79] Malory's stately prose, however,
dignifies the account, although it does not moderate any of its
extravagances. Malory varies the narrative by placing greater
stress upon the queen-religious' holiness, stating that all marveled
at how " vertuously she was chaunged ",[80] and by recording that
ultimately she was made " abbesse and ruller as reason wolde." [81]
The stories are, in fact, with these exceptions, almost parallel up
to the point in the stanzaic version where Lancelot's death is
related.

In *Le Morte Darthur* Lancelot survives the queen. In a vision
granted him " thryse in one night " he is charged in " remyssyon
of his synnes to haste hym unto almysbury ". He will find Guinevere dead, he is informed. He must, with his companions, convey
the body to the tomb of King Arthur and bury it at his side.
Lancelot reaches the nunnery to learn that Guinevere has died but
an half hour earlier. The nuns tell Lancelot that the Queen had
been aware of all that was revealed to Lancelot and that she had
informed them of his approach and the purpose of his coming.

---

[76] *Ibid.*, st. 466-477, p. 113.
[77] Cf. *op. cit.*, st. 468-488, pp. 113-118.
[78] *Ibid.*, st. 497, p. 121.
[79] *Loc. cit.*, 851-857.
[80] *Ibid.*, 851.
[81] *Ibid.*

They tell him also that, for two days now, she had prayed no more to see him with her bodily eyes.

Lancelot sighs on beholding her countenance, recites the *Dirige,* offers Mass, and goes on foot from Almsbury to Glastonbury, where, after further obsequies, they bury the body of the queen. When she is being lowered into the earth, Lancelot swoons, remaining insensible until revived by a hermit who reproaches him with displeasing God by " suche maner of sorow makyng ".[82]

Le Morte Darthur is the last example of medieval English Arthurian literature. There is nothing creative in Malory's version;[83] he is thoroughly faithful and representative of the period in which the Arthurian legends took their traditional form in England. He is the final summing up of the growth of that tradition on English soil. Because he is so faithful and so comprehensively representative, he clearly belongs to the medieval rather than to the modern epoch. There is no development in the Arthurian legend in England after his time, and all later English writers who treat Arthurian materials borrow from Malory [84] rather than from those from whom Malory himself borrowed. Moreover, although the last of the medieval Arthurians, he was the first of them to be printed.[85] Caxton published *Le Morte Darthur* in 1485 and it enjoyed an enormous vogue in its own day among all readers of chivalric tales and an exclusive vogue in later times among those who enjoyed Arthurian romance. Beyond him we do not need to proceed in establishing the Arthurian aspects of the nun tradition. With him this part of the nun tradition is fixed. It is only repeated thereafter in the various combinations which later writers elected.

[82] Cf. *op. cit.*, 856-857. Cf. Giraldus Cambrensis, *Opera*, 8; 126-128; Higden's *Polychronicon* 5; 330-332, and John Capgrave's *Chronicle of England*, 140-141, for an account of the discovery of Arthur and Guinevere's tomb. Cf. also *Perlevaus*, Potvin 1; 262-263 for a different version. Lancelot mourns at the tomb of Guinevere who, however, has not in that romance become a nun. Cf. also *Assertio Incomparabilis Arturii*, Mead, 108, 129.

[83] Cf. Nutt, 236, and note. Cf. also Gurteen, 84.

[84] Cf. Nutt, 236. For the subsequent treatment of Arthurian materials, particularly in the seventeenth century, cf. Brinkley, passim.

[85] Cf. Gurteen, 5.

13

VI. *Incidental References to Nuns*

Throughout the Arthurian materials there are many references to nuns and communities of nuns. Among these incidental references are some of a wholly romantic character. Others—by far the greater number—unconsciously reflect the contemporary social and cultural background without any romantic strain. The brief reference to Merlin's mother becoming a nun after the birth of her preternatural child [86] and the weird and cryptic account in *Perceval le Gallois* of Brangmore, mother of a King Pinagrés, becoming a nun in the chapel of the " Destroying Hand " [87] seem typical. The two nuns who carry food from the depleted store at the monastery to the maiden of the castle, as related in *Peredur ab Evrawc,*[88] and the description of an abbess and community of another convent, *l'abeïe saint Domin,*[89] in Gerbert's addition to *Perceval le Gallois* seem to represent the latter. There are numerous allusions to the entertainment of knights [90] and ladies at a convent during pauses in their journeys as well as to care afforded them by nuns during illness.[91] The reference to Morgan the Fey's [92] education at a house of religious and the hint of how the false Guinevere [93] was consigned to an abbey for security seem the most undoubted reflections of environment.

These references, though numerous and widely distributed through the Arthurian materials, neither reflect nor contradict the traditional nun-figure. They are too brief and colorless to be significant for this study and are only mentioned to be eliminated.

---

[86] Although the reference to Merlin's mother as a nun is comparatively slight, it is very often repeated. It is rarely omitted from an account of the mage Merlin. Cf. *Historia Regum Britanniae*, 380-381; Wace's *Brut* 1; 354-356; Layamon's *Brut*, 228, 231-235; Robert of Gloucester's *Chronicle*, 1; 128-130; Robert of Brunne's *Chronicle*, 1; 282-283, etc. Cf. also *Arthour and Merlin*, 36, 39; the prose *Merlin*, 121; Lovelich's verse *Merlin*, 228; and " Merline " in *Bishop Percy's Folio*, 1; 459; *Dial. Mir.*, I; Dist. III, No. xii, p. 124.

[87] Cf. Potvin 3; 166.   [88] Cf. Lloyd-Ellis 2; 92.

[89] Cf. *op. cit.*, 2; 67-68. Cf. also *ibid.*, 99 and the French beginning prefixed to *The History of the Holy Grail, Englisht by Lovelich*, 19-20.

[90] Cf. Sommer (4) 4; 151, 293; 5; 97, 98.

[91] Cf. *ibid.*, 5; 127, 256.

[92] Cf. Wheatley 1; 86.   [93] Cf. *ibid.*, 3; 468, 470.

VII. *Summary*

The Arthurian nun represents a combination of *amour courtois* and of local environment both within and without the monastery as that environment is reflected in the historiographical materials. It is a bizarre combination but a tradition, nevertheless.

Amour courtois, unknown in literature before the twelfth century,[94] essentially unreal and conventional, contributes the stress upon beauty, human love, and saccharine sentimentality transferred from the damsel of romance to Perceval's sister in *La Queste del Saint Graal,* to Elaine in the *Enfances* of *Lancelot,* and to Guinevere in *La Mort le Roi Artus.* The abbess of these materials, however, exercises in monastic affairs the calm judgment and keen intelligence characteristic of the abbess of historiography, as the nun of her community also conforms to the typical simple nun tradition. The retirement of royal women of the world into the cloister, as depicted in this romance literature, in also an echo of historiographical literature. So also are the various incidental references throughout the tales to hospitality offered, usually for the night, frequently for a longer period, to knights and ladies stopping at monasteries on their journeys; to the care given by the nuns in their monasteries to sick and wounded transient guests, and to the education of young women in monastic halls. The recluses,[95] moreover, upon whose secluded establishments Perceval and Lancelot come in the *Queste,* are another familiar institution carried over realistically into Arthurian romance. Their conduct, their mode of life, the sentiments they express, as revealed in the romance, are in general conformity with, for instance, the principles and practices laid down for such women in the *Ancren Riwle.*[96]

" There is no more strange fortune in literature ", one commentator upon this material observes, " than that which blended . . . a monastic theory of the saintly life, with all of chivalrous adventure . . . that the Middle Ages could conceive, and handed it on to the delight of the changing ages ".[97] This monastic theory,

---

[94] Cf. Lot-Borodine, Introd. 13.

[95] Sommer (4) 6; 52-59; Pauphilet (2) 56-57, 71-79, 142-145; Sommer (1) I; 642-643; Potvin 1; 318.   [96] Cf. *op. cit.,* 50, 64, 68-70, 96, 412-414.

[97] Lang in Sommer (1) 3; xiv.

the third element of the composite Arthurian romance nun, is externalized, apart from incidental references,[98] in the detailing of Elaine's religious practices at the monastery where she and her sister are nuns; in Guinevere's looking upon her religious life, not as an escape from condemnation or as a refuge in abandonment, but as a means of pleasing God and obtaining her soul's " hele ". Finally, if Perceval's sister be symbolic of a nun, her virginity [99] and the lofty mission it enabled her to perform reflect the esteem of this virtue expressed throughout all medieval literature from which the nun tradition most copiously developed.

Arthurian romance reflects in a remarkably realistic fashion the figures of the abbess and of the simple nun as depicted in the historiographical literature. Its peculiar contribution to the literary tradition of the nun is the nun-figure exclusively romantic. This figure is an extremely sentimentalized, theatrical creation, as true to the nun of religious life as Blanchefleur, or the more recent " Elaine, the fair, . . . the lily maid of Astolat ", is to the normal young woman. The figure is symbolized in Perceval's sister as represented in the *Quest* romances, but its perfection is embodied in the nun Guinevere. Guinevere, as a nun, is the incarnation of romance. No monastic shade can eclipse the radiant creature. The cloister and the raiment of a nun seem but an effective background against which the queen retires, all the more strikingly to set off her peerless beauty and personal charm. Somehow, despite her new surroundings and her renunciation of Lancelot, she seems to remain the courtly lady who was the mistress of Lancelot's affection. Of these points, not of her religious character, the reader is aware throughout her whole story. Not even Malory's pathetic effort to destroy this impression by stating " how virtuously she was changed " dispels the illusion. This sentimental type — neither sentimental, artificial, nor theatrical, of course, in its proper milieu where the laws and attitude of *amour courtois* prevail as they do in Arthurian romance—is represented in various degrees by each of the heroines presented in this chapter, but it reaches its climax of development in Guinevere, and through her, proceeds by way of the pages of Malory into modern English literature.

[98] Cf. for instance, Gerbert's addition 2; 9153-9157, p. 70.
[99] Cf. Pauphilet (1), 118. Cf. also Nutt, 245, 247.

CHAPTER V

THE NUN IN THE SATIRICAL MATERIALS, C. 1180-1540

I. *Introductory Survey* [1]

As we have seen in the preceding chapters, Anglo-Saxon and Anglo-Norman didactic writers were not in the least hesitant about exposing contemporary abuses and endeavoring to annihilate them thereby. But they did not write satires,[2] and except in the case of a few late Anglo-Normans no passages are to be found in their works which can properly be termed satirical. They were deadly serious in their purpose, but they—and here I include even the few Anglo-Normans of properly satirical bent—revered the institution whose abuses they attacked.

The beginnings of English satire, therefore, cannot be traced back as a distinct phenomenon much beyond [3] the twelfth century, when the Latin strain from Normandy had leavened the native seriousness and English students at Paris had caught something of the continental manner. Only then does a genuinely satiric purpose and the authentic satiric manner—wherein denunciation develops into ridicule and the aim to correct coalesces or is lost in the effort to amuse or exercise or destroy—become clearly manifest in literary remains. Only then is the writer detached sufficiently from the institution he berates to venture at least some fun at its expense. In this instance fun-making may be his only motive and certainly nothing more radical than correction inspires his banter at first. Latin-like, he still reveres, though mocking. But from the twelfth century satiric materials begin to multiply and motive and

---

[1] This summary is based chiefly on my own reading of all the materials, with such hints upon them as are noted in the footnotes. There is no adequate survey of English satire known to me.

[2] Cf. Walker, 1; Tucker, 35; Brandl, 1113.

[3] Manitius dates the MS. of the Cambridge Songs at the mid-eleventh century. Cf. Manitius (4), 3; 996. Cf. Giesebrecht, 25-26; Haessner, 12-13.

manner begin to change. The querulous note enters, the humor-less protest against an institution no longer revered and regarded as something of a pest. Soon writers are found, in numbers always increasing, who are openly glad of the opportunity afforded them by the existence of an abuse to strike at the institution through striking at the abuse. But their assaults are occasional and in-formal and, with one brief exception, parenthetical, for all their growing ill-will, and are found inserted in works called forth by some larger purpose than the iconoclastic passages which they in-clude. And thus the satiric spirit grows slowly in bulk and vehe-mence through the better part of three centuries and has its place—though always a secondary, subordinate place—in Anglo-Norman and Middle English verse-forms and in many Latin and Norman-French verse and prose works of medieval England. It is a period of satiric beginnings and we must speak of satiric asides, satiric parentheses, satiric digressions rather than of formal, independent satire. The latter makes its appearance only on the eve of the Reformation.

Except in the hands of the artist—and throughout this time of beginnings the artist who employs satiric materials is rare and draws his inspiration, for the most part, directly from France—denunciation of abuse remains crude and cumbersome, unpolished, and downright vulgar. Irony seems too delicate an instrument for novices. The favorite typical native weapon is blunt invective, a head-on collision, always forceful and sincere, even when outrage-ously over-done. Parody and burlesque are imported from across the Channel, but they lose nothing of their contemporary conti-nental grossness in their new home. The mocking irreverence of the Goliard and the unrestrained humor of the fabliau are the closest approaches to delicacy in ridicule.[4] The earnestness of expression characteristic of informal satiric beginnings is due undoubtedly to the personal immediacy of the author to the abuse against which he inveighs. To the men of Norman and early Tudor England contemporary life seemed to offer an abundance of

---

[4] And this delicacy, insofar as the fabliau is concerned, is an advance in style solely. The licentious note in English satire comes in with the fabliaux. The Goliardic contribution is chiefly distinguished by clever irreverence.

matter for satiric treatment. Social inequality and distress, political ills, ecclesiastical derangements kept satiric outbursts bitter. It is noteworthy, however, that a class [5] rather than an individual representative of the class is the object of satiric attention. Cardinal Wolsey—who post-dates this period of beginnings—is probably the first individual other than a king to win a specific attack.[6] Before him it is royalty, the ecclesiastical order, religious and secular, or crafts and tradespeople or womankind who are held up to reproach and scorn and ridicule. The closest approach to personal portrayals are Chaucer's peerless characterizations [7] in the *Canterbury Tales,* but even these are types.

To this point the English satiric spirit progressed by the end of the fifteenth century and the eve of the Reformation. The nihilism let loose thereafter had swift results in satire. The informal gave way to the formal; the parenthesis to the monograph. The bilious intensity of the times sought surcease in philippics that were Anglo-Saxon in their humorlessness and Latin in their subtlety and malevolence and that were dedicated frankly and for the first time wholly to destroying abuses by destroying the institution which bore them, and not only to destroying it physically but to destroying the intellectual foundation that had given the institution a primary reason for being. At the same time the Renaissance spirit seized upon the evils of the day as an occasion for reviving and cultivating just one more genre perfected in Classical Antiquity, and thus Horace came to England through the imitations of Wyatt.[8]

Throughout the period of beginnings a crescendo of wrath against the ecclesiastical order is reflected in the satiric materials. There is no question, of course, that the Church was the chief object of literary attack during the high-tide of the Reformation, when formal satire enters. There is little question, too, that of all classes of society the ecclesiastical [9] incurred the most virulent reproach in every stage of informal satiric development before the

---

[5] Cf. Alden, 47-48.

[6] Cf. "Rede Me and Be Nott Wrothe" and "Colyn Cloute" by Roy and J. Barlow and John Skelton respectively.

[7] Cf. Wolfe, 34; MME 691.

[8] Cf. Tucker, 227; Legouis-Cazamian, 219.

[9] Cf. Giesebrecht, 26-27.

Reformation. Precisely because priests, monks, and friars were avowedly obliged to righteousness, their vices became the more flagrantly exposed and attacked.[10] Inconsistency, incongruity, contrast between profession and performance, even the slightest semblance of hypocrisy aroused satiric comment.[11] And a sense of injury against the reputed wealth [12] of the ecclesiastical order kept feeding class-conscious resentment with a persuasiveness all its own until it reached its Reformation fury.

The nun has a relatively small part in either informal satiric beginnings or in the satire of Reformation times. She is treated satirically here and there in the earlier period but always incidentally, the major force of the satiric digression being directed against monks and friars.[13] Even in the fifteenth century and in the sixteenth, at least to the close of my period, only three works [14] of the kind are known to attack her chiefly and solely. The satiric effort of either period, when launched against monasticism, is rather, as in the case of other institutions held up to ridicule, a class-conscious effort, an assault upon monastic institutions generally rather than upon a given monastic institute. As a rule, therefore,—a rule admitting of no known exceptions in the informal materials—the nun is treated satirically not so much for her own sake as for the sake of the institution which includes her. She belongs to the standing ecclesiastical order. She cannot be ignored without creating the impression of incompleteness. Therefore she is treated.

It is finally worthy of note that in the general assaults upon womankind she has no place during the period of satiric beginnings and, as far as I have been able to discover, she is associated in such an attack only once [15] after the period of formal satire sets in.

[10] Cf. Alden, 47.

[11] Cf. *ibid.* 4, 15, 50; Tucker, 10.

[12] Cf. sketch of conditions particularly in the 13th century in Brewer, (1), xiii; cf. also A. Jessopp (2), 31-32; Fr. Cuthbert, 2-9.

[13] Cf. Howlett, *Monumenta Franciscana* 2; xxx.

[14] " Why I Cannot be a Nun ", anon. in Furnivall (1), 138-148; Erasmus, *Colloquia*, 168-178 and 178-181; Lindesay, *Ane Satyre of the Thrie Estaits.* Cf. below, p. 174 ff.

[15] Cf. Sir David Lindesay's *Ane Supplication in Contemptioun of Syde Taillis* in Murray, 574-579. In his *Anglo-Irish Literature,* 116-117, Seymour cites a Goliardic piece against women, one stanza of which refers

Regardless of the part she plays in other genres of England, or even in the satiric genre in other countries, the nun in English satire down through the sixteenth century has decidedly a minor rôle. This is not to assert, however, that it is not a necessary rôle for the purposes of this study. It is the source, as we shall see, of one phase of the traditional nun-figure of English literature.

II. *From the Twelfth to the Mid-Fifteenth Century*

Two twelfth-century Anglo-Latin works refer satirically to the nun: *De Nugis Curialium* [16] of Walter Map and *Speculum Stultorum* (c. 1180) of Nigellus Wireker. The first, a work of prose tales and personal reminiscences,[17] has a few allusions to the inefficacy of prayer by consecrated religious, who, despite their numbers, are ineffectual because of their very solicitude in the performance of good works.[18] Just why this is so is not clear. Map happens to be the first extant writer in this genre to express fears over the supposed proximity [19] of religious men and women in the monastery [20]—the recent founding of the double society at Sempringham being the occasion for his remarks. Other writers, one in this century,[21] one in the next,[22] irresponsibly imply the same proximity within the congregation at Sempringham by referring to that establishment as the model upon which they form the preposterous communities of their respective literary creations. In one passage —and it is the only one of its kind in Map's work—a nun is made to make, in circumstances that are utterly gratuitous, a degradingly coarse remark [23] Although there is but this one instance of the kind in Map's work, his attributing the expression to a nun seems but a typical sally of his typical impudence.

to the nun. The verses, however, are from the *Red Book of the Irish Exchequer*, as Seymour states, *ibid.* 116.

[16] James.

[17] Cf. Hartland, xvi.

[18] Cf. *op. cit.*, 24-25.

[19] But cf. Heimbucher 1; 404; Helyot 2; 405-406. Cf. also Munro, 92.

[20] Cf. *op. cit.*, 55. Cf. also Holkot, *Super libru(m) Sapientie* III, Lectio xxxvii, col. III.

[21] Nigellus Wireker, cf. p. 166, below.

[22] The anonymous author of "The Order of Fair Ease."

[23] Cf. *op. cit.*, 82.

Almost contemporary with Map's *De Nugis Curialium* is the *Speculum Stultorum*,[24] a comprehensive parody with many satirical passages. It contains the first downright burlesque on monachism in the literature of England.[25] It is the story of the ass Burnellus that becomes such a figure in subsequent medieval literature. Burnellus, having examined religious orders and having found them in the main wanting, decides to found his own institute, which is to be a compound of all traits which appeal to him and which the religious orders by their profession strive to avoid. The opportunity for satire in this device is obvious.

In the course of his description of a society of nuns (he has already reviewed with unmerciful wit Hospitalers, black monks, white monks, the Order of Grandmont, Carthusians, black canons, and secular canons) the satire is broad and pushed to the extreme of exaggeration. The voices of the nuns at the solemn chanting of the office, he notes, are like those of sirens. Although they have the appearance of Susanna, they have the body of a serpent and the heart of Paris. They easily obtain pardon for their wrong-doing, because they can so readily and copiously shed tears. They do not quarrel " unless time and place demand," and they strike each other " only for grave reason." They clip their hair and wear the regulation black veil and robe, but the externals of the habit are but deceit. About their dress Burnellus makes scurrilous remarks and imputes immorality to the entire community.[26] Taking a hint perhaps from Map, he affects suspicion of the double order of Sempringham,[27] and in drawing up the rules of his own order, Burnellus adopts both the mode of dressing of the nuns and the Sempringham arrangement, as he sees it, as quite in conformity with his taste.[28] Satirical material on the nun, then, begins in England by suggesting two evils, immorality and discord.

In the thirteenth century the philippics upon the nuns are almost as scant as in the twelfth and are equally the by-product of assaults

[24] Wright (12) 1; 2-145.
[25] Manitius, (4) 3; 810-812, has some illuminating remarks on the purpose of the *Speculum Stultorum*.
[26] Cf. *op. cit.*, 93-94.
[27] Cf. *ibid.*, 94-95.
[28] Cf. *ibid.*, 96.

upon the monk.[29] Thus in " The Order of Fair Ease " [30] and " The Land of Cokaygne " [31]—two devastating burlesques on the monks of thirteenth-century England which include several satiric passages—the nun receives a modicum of satiric attention. And yet even in this modicum the main force of the satiric effort is spent on the monk. The theme of the two works is sensual indulgence among the monks, and nuns seem to be introduced not as primary objects of satire but rather as accomplices in wrong-doing. " Of Men Lif þat Woniþ in Lond ",[32] also of this period,[33] is a bitter satirical piece in which nuns, friars, monks, priests, as well as merchants, tailors, skinners, and other tradesmen each receive a stanza of reproof.

The Order of Fair Ease will have " as at Sempringham " friars and sisters together.[34] But the Order of Fair Ease is to be an improvement upon Sempringham. Here there will be no wall separating the two halves of the community; there will be no obstruction to their intercourse. Monastic orders of England and the various ranks of extra-monastic ecclesiastics are surveyed and the various sensual malpractices which the writer attributes to them are adopted as the regular life in the Order of Fair Ease.[35]

" The Land of Cokaygne " is a Middle-English adaptation [36] of the clever French fabliau, " li fabliaus de Coquaine ";[37] but whereas the original is an amusing Utopia, having nothing to do with monks and nuns, its Middle-English descendant is a perverted Utopia, levelled first of all against the immorality of monks in their delectable monastery and then against the immorality of

---

[29] The *Ancren Riwle*, a strictly didactic treatise assigned by scholarship to the early thirteenth century (Cf. Allen, PMLA 33 (1918), 537 and 44 (1929), 640 for discussion of date), contains some passages that, while plainly didactic, are in decided contrast to the tone of the rest of the work and border on the satiric. Cf. Morton, 64-66; 82-84; 88-90; 100-102; 118; 128; 128-130; 134.

[30] Wright (14) 2; 64-77.   [33] Cf. MME 232-233.
[31] Furnivall (1) 156-161.   [34] *Op. cit.*, 66.
[32] *Ibid.*, 152-156.   [35] *Ibid.*, 66-67; 71-73.

[36] Cf. MME 228 on relation to the French work. But for a different view and an Irish claim, cf. Seymour, 5-8, 103. On Irish topography in the verses, cf. Heuser, Bonner Beiträge 14, 142.

[37] Cf. Barbazan 4; 175-181.

nuns.[38] The Middle-English version, like its French prototype, has charming descriptions. It tells, for instance, of the

> . . . . . . fair nunnerie
> Up a riuer of swet milke
> Whar is plente grete of silk.

On hot days in summer

> þe ȝung nunnes takith a bote
> And doth ham forth in that riuer,
> Bothe with oris and with stere,

and when far from the abbey

> Hi . . . . . .
> . . . . . . lepith dune in-to the brimme
> And doth ham sleilich for to swimme.[39]

" Of Men Lif þat Woniþ in Lond " is by no means so indiscrete as the two preceding, but it has a clumsiness, a downrightness, a lack of grace in treating of wickedness, which is absent in the two fabliaux. It has probably, therefore, not come under French influence as they.[40] It is also less specific. In treating of the nuns it mentions their fastidiousness and wrong-doing without being explicit and without distinguishing between the two.[41]

The fourteenth-century works from which satirical material on the nun is culled are more significant from a literary point of view than those of the twelfth and thirteenth centuries. The *Piers Plowman* of Langland exposes conventual evils through the confession of *Ira*. Having been a cook[42] for many months in the house where his aunt was abbess, Ira confesses that the abbess is

[38] Cf. *op. cit.*, 156-157, 160.

[39] *Op. cit.*, 160.

[40] Cf. Bédier, 30; Lanient, 30, 75. Furnivall contributed the title. In Wright-Halliwell, *Rel. Ant.* 2; 174-177, the stanzas are entitled "A Satire on the People of Kildare " and the composition of the work is attributed to Friar Michael of Kildare. Cf. also MME 232-233 and Tucker 59. But cf. Seymour, 4-5, 11, 52, and Heuser, *op. cit.*, 54.

[41] *Op. cit.*, 154.

[42] Cf. Gasquet (4) 202-3; 204-5; cf. " Item, a useless, superflous, quarrelsome, and incontinent servant and one using insolent language to the ladies shall be removed within a month. . . ." *Pontoise-Injunciones de Rumsey* 1302, Liveing, 101.

a lady who would " levere swouny oþer swelte þan suffry eny pene "; that the prioress and many of the nuns are immoral or of dishonorable birth or family, that the election of one to the office of prioress has been challenged on account of her evil connection [43] and her lapses of conduct. Repeating Wireker's charge of two centuries earlier, Langland, through *Ira,* accuses the nuns of disputing

"Til ' þow lixt' and ' þow lixt ' be lady over hem alle "

Wrath and revenge then lead to tears, to scratching with sharp fingernails, to biting and blows. To such excess does anger betray the nuns that those among them who " love any worship " loathe the vice.[44] Had the angry nuns, moreover, possessed knives " eyther had killed other ". Therefore Langland adds,

Seynt Gregorie was a gode pope and had a gode forwit,
þat no priouresse were prest for þat be ordeigned
þei had þanne ben *infamis* þe first day þei can so yvel hele conseille.[45]

In another place Langland states that Holy Church enjoins religious to observe their rules and to live under obedience day and night.[46] That they have departed from this ideal he infers in the prophecy,

Ac ȝut shal come a kyng and confesse ȝow alle,
And bete ȝow, as þe byble telleþ for brekyng of ȝoure reule,
And amende ȝow monkes moniales, and chanons,
And putte ȝow to ȝoure penaunce *ad pristinum statum ire.*[47]

John Gower more gracefully but no less clearly points out that which he considers reprehensible in the conduct of nuns. In *Mirour de L'Omme* he remarks a class of women, among whom he may include some nuns (the context does not allow us to be certain here), who, for one reason or another but not for the love of God, have assumed the obligation of a vow of chastity. They chafe under the yoke and, unable to live in retirement, wander about the city, blaming the " apostre ".[48] Gower's primary purpose, however,

---

[43] Cf. *Mirour de l'Omme*, 237.
[44] Cf. Skeat (1) C., 102.   [46] Cf. C., 86, 170, 440.
[45] B., 65-66.   [47] *Ibid.*, 91.
[48] Cf. Macaulay, 3; 207. What Gower means by the " apostre " is not

is by no means that of a satirist. He is preëminently didactic, and, although his observation of religious abuses can, for the most part, be classified as destructive criticism,[49] Gower is not hopeless of reform. His sympathy, moreover, is patently with the religious. Nevertheless, with the majority of those who lampoon monasticism, he exposes hypocrisy, singling out for attack those who

> *La fourme de Religioun*
> *Gardont, mais la matiere noun.*[50]

In *Vox Clamantis* he accordingly devotes a lengthy passage to "*mulieribus, qui in habitu moniali sub sacre religionis velo professionem suscipientes ordinis sui continenciam non obseruant*".[51] He explains at length the obligation of monks and the delinquencies into which many of them have fallen,[52] and then turns to nuns.

Professed nuns are as irrevocably bound to chastity as monks are, but, by nature, they are weaker. Should a nun err, therefore, the fault, Gower concludes, is not so grave.[53] They have neither the training, sense, constancy, nor strength of men; they fall into sin through simplicity, reading the text and neglecting the gloss of God's commands. Because Scripture has "*cuncta probare*", they feel they must try everything, because

> *Crescere nature sunt iura que multiplicare,*
> *Que deus in primo scripsit ab ore suo;*
> *Hecque dei scripta servare volunt, quoque iura*
> *Nature solit reddere mente pia.*[54]

Indulgence in banquets provided by the director of the convent, Genius, the priest of Venus, and indulgence in meat on Fridays by his concession, often prove fatal [55] to the nuns. With such state-

---

clear. It denotes, very likely, the authority of the Church which has sanctioned the vow and holds it binding. The nun out of the abbey was evidently an abuse. A thirteenth-century Goliard has a line indicative of the fact. Assuming to excommunicate various types of offenders, the poet includes

> "Juyf qui croit sainte Marie;
>   Et nonain qui est d'abeie ".—Wright (5) 1; 61-62.

[49] Cf. Tucker, 83-85.   [52] Cf. *ibid.*, 166-181.
[50] *Op. cit.*, 239.   [53] Cf. *ibid.*, 181.
[51] *Op. cit.*, Macaulay, 181-182.   [54] *Op. cit.*, 182.
[55] Cf. *ibid.*, 182. " The name of the priest, Genius, comes probably from

ments Gower lays responsibility for the guilt at the door of the priest of Venus, the confessor. Another long section, " *Hic loquitur qualiter ordinarii ex sua visitacione, qua mulieres religione velatas se dicunt corrigere, ipsas multociens officiunt deteriores,*[56] elucidates how the laws of the flesh prevail in the convent administered by such a person as Genius. His visits, Gower explains, corrupt the nuns, whose inherent feminine frailty and inclination[57] to evil Gower again stresses.[58] Gower thus in metaphors and incipient allegory laments, where Langland directly attacks.

In *The Romaunt of the Rose* (ante 1372), translated from the French[59] by Chaucer, hypocrisy hides under the garb of a nun. " Somtyme ", says *Fals-Semblant,*

> . . . . . . I am religious;
> Now lyk an anker in an hous.
> Sometyme am I prioresse,
> And now a nonne, and now abesse;
> And go thurgh alle regiouns,
> Seking alle religiouns.
> But to what ordre that I am sworn,
> I take the strawe, and lete the corn;
> To [blynde] folk [ther] I enhabite,
> I axe no-more but hir abite.[60]

Abstinence-Streyned, a boon companion of *Fals-Semblant,* also assumes the disguise of a religious habit. Dressed as a " Begyne ", carrying a psalter, a pair of beads " geven her, I wot wel . . . of a ful holy frere ", her " fader dere ", she sets out with *Fals-Semblant.* Fair and pale, the pallor arising from treachery and regret " of her estat ", *Abstinence-Streyned* can well impersonate the decorous nun, and, distressed and miserable, quite weighed down with a

---

the Romance of the Rose, although it appears in the *De Planctu Naturae* of Alain de l'Isle." Dodd, 44.

[56] *Ibid.*

[57] A medieval Latin epigram in dialogue form corroborates this view and shifts the guilt from the cleric to the nun. Cf. Wright, *Essays on Subjects Connected With the Literature . . . of England in the Middle Ages,* 2 vols. London, 1846, 1; 187-8. [59] Cf. Kaluza for the parallel texts.

[58] Cf. *op. cit.,* 182-184.

[60] *Op. cit.,* Skeat (3) 1; 237-238. Cf.

> " Sumtyme I can be a monke in a long syd cowle,
>
> Sumtyme I can be a none and loke lyke an owle ",

words of Sedwyson in Bale's *Kynge Johan* (c. 1548) Part 1, 8.

burden of theft and guile, she can, without much study, walk forth, as would a nun, full " sobrely." [61]

These satiric excerpts from *The Romaunt of the Rose,* present in the French original,[62] are Chaucer's only by adoption,[63] but through the translation and the widespread popularity of the *Le Roman de la Rose* they contribute their share to the formation of the English literary tradition of the nun.

The case of a nun-figure of Chaucer's own creation,[64] that of the prioress in *The Canterbury Tales,*[65] inevitably comes to mind. But despite an opinion of scholarship that the description of Madame Eglentyne is a specimen of Chaucer's satirical art, I do not hold it to be properly such.[66] Compared with the two nun-types

[61] Cf. *op. cit.,* 254.

[62] Cf. Kaluza, 362, 421-422.

[63] Whether Fragment C in which the passages cited from *The Romaunt of the Rose* are found is Chaucerian or not is a special problem and irrelevant here.

[64] Cf. MME 691.

[65] Cf. Skeat (3) 4; Prologue to *The Canterbury Tales,* 4-6.

[66] To state that the description of the prioress is not satirical is not, however, to maintain that it does not admit of satire. The problem becomes one involving the author's purpose, upon which, of course, there cannot be absolute certainty. Complete artist that he is, Chaucer produces characters as he sees them. The genuine Chaucerian manner is that in which he presents the prioress. So delicately balanced are reverence and quiet amusement in Chaucer's attitude toward her that to describe him here as " laughing without judging" (Cf. Wolfe, 35) is to jar the scale rudely. True as it is that Chaucer does not condemn (Cf. Power (2) 60), it is equally true that he is not laughing even to himself. He is respectful, reverent, and also unmistakably awestruck with the rest of medieval men in the company at the deftness and impeccable etiquette of Madame Eglentyne. But with all his esteem and courtesy, does Chaucer's perspicacity detect the inconsistency of courtly affectation with the religious habit? It may be nearer the truth that the lines,

> "And sikerly she was of greet disport,
> And ful plesaunt, and amiable of port,
> And peyned hir to countrefete chere
> Of court . . ."
>
> (*Op. cit.,* lines 137-140, p. 5),

indicate that Chaucer is tolerantly contemplating with a touch of masculine, philosophic satisfaction the abiding " feminine " observable even in the conduct of one who presumably had done with vanity. Root, 190, insists

that trace consistently through English historiography and didacticism from the seventh to the fourteenth century, the prioress represented in *The Canterbury Tales* is simply the unerring, undistorted, yet highly-colored picture—a literary masterpiece such as only a Chaucer could paint—of that particular medieval religious who in real life would be found upon a pilgrimage from London down to Canterbury. Since Chaucer's portrait is photographic rather than satiric, I do not consider Madame Eglentyne in this study.

upon the prioress' affectation. But cf. Kittredge, 176, and MME 705. The prioress' affectation does not consist in assuming polite behavior: that is hers. The effort to appear the court lady is the manifestation found inconsistent in a nun. Chaucer may, however, be commending the religious' pains to make herself agreeable to companions upon whom a less genial manner might pall. She must have been pleasing naturally, for to describe her appearance and smile, Chaucer selects Gower's—and many another medieval poet's—pretty phrase to his lady, " simple and coy " (line 119, p. 4. On the general popularity of the expression, cf. Lowes, *Anglia* 33, 440-446). Her " gretteste ooth ", " by seynt Loy ", is supposed, however, to have a touch of fashion in it. It had, at least, quite contemporary reference. (Cf. Manly, 203 and Skeat (3) 14, note 20) That Chaucer remarks the prioress' French as " after the scôle of Stratford atte Bowe " can hardly be construed as depreciation or ridicule, for the French of " Stratford atte Bowe " (Cf. Manly, 219-220) was that of contemporary court circles. (But cf. Root 190.) The " smale houndes ", however, for which Chaucer shows the prioress so solicitous, could draw upon their mistress authoritative reproof, although their possession might possibly be condoned by custom and concession. It was not a dog or two but *canum numerositas* that brought upon an earlier religious an admonitory word. Cf. p. 127 above. Nor does the description of the prioress' garb indicate that Chaucer implies its wearer to be a worldly religious. Her clothing is to be understood in the light of her rule (Cf. Sister Madeleva, *Chaucer's Nuns.* But cf. Power (2) 79). A religious would find reprehensible in the prioress, consequently—whether Chaucer does or not is a question—only affectation and the possession of pets. That Chaucer is equivocal to satirical intent in the motto inscribed on the prioress' rosary-medal, can, despite the cavalier spirit and literary convention of the age, hardly be accepted as compatible with Chaucer's general attitude toward the nun. But cf. Lowes, *op. cit.*, 441, on this point. The very presence, however, of the religious, although accompanied by her retinue, among the pilgrims borders, whether Chaucer is aware of the fact or not, upon the satirical, because, from as early as the eighth century, as the study of the historical material of the nun has indicated, ecclesiastical authority was adverse to religious women

14

John Lydgate († 1451), although not specifying nuns, writes of envy as general in religious houses. He is the first [67] writer in the vernacular and in this vein to impute this vice to religious, as he is perhaps the first in this restricted genre to try his hand at conscious irony.

> "Relygyous", he writes "of varaye holynesse
> With vertuous bene on heyght up borne.
> Envye in cloystres hathe none entresse,
> Conveyede by lyne ryght as a rammes horne ".[68]

III. *From the Mid-Fifteenth Century to 1540*

The satiric material on the nun thus far gathered consists of excerpts and fragments. The nun is treated as only one of a number of institutions deserving reform or censure. In the fifteenth century, very likely toward its close, appears the first polemic devoted exclusively to nuns in the centuries covered by this dissertation—the long and comparatively elaborate poem, "Why I Cannot Be a Nun ".[69] It is the only composition devoted in whole or in part to criticism of nuns in all this period that has at once a quality of beauty,[70] gentility of tone, and an air of refinement.

leaving their monastery to journey on pilgrimages. Chaucer might, then— although I hold that such is not the case—have placed the dainty Madame Eglentyne in such motley company for a purpose ulterior to artistic variety and the attainment of a complete assembly of medieval types as contemporary society actually presented them to the poet. But to accredit Chaucer, or, in fact, any English writer of this early age of English literature with an innuendo so tortuous would be, I think, as anachronistic generally as it would be to despoil Chaucer particularly of his greatest narrative gift—artless objectivity.

[67] Alexander Neckam (1157-1217) writes in the chapter, "De Invidia" of *De Naturis Rerum; "Proh dolor! septa claustrorum intrat fidenter"*, 339.

[68] Halliwell, *Lydgate's Minor Poems*, "As Straight as a Ram's Horn", 172. Cf. also the humorous verses, "The Tale of the Lady Prioress and her Three Suitors," *ibid.*, 107-117.

[69] Furnivall (1) 138-148.

[70] "The Land of Cokaygne", the audacious little thirteenth-century fabliau, the happiest artistic achievement in this genre hitherto, is the only composition in all the informally satiric materials on the nun that can, like the pious, thoroughly earnest treatise, "Why I Cannot Be a Nun", lay claim to beauty.

The author employs the familiar medieval devices, the dream-vision
and the allegory of a spiritual abbey, and puts the account on the
lips of Catherine, an attractive young girl.

Catherine wishes to become a nun. Her father's couriers have
scoured England only to find all convents in the same condition.
He accordingly refuses his daughter his consent. She submits but
does not understand. One fair "mornyng of may", still intent
upon consecrating herself to God, Catherine prays ardently and
then falls asleep. In her dream a lady, "Experience", conducts
Catherine to a "howse of wommen regular", a

> . . . . . . ryalle byldyng . . .
> Hyt schyned wythe-owte so fayre and clere,
> But syn had made hyt fulle vnclene
> Wythe-in. . . .[71]

She beholds here a community of nuns of different orders, old and
young, poorly governed, the precise antithesis of the ideal community personified in the fourteenth-century allegory, the "Abbey
of the Holy Ghost".[72] "Dame Pride" is held in great repute;
"Dame Mekenes" is set aside; "Dame Ypocryte" looks

> . . . . . . vp-on a boke
> And bete(s) her selfe vp on the brest.[73]

"Dame Devowte" has been expelled by "Dame Sclowthe" and
"Dame Veyne Glory". "Dame Envy", "the whyche can sethe
stryfe in euery state",[74] has care of many things and carries "the
keyes of many a dore".[75] Dwelling there are also Dames "Loue
Vn-ordynate", "Lust", "Wantowne", and "Dame Nyce".
"Dame Chastyte" is "oft in poynte to go her way, sche is so lytelle
beloved there".[76] Some love her with "hert fulle dere", but some
set "no thyng by her" and grant her "gode leue for to go".[77]
Catherine refrains, in accordance with "a poynte of curtesy",
from describing all that she witnesses, insinuating thereby greater
evils.[78] She seeks "Dame Pacience" and "Dame Charyte" and

[71] *Op. cit.*, 143.
[72] Cf. Horstman (15) 1; 321-337. Cf. also Allen (3), 335-343.
[73] *Op. cit.*, 144.   [76] *Ibid.*, 144.
[74] *Ibid.*   [77] *Ibid.*
[75] *Ibid.*, 145.   [78] *Ibid.*

finds them withdrawn to an outer chamber where they may dwell without strife and where good women have joined them.[79]   In the convent, to which Catherine again turns her attention, she notices "Dame Dysobedyent", who sets the prioress to naught.   The presence of disobedience is most influential in causing Catherine to change her mind.   As she expresses it:

> . . . . . . alle was shent,
> For suggettys schulde evyr be dylygent
> Bothe in worde, in wylle, and dede,
> To plese her souereynes wyth gode entent,
> And hem obey, ellys god forbede.
> And of alle the defawtes that I cowde se
> Thorow3 schewyng of experience,
> Hyt was one of the most that grevyed me,
> The wantyng of obedyence.
> For hyt schulde be chese in consciens,
> Alle relygius rule wytnesseth the same.
>
> .   .   .   .
>
> And than I sped me thens a grete spede,
> That couent was so fulle of syn.[80]

At Catherine's request "Experience" explains that she has shown her this nunnery to dissipate the desire she cherishes to become a nun.   Some nuns, "Experience" concedes, are devout, holy, and manifestly on the path to heaven, but others are "feble, lewde, and frowarde", and convents generally are in the condition in which she has just seen this one to be.   Catherine awakes, determined, as a result of the abuses she has witnessed, not to become a religious, unless there be a general amendment; for the dream, she remarks, was no phantasy.[81]   The condition qualifying the young girl's resolution indicates that the author was not hopeless of monastic reform.   A didactic discourse, moreover, with which the treatise is resumed after a break in the manuscript at this point, further removes the allegory from the realm of destructive criticism, to which satiric materials on the nun converge with the approach of the Reformation.

The instruction appended to the narrative draws the moral of the tale.   It alludes to the danger of nuns' trespassing the limits of their cloister, by referring to Dinah's (Gen. xxiv) going out to

---

[79] *Ibid.*, 145.   [80] *Ibid.*   [81] Cf. *ibid.*, 146-147.

"see thynges in veyne".[82]   Then follows a disquisition on the salient point of all this critical material—the hypocrisy of nuns whose inner life and conduct belie their holy habit.[83]   The treatise closes with a traditional homiletic device, an exhortation addressed to nuns, urging them to imitate the virgin saints and religious, among whom Saints Scholastica, the Anglo-Saxon Queen-religious Etheldreda ("Audre"), Saints Sexburga and Ermenilda [84] are mentioned.[85]   Thus the fifteenth-century dream-vision is linked to the original material written about and to nuns in Anglo-Saxon England as early as the eighth century.

The first formal satire in England upon nuns dates from the second decade of the sixteenth century and owes its origin to Desiderius Erasmus.   Two of his *Colloquia* [86] (c. 1518), strikingly similar to "Why I Cannot Be a Nun" in plot, are, however, absolute satire.   The intention of Erasmus' work is utter destruction and its aim, is directed against the very foundation of the religious life.   From his pen Reformation satire begins to flow at its bitterest.   Censure and ridicule to this date had been curative in intention, at least not purely destructive.   Erasmus proposes to annihilate.

Both colloquies are carried on by another Catherine and a certain Eubolus with whom she discusses her intention to become a nun. In the first, Erasmus presents Catherine as a maid, attracted to the convent by the mere accidentals of the religious life; a girl, caught by externals that had appealed to her childish mind.   As a child she had visited a convent where the charming manner and sweet converse of the nuns, the presence of two of her former playmates, the exquisite order reigning everywhere, the neatness and perfume of the chapel had captivated her fancy.   Now in her seventeenth year she longs to follow her inclination to join the religious, but her parents object.   She is told that she can lead a consecrated life more safely in her home than in a cloister; that

[82] *Ibid.*, 147.

[83] Cf. *ibid.*, 147-148.

[84] Cf. *ibid.*, 148.

[85] Religious treated by Aldhelm, Venerable Bede, and others.   Cf. p. 84 ff., above.

[86] Frobenius, *Colloquia Familiaria*, "Virgo Μισογαμα", 168-178; "Virgo Poenitens", 178-181.

baptism has made her the spouse of Christ, and that religious profession can add nothing to her union with God.   Intimate acquaintance with monastic life will dispel her lofty ideals of that institution
and its members.   Moreover, should one attempt to leave, after
joining the society, she is compelled against her will to remain.

The second colloquy takes place in the convent parlor.   Catherine,
having been aided by the persistent solicitations of monks and nuns,
has gained her parents' consent to enter the religious life.   Not yet
professed, but having had sufficient trial of the life, she, weeping,
reveals to Eubolus that she had been deceived by appearances and
states her determination to leave the convent in order to escape
evils, the enormity of which Erasmus succeeds in insinuating to
greater effect by the incoherent remarks of the weeping novice than
he could have achieved by the most open denunciation.   Two evils,
which he would impute, are made plain; that religious are immoral
and that greed prompts them to exact large sums from the parents
of those who embrace the monastic life.

In Reformation satire the traditional assaults upon monastic
immorality are combined with an emphasis on monastic greed.
Monastic greed is implied in most of the satire of the preceding
time, but it does not receive elaborate emphasis until the Reformers
seek a political-social justification for their activities against
religious orders.   The satire of this new time is frankly bent upon
the destruction rather than the correction of monasteries, and
monastic greed and immorality are the chief missiles in the polemics
of the Reformers.   Erasmus — howsoever little he may have wished
later on to be associated in men's minds with the anti-humanistic
Reformers [87] — certainly inaugurates in two of his colloquies the
first appearance of the Reformers' peculiar vituperation of the nun
in England.[88]

---

[87] Cf. *CMH* 2; 697-700.

[88] Invective and abuse, however, are hurled from both sides.   Some, who
resent and deplore the evils of the Reformation, scoff and jeer at the Reformers, but in the course of their onslaughts they attack the contemporary
nun.   For example, in *Colyn Cloute* (Dyce, *The Poetical Works of John
Skelton*, 2; 125-169), a lengthy and exclusively ecclesiastical lampoon by
John Skelton, every order of clergy and religious is held up for reproach.
Exposing, of course, only "them that do amys" and among whom he
"escryes" no "good nonne" (*Op. cit.*, lines 1097-2004), he nevertheless

John Skelton (d. 1529) 'the first Englishman to win the name of being primarily a satirist ",[89] reverts in *Magnificence* to the traditional charge against religious — that of hypocrisy. But whether or not he would implicate nuns, to whom he alludes in the brief passage in point, is not clear.[90]

observes that the example of religious men wandering about outside the monastery "*contra regulam morum*" has influenced nuns to do the same. He then severely blames those who expel nuns from their convents and confiscate their property.

> "My Lady ", he states, "now she ronnes,
> Dame Sybly our abbesse,
> Dame Dorothe and lady Besse,
> Dame Sare our pryoress,
> Out of theyr cloyster and quere
> With an hevy chere,
> Must cast up theyr blacke vayles
>
> . . . .
>
> And all the fawte they lay
> On you prelates, and say
> Ye do them wrong and no ryght
> To put them thus to flyght;
> No matyns at mydnyght,
> Boke and chalys gone quyte;
> And plucke away the leedes
> Evyn over theyr heedes,
> And sell away theyr belles
> And all that they have elles."   (*Op. cit.*, 137-139).

The second instance of a reference of this kind (and I have discovered only two) is found in an anonymous ballad "Against the Blaspheming English Lutherans and the Poisonous Dragan Luther ". The twenty-seventh stanza runs:

> "Thei say that . . . . . .
> fryers with nones may wel mary;
>   Mans law is but a vanyte:
> no superior nor obedience;
> agaynst mysdoers say no violence;
>   this call thei christen libertye."

[89] Alden, 25.   (Furnivall (7) I; 287).

[90]   "To counterfet this freers have lerned me:
> This nonnes nowe and then, and it myghte be,
> Wolde take, in the way of counterfet Charyte,
> The grace of God under *benedicite*."
>
>   (*Op. cit.*, Ramsay, 2; 16).

Nuns are drawn in incidentally and without comment as party to the general hypocrisy of ecclesiastics in another invective against abbots, priors, canons, and monks. The work is called " *The Image of Ypocresye* " [91] and was written about 1533.

In *Cock Lorell's Bote,* a buffoonish travesty on society of this period, nuns are grouped again with ecclesiastics and accused of general folly. Representatives of almost every trade and pursuit are in the " bote ", a device imitated obviously from Barclay's *Shyp of Folys.*[92] Eager to board the vessel, but arrived too late, are

> . . . . . . ermytes, monks and freres,
> Chanons . . .
> And many whyte nonnes with whyte vayles.[93]

Finally, the medieval informal satire of England, and with it the satiric materials upon the nun, culminates in *Ane Satyre of the Thrie Estaits,*[94] an elaborate morality play written by Sir David Lyndesay and performed before James V of Scotland in 1535, the very year of the royal visitation of English monasteries preparatory to their dissolution.[95] Five years earlier (1530) Sir David Lyndesay had given expression to the same theme, insofar as it concerns the nun, in a less significant work, *The Testament of the Pepyngo.*[96] Comparatively inconsiderable and ineffectual in the context of the *Testament,* the theme of the moral decay of religious resulting from wealth is prominent and — whether so intended or not — predominant in the drama. The preëminence of the vilification of nuns in a work purporting to present the necessity of a general reform of " King, Commons, and Spiritualitie " will not surprise anyone familiar with the contemporary literature of protest in Scotland. This is evidently what the audience, the place, and the time demanded. So constructed is the prioress' part in the play and so compelling is her personality that she carries the action to a point where it is concluded that in church and in state the nun is unnecessary.

This satire, like that of Erasmus' colloquies on the nun, is absolute. It is without relief of any kind. The religious whom the

[91] Furnivall (7) 1; 181-266.
[92] In turn an English replica of *Narrenschiff* by Sebastian Brandt.
[93] *Op. cit.,* Rimbault, 14.   [95] Cf. *Cambridge Modern History,* 2; 444.
[94] Hall.   [96] Small.

prioress represents are all reported as wholly immoral and as encouraged in their evil life through the luxury made possible by
their practical immunity from taxation.[97]   Although they pro-
nounce a vow of chastity, they do not observe it.   They are dominated, on the contrary, to such an extent by sensuality that the
monastery is notorious for sin.   The prioress, in whom are illustrated Lyndesay's most execrable allegations, is, as she avows,
utterly disinclined toward the religious life; she has been forced
by the greed of her friends to embrace the state " nocht for Christ
Jesus Our Lord " but to acquire an abbacy.   Arraigned at last
before the tribunal at which the three estates are tried, and where
she is convicted of hypocrisy, despoiled of the religious habit " of
fein3eit holines ", and revealed robed in silk, she proclaims:

> Howbeit . . . Nunnes sing nichts and dayis,
> Thair hart waites nocht quhat thair mouth sayis;
>   The suith I 3ow declair.
> Makand 3ow intimacioun
> To Christis congregatioun
>   Nunnis ar nocht necessair.[98]

This type of material represents Reformation satire at high tide.
Not so mordant or so sardonic but clumsy and coarse where
Erasmus is subtle and artistic, Lyndesay, nevertheless, is as veno-
mous in intent.   He even extends the objective of satire to embrace
an attack upon monasticism for women, not only as spiritually
useless but as politically and socially unnecessary as well.

Although the materials employed by Erasmus and Lyndesay are
practically the same as those used in satiric beginnings throughout
the four centuries during which the genre was developing in England, the spirit in which the materials are utilized removes both
Erasmus and Lyndesay from the class of informal satirists in
whose hands the English tradition of satire on the nun took shape.
Those in the tradition of Map and Wireker wrote to exasperate, to
startle, to amuse, and to cure.   Erasmus and Lyndesay write with
the unqualified intention of presenting irrefragable evidence in
favor of the destruction of convent life.   To this end Lyndesay
concludes in *Ane Satyre of the Thrie Estaits:*

---

[97] Cf. *op. cit.*, 489-490.

[98] Cf. *ibid.*, 421-422; 423-444; 495; 504; 506; 514.

Thir wantoun Nunnis ar na way necessair
Till Common-weill, nor ȝit to the glorie
Of Christ's Kirk . . .
And . . . that fragill ordour feminine
Will nocht be missit in Christ's Religioun:
Thair rents vsit till ane better fyne,
For Common-weill of all this Regioun.[99]

Because absolute and unqualified in destructive intent, this drama, although written by a Scotchman and belonging primarily to Scottish literature, marks, nevertheless, the climax of the satiric materials of England on the nun. It is again a Scotchman, the same Sir David Lyndesay, who, three years later, pens a brief satire upon womankind in general and includes in the attack the nun, — his *Ane Supplicatioun in Contemptioun of Syde Taillis "*.[100] The short work abusing women for wearing long trains to their gowns is coarse with Lyndesay's characteristic vulgarity. The work is significant because it is the first [101] extant example, so far as I can discover, of a composition of this familiar medieval kind in which the nun is attacked in a manner not to be distinguished from attacks upon other women.

IV. *Summary*

Satiric materials upon the nun produced in England during the period from the twelfth to the mid-sixteenth century are remarkably scant, are for the most part nondescript and fragmentary. With a few outstanding exceptions they represent the work of mediocre and decidedly inferior talent. The sophisticated art of satire did not appear in England until the sixteenth century. And even then, when utilized against the nun, it was not written by Englishmen. Neither Erasmus nor Lyndesay was born in England. Satiric expression against the nun — except when touched, like the Anglo-Latin parody of the twelfth century and the Middle English and Anglo-Norman fabliaux of the thirteenth, by a foreign grace—is lumbering, downright, and blunt. Until Langland it is general in its reproach, censuring nuns because of their common membership with monks and friars and ecclesiastics in an order usually attacked. The Anglo-Latin of Map and Wireker and the Norman and Middle

[99] *Op. cit.*, 521.　[100] Cf. Murray, 575.　[101] But cf. p. 164, note 15, above.

English verses of the next century, in which are strains, respectively, of the pagan inheritance [102] of the Goliard and the French ancestry of the fabliaux, impugn the moral character of nuns. Yet their unrestrained imputations reflect but little upon the nun in reality, for they seem rather exercises of wit than serious exposures of wickedness. Native seriousness also has hardly more effect, expending its growing wrath in denunciations that are as vague as they are violent.

It is a period, it must be borne in mind, of satiric beginnings. Genuine satire of the formal type is not represented by a single example. Many of the works from which materials of a satiric purport are selected are, strictly speaking, not satire at all. These selections, nevertheless, because they are selections, are important in the study of the genesis of the genre. Such are the excerpts from the works of Chaucer and Gower. These men are articulate, and the portions of their works approaching satire of the nun are illuminating both by the light they cast on the meaning of contemporary obscure works and by the more complete outline they disclose of the nun-figure becoming definite in the satiric writings. While they do not deny the charge of immorality hurled against nuns by earlier writers in this material, they place greater emphasis upon the discrepancy between profession and practice. Nuns acquire from these writers, particularly from Chaucer's translation of the *Roman de la Rose*, the name of being fair hypocrites. The religious habit becomes suggestive both of a pose and of a disguise— a pose of virtue and a disguise of vice.

The fifteenth century marks the first complete work derogatory to the nun. But it is not yet satire of a formal kind. It is more closely akin to traditional didacticism. It finds its proper place here, however, in the gradual development of satire upon the nun. This work *Why I Cannot be a Nun,* anonymous and devoid of vernacular crudities and censoriousness, as well as of continental pungency, most effectively reveals the defects in nuns which it would correct. Insubordination is added to the traditional reproaches against nuns. Their disobedience and disregard for their superiors is remarked as the most fatal of their defects. The work, moreover, connects the nun of satiric materials with her of traditional his-

---

[102] Cf. Lehmann (1) 9, 19-20; Manitius (4) 3; 812.

toriography. The corrective of present abuses, it states, is the imitation of Scholastica, Etheldreda, Sexburga, and Ermenilda. The points it makes in correction are a perfect and complete antithesis to the traits emphasized of these and other saints and model religious by Venerable Bede and his successors.

The Reformation brought formal satire on the nun into being. Erasmus and Lyndesay cast into oblivion the contemporary balladist who occasionally refers to the nun. They depict the nun in the most unfavorable light possible. Erasmus, with consummate art, puts her condemnation on the lips of one who, having supposed the nun to be ideal (the traditional traits are implied), learns by experience that she is the unmitigated opposite. He insinuates, moreover, unnamed evils beyond the violation of the traditional virtues. He would destroy monasticism at its source. Lyndesay, less subtle and more gross, illustrates and dramatizes what Erasmus suggests. Erasmus destroys the ideal: Lyndesay covers it with ignominy. To the vices hitherto imputed to the nun, both add that of greed, covetousness of monastic wealth and property. Which of the two satirists depicts a more evil nun-type, it is difficult to judge. The nun in this material has been lowered from the high estate she occupies in every other literary form. It is very significant that after such degradation the nun, as never before, I believe, in the literature of England, is ridiculed and reproached in a little satire, attacking, as was the medieval custom, womankind in general.

The lethal type of Reformation satire died out with the dissolution of monasteries, but the suggestion of greed, the conviction of luxury and immorality, and the suspicion of hypocrisy, associated in varying degrees with the religious habit almost constantly since the twelfth century, clung to the nun in literature. Five centuries of unlovely, quasi-literary tradition must be taken into account, accordingly, when approaching a study of the nun-figure in English literary tradition.

CHAPTER VI

The Nun in the Exempla

I. *Introduction*

Both the term exemplum and the type of composition [1] commonly designated as such in the twelfth and later centuries in England [2] are the result of long traditions. The type—a brief tale in a larger literary unit to illustrate a point—is among the oldest devices of literature. It is one of the recognized instruments of emphasis considered by ancient systematic rhetoric.[3] Christianity adopted it, as it adopted so many other ancient forms; the Fathers employed it abundantly in their homilies. Thus become a part of Christian homiletic practice, it finally passed, as did so much else that is patristic, into medieval Christian England.[4] The earlier history of the term need not concern us. Toward the end of the twelfth century Alanis de Insulis (d. 1202) seems to have considered any illustration as an exemplum. Other writers of the time applied the term to figures of speech and analogies.[6] But it was already becoming restricted for the most part to designating that device which interests us here—the anecdote in illustration of a general statement, told ordinarily, though not necessarily,[7] in the course of a homily or sermon.[8]

[1] With which I associate "Miracles of the Virgin". Cf. Frenken, 46.

[2] Cf. *ibid.*, 13; Crane (1) xviii, xix. But cf. Schönbach, 12-13 and Crane (6) 231-232.

[3] Cf. Frenken, 6, 15. Cf. Wünsch, "Exemplum", Article in Pauly-Wissowa, 6, 1586-1588.

[4] Cf. *ibid.*, 17-18; Gerould, 14.

[5] Cf. *Summa de Arte Praedicatoria*, PL 210, col. 114. Cf. Crane (1) xix; Smith, L. T. 27; Frenken 14.

[6] Cf. Mosher, 5.

[7] Cf. G. R., I; 231-235; 253-259; Giraldus Cambrensis, *Gemma Ecclesiastica*, 2; passim. Preachers drew illustrative material also from *De Naturis Rerum* and *De Laudibus Divinae Sapientiae* of Alexander Neckam (1157-1217), Wright (10); cf. also Owst, 300 and Mosher, 72-73.

[8] Cf. Frenken, 5.

The English beginnings of the type cannot be recovered in detail. We can point to Saint Gregory the Great, however, as a patent source for England. Abbot Aelfric made use of his materials to lend point to his Anglo-Saxon homilies.[9] The translation of the *Liber Dialogorum* into the vernacular at the time of King Alfred is considered [10] to have been a lively incentive to the production of exempla in England before the efflorescence of the type. Aelfric, undoubtedly, resorted to the original. But whatever rendition he employed, the borrowing represents only one definite instance of the use of patristic sources for exempla. The writings of the Fathers, however, were in abundant [11] and constant circulation among churchmen throughout the subsequent Middle Ages. The great continental collections of exempla, formed for the convenience of preachers, found their most staple and popular materials in these familiar patristic sources. The most inexhaustible of these seem to have been the *XL Homiliarum in Evangelia, Libri Duo* [12] and the *Liber Dialogorum* [13] of Saint Gregory and the *Vitae Patrum;* [14] they were by no means the exclusive patristic sources, as numerous anecdotes, some attributed to their author and some unacknowledged, throughout the texts reveal. The representative and stock continental collections are the *Sermones De Tempore* and *Sermones Vulgares* [15] of Jacques de Vitry [16] (c. 1180-1240, 60), the *Dialogus Miraculorum* [17] of Caesarius of Heisterbach (1220-1235), and the *Alphabetum Narrationum*,[18] once attributed to Etienne de Besançon, but now ascribed, although still with some degree of uncertainty, to Arnold of Liège. [19] Alongside the cos-

---

[9] Förster (1) 37 and passim.

[10] Cf. Mosher, 24.

[11] Cf. Manitius (3) v-vi.

[12] PL 76, col. 1076 ff.

[13] *Ibid.*, 66, col. 126 ff. (for Liber II), and 77, col. 149 ff. Cf. Meyer (4) 269; Mosher, 11-12.

[14] Butler (1). Cf. Crane (1) lxx and Mosher 15.

[15] Crane (1); Frenken; Greven.

[16] Cf. Lecoy de la Marche 299-300; Crane (1) xli, xlvi.

[17] Strange; Herbert (2) 348 ff.

[18] Cf. Banks.

[19] Cf. Herbert (1) 101; Crane (5) 377, 378; Schröder, *Beiträge z. Geschichte d. d. Spr. u. Lit.*, 43 (1918), 545-548.

mopolitan collections, which seem to have been popular and prolific everywhere, the native exempla of Odo of Cheriton (1175-
1247) were popular and also comparatively prolific.[20]

Whilst the multiplication of these sources indicates a growing
use of the type on the Continent, it was the coming of the preaching
friars,[21] the Franciscans and the Dominicans, to England in the
first quarter of the thirteenth century which gave the exempla their
greatest English vogue.[22] From now on collections of exempla
became more numerous. The force of tradition and the uniform
purpose of compilers, however, precluded originality either in
content or in form. The exemplum, in fact, never acquired any
distinguishing national features,[23] although a few bear the traces
of a clumsy touch of local color.[24] Standard tales from the Fathers,
incidents from the life of a saint, from history, from fable, and
sometimes from contemporary life [25] were repeated and assembled
in greater or less numbers with more or less elaboration of detail.
Style was a negligible factor, since effect depended upon the ability
of the particular preacher to adapt the comparatively bald outline
of the exemplum to his purpose and to render it appealing to his
particular audience.

The audience was usually gathered from the masses. It was
made up ordinarily of the inhabitants of the medieval town, the
lower classes, and the heterogenous medieval strata who were
coalescing into the middle class. To reach the average intelligence
of this group, the preaching friar necessarily supplanted dialectic,
subtlety, and involved figures with convincing, interesting, and, at
times, amusing illustrations or applications of the virtue or vice of
which he was speaking.[26] To drive the lesson home, to grip the

---

[20] Hervieux 4; cf. Herbert (2) 2-3, 33, 52-56; 57-78; Frenken 18, 42-46;
Crane (4) 231. Before Odo of Cheriton, Bishop Herbert de Losinga (c.
1050-1119) employed the exempla in sermons which are extant. Cf.
Goulburn-Symonds, 2; 31, 71, 89, 109, 319, 387. Undoubtedly their meager
number in contrast with the many exempla in the works of Odo of Cheriton
accounts for the slight attention given the former.

[21] Cf. Brewer (1), pref. 11. Cf. Luard (1) ep. 58, 180. Cf. Owst, 255-256.

[22] Cf. Owst, 299-300; Frenken, 16-17. For an observation on earlier
preaching, cf. Owst, 48; 49-50.

[23] Cf. Mosher, 112.

[24] Cf. R. Bond, 239.

[25] Cf. Lecoy de la Marche, 302-304.

[26] Cf. Frenken, 17.

audience with awe or fear he would sooner or later, and without respect of persons, embody the virtue or vice in a character-creation which was an unrelieved paragon of the one or the other. He would thus lead the audience to a vivid sense of the odiousness of evil or the beauty of virtue. For the same reason the narrative strokes were usually bold, extreme, and vigorous; the colors glaringly lurid; and the action rapid and melodramatic. [27] Preachers were supposed to use discretion in the choice of exempla. Authorities suggested discrimination [28] and designated material proper to audiences of different classes of society,[29] and exempla-books often indexed [30] the stories suitable to particular groups. It must be confessed, however, that the medieval standard of appropriateness in such matters is lost upon us in this instance, for to the modern mind exempla, generally speaking, are frank to the point of repulsiveness. Many exempla on the nun even seem indelicate to us.

With the fifteenth century the vogue of the exempla began to wane.[31] Naturally material of this type was open to abuse and the story or picture gradually became more important than the sermon which embodied it. Although from the fourteenth century particularly, measures had been taken [32] and legislation directed against the inclusion of inappropriate narratives in sermons, by the time of the Reformation exempla had fallen into " general disrepute and . . . had long since become associated with facetiae, jests, and secular tales ".[33] With the destruction of books at the hands of the Reformers " it is very likely that many works containing exempla have been destroyed ".[34]

[27] Cf. Owst, 243; Mosher, 16.

[28] Cf. Little, 56, 94-95, 98, 115-116, 120-121, and Small, *Isti versus omittantur a lectore quando legit Anglicum coram laycis*, 26.

[29] Cf. *Summa de Arte Praedicatoria, Quibus proponenda sit praedicatio, op. cit.*, cap. xxxix.

[30] Cf. *An Alphabet of Tales*, Banks, 345 and *Moniali, possunt adaptari multa que dicuntur infra de muliere, ibid.*

[31] Cf. Mosher, 114; Paul, *Grundriss* 2; part 2, 739; Caplan, " The Four Senses of Scriptural Interpretation and the Mediaeval Theory of Preaching ", *Speculum* 4 (1929), 289.

[32] Cf. Mosher, 18; Crane (1) lxix-lxx.

[33] Mosher, 19. Cf. Krapp, 170-184.

[34] *Ibid.*, note 16, 87. Cf. Gerould, 314.

The exempla that remain,[35] however, are found for the most part in four kinds of works: collections of sermons or of sermon material; exempla-books, among which collections of " Miracles of the Virgin " are included; religious treatises; and " instruction books." Material on the nun is derived from the exempla of the first, second, and third classification, but not from those of the fourth. We are interested here in the subject-matter of the exempla rather than in the types of compilation in which they happen to be preserved. The treatment of the nun in any of the compilations is the same. It is only the subject-matter of the story that may differ. Frequently enough the same exemplum on the nun is repeated in several types of compilation. It is employed for one purpose in one collection and for another and far different purpose in another, while sometimes the application is left wholly to the discretion or choice of the preacher.[36] Classification according to the most obvious purport of the various exempla considered individually and apart from accidental context seems the most practicable method of presenting the material. The method, moreover, will throw into relief the static, impersonal nature of the figure and reveal both the constant repetition and utter want of development of the type. Hence, the exempla on the nun in the literature of England are treated here under the following headings:—[37]

> Romula.
> The Need of Guarding the Eyes.
> Prayer: Its Manner, Efficacy, and Necessity.
> Portraits of Edifying Nuns.
> Punishment of Evil.
> The Renegade Nun.
> Exempla in Which the Nun is Incidental.

---

[35] There are undoubtedly exempla of English origin or compilation in MSS. that have not been printed or catalogued.

[36] Cf. p. 209, below.

[37] I regret not having had access to the forthcoming bibliography, *Motif-Index of Folk-Literature: A Classification of narrative elements in Folk Tales . . . Medieval Romances, Exempla, Fabliaux* . . . by Stith Thompson, referred to by George R. Coffman in his " Note on Saints' Legends," (*Studies in Philology*, 28 (1931), note 2, 581).

II. *Romula*

Among the homilies of Aelfric written two centuries and more
before the rise of popular preaching in England is a passage from
Saint Gregory the Great which Aelfric employs as an exemplum.
The "bysne",[38] as the illustrative tale is designated in the vernacular of Aelfric, constitutes the starting point for the study and
survey of exempla about the nun. It is a verbal [39] translation of
Saint Gregory's portrayal of the deathbed scene of the patient
virgin, Romula.[40] In illustration of his remarks on patience
Aelfric, in this "bysne", presents the "mynchen" Romula, patient,
obedient, silent, prayerful. Stricken with paralysis, she improves
her time by assiduous prayer and the practice of virtue. One night
as she lies crippled upon the bed, a brilliant light floods the cell
and a winsome fragrance fills the air with sweetness. A noise is
heard at the door as if a multitude were seeking entrance. Redempta,
Romula's spiritual mother, and another sister who is present become exceedingly terrified. "Fear not, my Mother", Romula calls
out, "I shall not die yet". With her words the light fades. The
perfume, however, lingers about the cell. Four nights later
Romula requests "housel". After she has received the last sac-
raments two heavenly hosts stand before the door, singing a celestial
song in double choir, the male voices intoning and the women's
responding. During the heavenly melody Romula's spirit passes
to heaven. With the song her soul goes upward, the harmony
growing fainter and fainter until it dies upon the air.[41]

Romula manifestly represents the ideal simple-nun type of traditional didactic materials. She appears again as the subject of an
exemplum in a manuscript dated from the second half of the
twelfth century.[42] Nuns suggestive of this type appear, moreover,
in exempla belonging properly to the heyday of the genre. They
are the only ones, however, of their kind. The nun-figure, pecu-
liarly and distinctively characteristic of the exempla material, is,

[38] *Op. cit.*, Thorpe (2) 2; 546.

[39] The few omissions in the Anglo-Saxon are negligible.

[40] Cf. PL 76, Hom. xl, cols. 1310-1317. The description is given more
briefly in *Liber Dialogorum* IV, PL 77, cols. 344-345.

[41] Cf. *op. cit.*, 546-548.   [42] Cf. Cotton, Vesp. D. f. 43 b. Herbert (2) 454.

as we shall see, something quite different. It bears the marks of its proper matrix.

III. *The Need of Guarding the Eyes*

Among the works of Giraldus Cambrensis, who wrote at the close of the twelfth century, typical exempla are copious. Only in his *Gemma Ecclesiastica*,[43] however, are there exempla on the nun. They present the nun in the manner that is typical of exempla material generally. Two of them, illustrative of the need of guarding the eyes, are told in order to reinforce a preliminary instruction on the necessity of virtue among ecclesiastics. Having cited various instances of notable resistance to temptation and passing to concrete examples of the danger which those incur who do not observe caution, Giraldus relates the story of a nun who, failing to guard her eyes, brings upon herself severe temptation; is visited by a demon whom she recognizes as such, and whom she succeeds in putting to flight only after vigorous measures and excessive labor.[44] The second refers to a member of the double monastery of Sempringham. A consecrated maid there, having allowed her eyes to wander, becomes the victim of a violent and evil passion, of which she is cured only by the sight of her beloved's revolting person.[45]

At the close of the homily [46] on the Gospel of *Dominica infra Octavam Nativitatis Domini secundum Lucam*,[47] the verse, " This child is set for the fall, and for the resurrection of many " (Luke II, 34), is explained by the story of the " fall and rise " of

> Ane ersbisschope be3onde the se,
>
> .   .   .   .
>
> A hali man and gude. . . .[48]

---

[43] Brewer (2) 2.

[44] Cf. *op. cit.*, Dist. II, cap. xi, 222-223.

[45] Cf. *ibid.*, cap. xvii, 247-248. The exemplum is repeated in *Dial. Mir.* I, Dist. iv, cap. 103, pp. 273-274, and in Herbert (2), no. 68, 356.

[46] Small, 74-93. The homily is included in the North English Homily Cycle. Cf. MME 290; Gerould, 164-176; Horstmann (7) lvii-lxxxix. Parts of the cycle, including the archbishop's tale, have been printed by Small in *English Metrical Homilies* (Edinburgh, 1862) and by Horstmann in " Die Evangelien-Geschichten der Homiliensammlung des Ms. Vernon ", *Archiv* 57 (1877), 241-316. Herbert (2) states that it seems to have been composed originally at the beginning of the fourteenth century. Cf. *op. cit.*, 320.   [47] *Ibid.*, 74.   [48] *Op. cit.*, 78.

In the " contree " where the " ersbisschope " dwells is a " non-
nery ", the exemplum begins. From the convent candidates for the
veil are sent to the archbishop to receive their insignia. For this
ceremony

> Thi maydens came befre the autere,
> And toke thaire vayles on gude manere.
> And this bisschope his eye uppe kest
> To one of thaim that was fayrest,
> And sone on hir his lufe was fest [49]

He summons the abbess of the nunnery to which the newly-
invested religious have returned. The abbess, coming as she thinks
" The nedes of hir house to do ", is bribed by the dignitary to send
him the nun. Thinking of the good he had done her and her house,
fearing his wrath, and preferring to incur that of God rather than
to occasion the archbishop's " dethe ", she consents. The young
nun also consents for the sake of the abbey, not understanding—
the homilist observes with a rare regard in this material for the
religious character —

> How Criste, that boght hir on the rude,
> Had tane hir als his leeve spouse,
> And broghte hir to his awne howse.[50]

" Bot ", he adds, after the fashion of Gower,

> . . . for scho was als wommane waike
> Scho heldid sone to synfull layke.[51]

With the fall of the ecclesiastic accomplished, the homilist does
not concern himself further with the nun or her abbess. He merely
adds the moral :

> . . . all that will this tale here,
> Gode ensaumpil may thai lere
> Unsikir of thaim self to be,
> If thai will understand and se,
> How wyse man this bisschope wasse,
> And sithen to foly gon he passe,[52]

and then relates the remarkable " rise ", extraordinary penance,
and future surpassing sanctity of the humbled archbishop.[53]

---

[49] *Ibid.*, 78-79.   [50] *Ibid.*, 82.   [51] *Ibid.*, 83.   [52] *Ibid.*
[53] Cf. *ibid.*, 85-90. Cf. MSS. Add. 30358, Herbert (2) 320-322; MS.
Harley 2391, f. 160, *ibid.*, 333-334, and MS. Add. 38010, f. 23b, *ibid.*, 716.

IV. *Prayer: Its Manner, Efficacy, and Necessity*

Under the designation, prayer, its efficacy and necessity, can be grouped an assembly of miscellaneous exempla on the nun derived from various sources, all emphasizing some marvel effected by prayer or an exceptional occurrence associated with prayer. At least one-half the number are " Miracles of the Virgin ".

The first of these, printed in the *Speculum Laicorum* (1279-1292), an alphabetical treatise, the author of which is not known, is included in the chapter *De Oracione*. It states that a certain nun of England honored the Blessed Virgin by saying the angelical salutation as often as she could every day. The glorious Virgin appears to the nun and says, " Your salutations are very gratifying to me, but they would please me much more, were they pronounced more slowly ". Henceforth the nun says fewer prayers in a day, but that number she offers with greater devotion.[54] This exemplum is repeated from the twelfth to the fifteenth century.[55] Somewhat similar is the nun-figure suggested in the following brief anecdotes. In one a *quedam devota monialis*, standing before the statue of the Blessed Mother and the Divine Child to say an " Ave ", is asked by the Infant sometimes to say an *Ave benigne deus* to Him.[56] In another a nun prays to the Blessed Mother for the release of her brother, a knight, from captivity. The Blessed Mother informs the nun that in answer to her prayers the knight shall be set free. The nun herself shall die, however, for in her prayer she has reminded the Blessed Mother solely of her sorrows, neglecting to commemorate her joys.[57] The Blessed Mother's grief at the loss of

[54] Cf. *op. cit.*, Welter, cap. lix, ex. 433, p. 84. Cf. MS. Add. 11284, f. 63 (14th cent.) Herbert (2) 397.

[55] MSS. Cotton Cleop. C. x, f. 136b-137b (late 12th cent.), Ward, 614; Royal 6B. xiv, 97b (c. 1200), *ibid.*, 641; Arundel 407, f. 43 (13th cent.) *ibid.*, 655; Harley 4401 f. 59b (French; mid-13th cent.), *ibid.*, 721; Harley 2385, f. 54b (early 14th cent.), Herbert, 523; Add. 18346 f. 56b (14th cent.), Ward, 647; Harley 495, f. 58b (early 14th cent.), Herbert, 535; Add. 18349, f. 64 (14th cent.), *ibid.*, 605 and Sloane 4029, f. 192, c. 1456, *ibid.*, 697. Cf. Dexter, 35-36.

[56] Cf. MSS. Add. 32248, f. 4 (13th cent.), Ward, 697, and Arundel 506, f. 2b, col. 2 (14th cent.), Herbert, 543. The same anecdote is told of a clerk in MS. Add. 18364, f. 49, *ibid.*, 614.

[57] Cf. MS. Royal 6B x, f. 40 (13th cent.), Ward, 645. The same " miracle "

her Divine Son is, on the contrary, incomprehensible to another
nun.[58] In a dream this religious experiences similar sorrow. She
thereafter believes in and can compassionate the sorrows of the
Blessed Virgin. Closely associated with the nun-figure in narratives of this kind is that of the anchoress who, as is recounted in
various manuscript collections of exempla,[59] learns by a miraculous
voice, the number of Christ's Sacred Wounds. The voice also
instructs her how to venerate the Holy Stigmata. A hermit com-
municates the information learned from the anchoress to the nuns
of a nearby abbey. The nuns, accordingly, practice the devotion
to the Sacred Wounds, and the anchoress perceives in a vision the
salutary effect of their piety.

Many brief exempla taken from various continental collections
and assembled in *An Alphabet of Tales,* a mid-fifteenth century
Middle-English translation of the *Alphabetum Narrationum,*[60] also
have to do mainly with the power of a nun's prayer. One of these,
delightfully representative of the private devotions of some religious, is entitled "*Petrus monialem absentem sanavit*".[61] It
relates how a nun "in Lombardye þat had þe gutt grevuslie in hur
kne", of which malady "she cuthe not be helid with no medcyn",
made a spiritual pilgrimage to "Mylayn" in honor of St. Peter.
The "iorney fro hur place vnto Mylayn" being one of fourteen
days, for fourteen days she says so many prayers. The last day
of the pilgrimage she kneels in spirit at "hys tombe", and when
she has completed the spiritual journey back, she is cured.[62]

is contained in a twelfth-century continental MS. in the Bibliothèque
Nationale. Cf. *ibid.*, 42 and Mussafia, "Studien zu den mittelalterlichen
Marienlegenden", I, *Wiener SB* 13 (1886), 917-994 where the MS. is
designated as SV.

[58] Cf. Add. 33,956, f. 75 (early 14th cent.), Ward 675.

[59] Cf. Arundel 506, f. 28, col. 2, Herbert (2) 552. Herbert mentions
MS. Add. 37787 f. 71b, Harl. 2869, f. 204, Add. 33381, f. 152, and Harl.
211, f. 130 as containing this exemplum. Cf. *ibid.* Harl. 211, f. 130, an
English MS., relates the incident of St. Bride of Sweden. Cf. *ibid.*

[60] Cf. p. 186, above.

[61] *Op. cit.*, no. DCXXIX, 420.

[62] *Ibid.* An exemplum somewhat similar to this one is found in *Dial. Mir.*
II, Dist. vii, cap. 48, pp. 68-69, and repeated in the *Promptuarium de
Miraculis B. M. V.,* compiled by Herolt in the fifteenth century. In this
exemplum a nun who has injured her knee by too much kneeling is healed

Under the heading, *Raptus spiritualis. Rapitur aliquando anima extra se,* among illustrations of ecstasy in prayer is given, on the authority of Jacques de Vitry,[63] the instance of a nun " nerehand of xxx^{ti} yere old ", who " was kepyd with so grete luff be hur spowse in þe clostre, at sho mot be no ways go furth þeroff. And neuer so many men had drawen hur to þe hand, ffor oft tymys ", the exemplum explains, " sho was enforcid to be drawen oute, bod it was in vayn bod if þai would hafe rugid hur in sonder . . ." [64]

Another exemplum on the power of the salutation, " Ave Maria ", to dispel phantasms and put the demon to flight, represents an anchoress deceived by a fiend who appears to her in the form of an angel of light. The evil spirit, having succeeded to a certain extent in deluding the recluse, her confessor advises her to request the spirit to present the Blessed Mother before her, and at her appearance to salute the figure with the words, " Ave Maria ". The anchoress follows his advice and foils the evil spirit.[65]

To indicate the value of devotion to the Blessed Virgin an exemplum of a thirteenth-century collection [66] describes a nun as appearing thirty days after her death to a sister-religious in fulfilment of a promise made on her deathbed. She assures the sister of the heavenly reward for devotion to the Mother of God and leaves her celestial flowers of exquisite fragrance.

The efficacy of prayer is shown also in two exempla in which a thirteenth-century Béguine, Mary of Oigniez, is mentioned. Originally from the works of Jacques de Vitry,[67] they are repeated in the *An Alphabet of Tales* under the legends " *Demones insistunt Morientibus* " and " *Orationibus iuuantur anime in purgatorio* " [68] respectively. In the first, Mary puts to flight a " multitude of

by a fragrant ointment given by the Blessed Mother. Cf. Ward, 684. An actual pilgrimage undertaken by a Béguine is described in an exemplum from a fourteenth-century collection, the unfamiliar anecdotes in which are undoubtedly of German origin. The Béguine, having served God for eighteen years, goes to Rome to complain to the Pope that in all that time she has never been comforted by a vision. On the night of her arrival Christ appears to her and in the morning she dies. Cf. MS. Add. 15833, f. 113, Herbert (2) 585.

[63] " Iacobus de Vatriaco says ", *op. cit.,* 446.

[64] *Ibid.*   [66] Cf. MS. Add. 18,929, f. 80b. Ward. 657.

[65] Cf. *op. cit.,* 320-321.   [67] Cf. *ibid.,* 174, 391.   [68] *Ibid.*

fendis rumyand aboute hur (dying) sister bed " by offering to
assume any guilt the sister—who is herself praying fervently for
help—might have incurred through negligence or ignorance. In
the second, Mary beholds about her in her cell a "multitude of
handis haldyng vp as it had bene to pray vnto hur". Beseeching
God to let her know what it means, she learns that the hands
represent the souls in purgatory imploring her prayers.[69]   An
exemplum very much like the first of these presents the dying nun
as obtaining peace through the sacrament of extreme unction.[70]

In all the exempla materials of England on the nun there are
four exempla that are particularly charming. They perhaps derive
their singular appeal from the fact that they present a little girl
in conventual environment. The three most attractive of these
exempla depict the value of prayer and devotion, and are, accordingly, properly treated here.

"A certain nun", according to the *Speculum Laicorum* wherein
the first of these exempla is found, has charge of the education of
a little girl. She teaches the child—her cousin, in the Middle English version [71]—to salute the glorious Virgin Mary so many times a
day and to calculate the number of her prayers on the joints of her
fingers. Shortly after, however, the little girl dies and the nun,
her mistress, "ceases not day and night to lament her". But she
who is the Mother of Mercy, appearing to the grieving religious,
inquires,

> Why so many tears?

To whom the nun,

> Oh, my Lady, for my little pupil who has recently died.

Then the Blessed Mother declares,

> "Behold the little girl whom you bewail! "

And before her the religious sees the child, the knuckles of her
hands gleaming as if so many precious jewels.[72]

[69] *Ibid.*
[70] Cf. MS. Egerton 1117, f. 183b. col. 2, Herbert (2) 473.
[71] Cf. Horstmann (6) 324.
[72] *Op. cit.*, Welter, ex. 386, 75-76; Herbert (2) 395.

That religious may pay heed to the devout recital of the *Te Deum,* the story of another little maid in a cloister of nuns is adapted from Caesarius of Heisterbach's version[73] and recounted with exquisite simplicity both in *The Myroure of Oure Ladye,*[74] (1408-1450), a treatise devoted particularly to the exposition of the religious services of the monastery of the Sisters of Sion, a " religious community near Isleworth on the Thames ",[75] and in *An Alphabet of Tales,* where the incident is localized to Essex[76] and told with many happy homely details. " In a monasterye of nonnys ", the exemplum in the *An Alphabet of Tales* begins.

> Þer was a litle damysell, and on a grete solempne nyght hur maistres lete hur com with hur to matyns. So þe damysell was bod a wayke thyng, and hur maistres was ferd at sho sulde take colde, and sho commaundid hur befor Te Deum to go vnto þe dortur to hur bed agayn.[77]

The child, loath to leave, lingers outside the choir to hear the rest of matins, and when the *Te Deum* is begun, she beholds the heavens open and the choir of nuns elevated to the company of the angels and saints. As each heavenly order is mentioned in the hymn, that order, chanting with the nuns, bows low and worships God. At the last verse, " *In Te, Domine, speravi* ", the child sees " þe quere of þe susters " descend again to earth " and hevyn sparryd agayn after þaim ".[78] " And by thys ye maye se ", the author of the *Myroure* appends to his version, " how moche owre lorde god and all hys aungels and sayntes are pleased wyth the deuoute saynge of thys holy hympne." [79]

Another little girl, " brought up as a nun, is taught above all to love ". " At first ", as the fourteenth-century collection of religious tales [80] explains, " the child divides her love between a bird and

---

[73] Cf. Dial. Mir. II, Dist. viii, cap. 90, pp. 157-158.

[74] Cf. *op. cit.*, Blunt, 116-117. *The Myroure of Oure Ladye* is attributed to Dr. Thomas Gascoign of Merton College, Oxford. Cf. *ibid.*, viii-ix.

[75] Mosher, 128.

[76] Cf. *op. cit.*, 496. The Latin MS. states " Saxonia " and *The Myroure of Oure Ladye* " the contre of Saxony " as the locale.

[77] *Ibid.*, 496.   [78] *Ibid.*

[79] *Op. cit.*, 118. The exemplum is included also in a thirteenth-century collection, MS. Egerton 1117, f. 191, col. 2. Herbert (2) 476.

[80] Cf. MS. Cotton, Cleop. D. viii, f. 109 as catalogued and described by Herbert (2) 638-639.

the abbess' dog ", but later, while standing before an image of the
Blessed Mother and the Infant Jesus, she decides to give all her
love to the Holy Child. She hears a voice promising to love her
in return. Afterwards she is rebuked by one of her elders for
having smiled during Mass. She explains that she smiled because
her Divine Love smiled at her as He was elevated in the hands of
the priest.[81]

More typical, however, of the genre are the many exempla of the
foiled nun. Among works produced on English soil the story seems
first to appear in the *Gemma Ecclesiastica*[82] of Giraldus Cambrensis.[83] In this anecdote the nun, intending to quit the convent
to live with a knight, finds her passage barred at every door she
tries, from the small door of the church to the main entry of the
monastery, by the crucifix which she has been in the habit of
venerating. Having struggled unsuccessfully for two nights to
evade it and to make her escape, she can resist no longer, but falls
down and adores God. Her customary devotion to the cross thus
proves salutary, the exemplum adds at the close, as well to the
knight as to the nun.[84]

Variants of this theme are frequent and common from the twelfth
to the fifteenth century. In the *Dialogus Miraculorum*[85] of
Caesarius of Heisterbach, perhaps the most common source of later
versions of the exemplum, the crucifix bars the doors and the
Blessed Mother's image, which the nun has always venerated, slaps
her face as she tries to depart. A late twelfth or early thirteenth-
century manuscript[86] has the nun labor in vain for two nights to
unfasten the convent door, to discover on the third night the
Blessed Virgin's hand upon the lock.[87] A mid-thirteenth-century
French[88] version and an early fourteenth-century Latin version[89]

[81] Cf. *op. cit.*

[82] Cf. above.

[83] Cf. p. 191, above.

[84] Cf. *op. cit.*, Dist. II, cap. xi, 224-225.

[85] Cf. *op. cit.*, II, Dist. vii, cap. 33, pp. 41-42.

[86] Add. 15723, f. 86b, Ward, no. 34, 634.

[87] Said to have been confided to Magister Serlo, a Cistercian abbot,
while on a visit to England. Cf. *ibid.*

[88] Harley 4401 (Gautier de Coincy, B. 1. no. 17) f. 55b, col. 2, Ward, 721.

[89] Arundel 506, Herbert (2) 546. Cf. Tryon, "Miracles of Our Lady

have the nun deterred by a vision in which she is dragged to the
mouth of hell by devils and rescued by the Blessed Virgin. Another
fourteenth-century variant [90] tells how the nun beholds in vision a
noisome pit of serpents and, in horror, resolves to persevere. Still
another [91] contains an exemplum in which the unfaithful nun is
the sacristan of the monastic church. Unable to withstand the
temptation to leave, she lays her keys on the altar with a parting
prayer to Mary. She swoons and revives repentant and determined
to remain. This same manuscript [92] contains another version of
the foiled nun story.[93] The religious in this exemplum is a secular
canoness in a convent in Germany. Casting two bundles of clothing
before her, she leaps out of a window; falls into the hands of
thieves; escapes, and loses her way in the woods. Robbed of her
few possessions and utterly defenseless, she prays to the Blessed
Virgin. After the prayer she goes to sleep and awakes safe in the
monastery dormitory, her two bundles of clothes beside her. She
becomes, thereafter, very holy and ends her days in sanctity.[94]

Recurring frequently also are exempla about a lapsed nun who,
having repented and devoutly undertaken the penance imposed upon
her by the abbess, dies before completing it. After her death she
appears to her superior and informs her that she is still undergoing
punishment for her sin, but that the Blessed Virgin had promised
to release her after a time.[95] Other versions [96] have the abbess

in Middle English Verse ", PMLA 38 (1923), 368, for John of Garland's
version.

[90] Add. 33956, f. 72 (early 14th cent.). Cf. Herbert (2) 673. Cf. also
Klapper (2) (MS. Breslau, c. 1485), 292; and Mussafia, " Studien zu den
mittelalterlichen Marienlegenden I ", *Wiener SB* 113 (1886), 971.

[91] Egerton 1117, f. 173, col. 2 (end of 14th cent.), Ward, 667.

[92] *Ibid.*, f. 171b, 666.

[93] The version is printed in Wright (2) 96.

[94] Cf. *op. cit.* Cf. also Klapper (1), no. 95, 70.

[95] Cf. MS. Arundel 346, f. 70, col. 2 (c. 12th cent.), Ward, 621. " Printed
by Duplessis in the introduction to Le Marchant's Miracles de N. D. de
Chartres (Chartres, 1885) ", xxi-xxvii. It is found also in Pez, cap. 42,
ibid. Cf. Miélot, 15.

[96] MS. Egerton 612, f. 61 (early 13th cent.). *Ibid.*, 715 and Welter,
cap. xxiii, " *De cura pro mortuis* ", ex. 173, 38; in Herbert (2) 384. Cf.
also MSS. Royal 20 B. xiv, f. 160b, col. 2 (French, early 14th cent.),
Ward, 733; Harley 2385, f. 57, col. 2 (early 14th cent.), Herbert (2) 523,
and Add. 18346 f. 68b (14th cent.), Ward, 648.

assign the unfulfilled penance to the other sisters of the community, and in these the nun appears to tell the abbess that the
Blessed Mother has informed her that their atonement will effect
her release. To the same end, in different collections, the exemplum
is cited in which the lapsed nun, having abandoned religious life
and spent years in evil, is struck with remorse and, praying fervently to the Virgin and Child, is assured by the Blessed Mother
that all her sins are forgiven.[97] Another exemplum to the same
purpose tells of the nun who is haunted by an incubus, sins once,
but, confessing, repents immediately.[98]

Undoubtedly the most striking exemplum on the nun, illustrating the efficacy of prayer, is also, judging from the frequency of its
occurrence in these materials, one of the most popular of the
medieval " Miracles of the Virgin ". In Latin, in Old French, in
Middle English, in prose and in verse, it is repeated now very tersely
and cursorily, now in great elaboration of detail. It is told in the
twelfth century and in the thirteenth, in the fourteenth and in the
fifteenth, recurring steadily with slight variations in sermons and
homilies, collections of " Miracles of the Virgin ", religious treatises — in short, in every variety of exempla material in which the
nun-figure appears. Found at the earliest almost contemporane-
ously in the sermons [99] of Odo of Cheriton (d. 1247) [100] on the
Sunday Gospels throughout the year; in the *Dialogus Miraculorum*
of Caesarius of Heisterbach,[101] and in early thirteen-century manuscripts,[102] the exemplum is told subsequently by many,[103] notably

---

[97] Cf. MS. Egerton 1117, f. 173 (end of 13th cent.), Ward, 667; Wright
(2) 95.

[98] Cf. MSS. Royal 7 D., f. 117 (end of 13th cent.), Herbert (2) 495 and
Harley 206, f. 112b (mid 15th cent.), *ibid.*, 700.

[99] *Exempla of Odo of Cheriton*, MS. Arundel 231, f. 47 (early 14th cent.).
Herbert (2) 69. Not in Hervieux, " *Odonis de Ceritonia Parabolae ex
Sermonibus super Evangeliis Dominicalibus Extractae* ", *Les fabulistes
latines* 4; 265. Cf. also Crane (4) 231. But cf. Aelred of Rievaulx, *De
Sanctimoniali de Wattun*, PL 195, cols. 789-796.

[100] For a discussion of the identity and the works of Odo of Cheriton,
cf. Hervieux 4; 3-31, and Herbert (2) 31-34.

[101] Cf. *loc. cit.*

[102] Cf. MS. Add. 15723 of the late 12th or early 13th century, no. 6, f. 71b,
Ward, 626, MS. Royal 6 B, xiv, c. 1200, no. 9, f. 87, col. 2, *ibid.*, 638.

[103] Cf. MS. Arundel 407 f. 41b, p. 655, 13th cent.;

by John of Garland (c. 1180–c. 1252) in the *Liber metricus qui vocatur Stella maris*,[104] by Nigellus Wireker in Latin elegiacs,[105] and by the anonymous compilers respectively of the *Liber Exemplorum*[106] and the *Speculum Laicorum*.[107] Outstanding among the numerous renditions, however, are the Middle English metrical version in the *North English Homily Cycle*[108] (which has been mentioned as the source of the most elaborate version of another exemplum[109] in which nuns have a prominent part) and the Middle English prose version in *An Alphabet of Tales*.[110]

In the Homily-Cycle[111] the exemplum is an illustration of the mercy of the Blessed Mother in response to prayer and a virtuous

MS. Egerton 612 f. 96, 98, early 13th cent. Old French, *ibid.*, 7, 17. (The MS., except this tale, is printed by C. Neuhaus, " Adgar's Marienlegenden ", Foerster's *Altfranzösische Bibliothek*, 9, 1886) ;

MS. Harley 4401, f. 45, col. 2 (Gautier de Coincy's), French, mid-13th cent., *ibid.*, 720;

MS. Add. 32248, Latin, 13th cent., *ibid.*, 697;

MS. Add. 18929, f. 79b, late 13th cent., *ibid.*, 656;

MS. Add. 33956, f. 72, col. 2, early 14th cent., *ibid.*, 673;

MS. Royal 20 B, xiv, f. 121b, French, early 14th cent., *ibid.*, 730. Cf. Kjellmann, 62-67.

Cf. MS. Harley 2385, f. 55, Latin, early 14th cent., Herbert (2) 523;

MS. Add. 18346, f. 61, Latin, 14th cent., *ibid.*, 647;

MS. Arundel 506, f. 20b, Latin, first half of 14th cent., *ibid.*, 547;

MS. Harley 268, f. 19b, Latin, second half of 14th cent., *ibid.*, 565;

MS. Harley 2316, f. 6b, second half of 14th cent., *ibid.*, 575. Cf. Neuhaus, 206.

Cf. MS. Vernon, published by Horstmann (3) 257-258;

MS. Harley 4196, f. 143, Middle English verse (printed by Small), early 15th cent., Ward, 740;

MS. Sloane 4029, f. 185b, c. 1456, Herbert (2) 696. Cf. also Brown, *A Register of Middle English Religious and Didactic Verse.*

[104] MS. Royal 8c, iv, f. 16b (late 13th cent.), Ward, 700. Cf. Tryon, 341, 369. Cf. also L. J. Paetow, *The Morale Scolarium of John of Garland* (Berkeley, 1927), 114-115.

[105] Cf. MS. Cotton Vespasian D. xix, f. 22b (13th cent.), Ward, 691, 694-695.

[106] Cf. Little, 32-33; Wright (2) 38; Miélot, 73-75.

[107] Cf. *op. cit.*, 75-76.   [109] Cf. p. 191, above.

[108] Cf. *loc. cit.*   [110] Cf. *op. cit.*, 95

[111] Parts of which, including this exemplum, have been published by Small, *op cit.*, and by Horstmann, *op. cit.*, *Archiv* 57 (1877), 241-316.

life, for the *narracio,* as the story is there designated, is appended
to the homily, *In Purificationem Beate Marie, secundum Lucam,*[112]
after the following introductory and explanatory lines:

> Bot scho [Mary] es moder of mercye,
> And til sinful men ay redye.
> Sche fayles neuer mar in nede,
> That mai we se bi many dede
> That scho dos oft for sinful man
> That haues igain hir son mistan.
> . . . .
> That mai ye se bi a lefdy,
> That was abbes of a nunrye.[113]

In the *An Alphabet of Tales* the anecdote is disassociated from
any matrix and is classified with two other exempla under the term
" abbatissa ".[114]

The story is briefly — for this tale is expanded beyond the usual
limits of an exemplum [115] — of an otherwise model abbess, " gude
of governans bothe in wurde & dede ". Her community she
guards zealously, loving all the sisters " with a spirtuall luf, . . .
& with grete aw & straytnes, þe congregacion att sho had gov-
ernan[s] of, sho compellid to kepe þer ordur ". Notwithstanding
her exemplary zeal and lofty virtue, " þurgh entysing of þe devull ",
she falls. But not in the least does she thereafter slacken in vigi-
lance for regular discipline. So " strayte " is she with her subjects
that, when her sin is known, they are eager to accuse her. They
denounce her to ecclesiastical authority. The abbess, in great
misery, casts herself in tears before an image of Our Blessed Lady.
She prays ardently, humbly, for help. Worn out with grief and
distress, she falls asleep. The Blessed Mother appears to her in a
dream; comforts her, and promises to save her from disgrace.
Miraculously saved from confusion, the abbess is exonerated the
next day at an assembly gathered to condemn her. Her child, of
whom she later informs the bishop, is carefully educated by this
dignitary and it, in turn, becomes a bishop.[116]

[112] *Op. cit.,* 153-171.   [113] *Ibid.,* 164.   [114] *Op. cit.,* 11-14.

[115] The " narracio " in the *North English Homily Cycle* tended to expand
out of all proportion to the homily proper. Cf. Gerould, 171.

[116] Cf. *op. cit.,* 11-12.

The North English Homily version has the abbess betrayed to the community and ecclesiastical authority by a foundling whom she has reared and " mad hir nunne in that nunrye ", and to whom, in her distress, she had given her confidence.[117]

An earlier form of the narrative gives the child the name Bonus,[118] who in another " Miracle of the Virgin " is identified [119] with Saint Bonus and is represented in later life as receiving an ecclesiastical vestment from Our Lady.[120]

V. *Portraits of Edifying Nuns*

Another arbitrary group of exempla may be designated portraits of edifying nuns. In one of these, quoted from *Vitae Patrum* by John of Bromyard (d. 1418) in the *Summa Praedicantium* [121] under the caption " Temptatio I " and translated with slight variants into Middle English in the *An Alphabet of Tales*,[122] an abbess valiantly withstands temptation. She prays not that the temptation be removed, but that she be given the fortitude to resist. After many years the devil appears in bodily form and admits that she has vanquished him. Not even by this avowal is the abbess deceived. She responds—as the Middle English version has it— " I hafe not overcommen þe, bod my Lord Iesu Criste hase ouer-commen þe ".[123]

Heroically valiant also is the nun of Fontrevault who, as Odo of

---

[117] Cf. *op. cit.*, 164, 165-167.

[118] Cf. MS. Add. 18929, f. 79b (later 13th cent.) Ward, *op. cit.*, no. 4, 656.

[119] Cf. *ibid.*, f. 18b, 657.

[120] Cf. Add. 15723, ff. 64-66, *ibid.*, 622-623.

[121] Cols. 3-4, 263.

[122] Cf. *op. cit.*, 13. Cf. also *Ancren Riwle*, 234-235.

[123] *An Alphabet of Tales* cites a similar exemplum, giving " Caesarius " (cf. *Dial. Mir.* II, Dist. viii, cap. 42, p. 114) as the source. In this a " religious mayden in Fraunce " prays to be freed of a temptation. Given instead doubts against the Faith, she beseeches the angel who questioned her that the first trial be restored as lighter. Cf. *op. cit.*, 501-502.

From Caesarius of Heisterbach (*ibid.*) also practically the same story is taken and told as of an " Anchoress in Friesland " in an anonymous collection of exempla, catalogued as MS. 18364, f. 56b (14th cent.) by Herbert (2) 616. In this exemplum the angel explains to the anchoress that temptation is necessary. Cf. *ibid.*

Cheriton observes, having learned that her eyes are a source of attraction for the King of England, plucks them out to present them to him.[124] In the *An Alphabet of Tales,* where the incident is also recorded and attributed to Jacques de Vitry,[125] the nun, having inquired of the delegation sent by the king to secure her, " whi þai tuke hur oute of hur abbay more þan hur other sisters ", and they having replied, " becauce sho had so fayr een ", " sho garte putt oute hur een onone, & layd þaim in a dissh & broght þaim vnto þaim & sayd; ' Lo! here is þe ene at your maister desiris, & bid him lat me alone, & lose nowder his sawle nor myne . . . ' & with-in iij yere after ", the story states at the close, " sho had hur een agayn als wele as euer had scho . . . " [126]

Another nun of whom Odo writes at comparative length in the same series of sermons answers the query, " *Quomodo sancta esset religiosa* " with the story of her parents. In imitation of her father who, silent and secluded, had lived meekly and laboriously, she has embraced a life of silence and labor. At her parent's death, she concedes, she had hesitated whether to adopt her father's mode of life or that of her mother, for, though garrulous, litigious, and wanting in virtue, her mother had died in great peace, while the father's death had occurred during such tempestuous weather that it seemed that even nature opposed his burial. A vision of her parents, however, dispelled her doubts, for she saw her father in bliss and her mother in torment. To obtain a reward such as she beholds her father enjoying, she embraces the religious life to live there as he had lived, in silence, retirement, and labor.[127] This story, taken from the *Vitae Patrum,*[128] is told with slight differences in other collections [129] of exempla.

Also from the *Vitae Patrum* [130] is the account of a very humble nun whose edifying life is described in verse in the *North English*

[124] Cf. Hervieux, 4; cxx, 311 and f. 107b.   Herbert (2) 72.

[125] The exemplum is no. lvii, in *Sermones Vulgares*, Crane, 22.

[126] *Op. cit.*, 95. Cf. also Little, 119.

[127] Cf. Hervieux, 4; no. clxix, 330-332.

[128] Cf. PL 73, col. 995.

[129] Cf. MSS. Cotton, Vespasian D. II, second half of 12th cent., Herbert (2) 455-456, and Royal 5 A. viii, f. 150b, 13th cent., no. 24, Ward, 654, and Arundel 506, f. 11. Cf. Little, 112.   [130] Cf. Butler (1) xxxiv, 98-100.

Homily Cycle [131] and in prose both in *Jacob's Well* [132] (a comparatively elaborate religious treatise in Middle English composed very likely during the first quarter of the fifteenth century [133]) and in *An Alphabet of Tales.*[134] Although the story is old and borrowed quite literally from its source, the homely diction and simplicity of expression of the Middle English prose redactions give it, as other exempla quoted from these two works, a timeliness and vigor that few traditional exampla possess. This " nunne ",

" for loue of crist, lefte pride, & toke lownes, & made here as a fool, & obeyid here to alle here sustren as here fool. sche wyssche here dyssches, & scouryd here pottys, sche turnyd here spyttes, sche lay in þe kechyn ny3t & day, sche sate neuere at borde, but eete of here trenchourys & of here broke mete þat was most abiecte. sche wente euere bare-foote, here heuyd was wryed wyth rente clowtys. þey in þe kechyn, for iape, pouryd on here hefd hoggyswasch; sche grucchyd neuere. Be steryng of an aungyl, an holy man, þat hy3t Pincerius, kom out of the desert to þat nunnerye, & clepyd aforn hym alle þe nunnys, saaf sche fayled þat made here as a foole. þe holy man seyde to hem. ' On of 3ow fayleth 3it here.' þe nunnys seyden, ' none fayleth but a fool '. þe man seyde, ' clepe here hyder ! ' sche com. þe holy abbot fell doun to here fete, & seyde to here, ' holy modyr, blysse þou me ! ' Sche fell doun to his fete, & seyde, ' holy fadir, blysse þou me ! ' here systryn seyde, ' Abbot, sche is a fool. Why do 3e here þis worschip ? ' þe Abbot seyde, ' 3e be folys ! for sche is holyere þan 3e or I.' þanne here sustryn cryedon here mercy of þe dyffoule þat þei dedyn here, & sche for3af it hem. In þis lownes sche dyed; & aungelys, with melodye, beryn here to blys." [135]

At the close of the exemplum the author of *Jacob's Well* adds the exhortation, " fforsakyth pride, takyth lownes, þat aungelys mowe bere 3ow to blyss ".[136]

Except for an even more colloquial expression or two, the version in *An Alphabet of Tales* is practically the same. The holy man who brings about the glorification of the lowly nun is called *Piterius* [137] in the source, " *Pincerius* " in the above account, " *Poyternus* " in the North English Homily Cycle,[138] and is " Saynt Patryk . . . a holie man & liffid in wildrenes " [139] in *An Alphabet of Tales.*

[131] Cf. Horstmann (3) 308-309.
[132] Ed. Brandeis, 81.
[133] Cf. *ibid.*, xi.
[134] *Op. cit.*, 223-224.
[135] *Jacob's Well*, 81.

[136] *Op. cit.*
[137] Cf. Butler (1) 98.
[138] *Op. cit.*, 308.
[139] *Op. cit.*, 223.

16

Kindred in spirit but of later origin is another exemplum in the *An Alphabet of Tales*. It is the story told by Jacques de Vitry [140] of the unexpected result of a visit to the edifying Béguine, Mary of Oigniez.[141] The traveling companion of the "chawntur of Cama- tensis", when invited by the latter to pay a visit with him to Mary of Oigniez, jeers, "For God, what seke ye þer? Will ye go kepp butterfleis as barnys duse?" Remaining outside where he pre- ferred to wait, the companion, however, grows tired and goes in search of the "chawntur" that they may be on their way. But meeting the pious woman, he is overcome in her holy presence; he weeps, and is unable to depart. The "chawntur", in his turn, retaliates with high good humor. "Go we! Whar-to sulde we stand here at kepp buttyrfleis?" The companion begs forgiveness for his incredulity and avows that he has perceived the virtue of Almighty God in the saintly woman.[142]

Another exemplum relates the remarkable incident of an entire community of nuns who, although ordered by the bishop to seek safety, refuse to leave the convent building when fire threatens to devour it. The conflagration, thereupon, miraculously turns aside and spares them.[143]

The portrait of a patient nun is drawn most effectively by con- trast with the description of an impatient one in an exemplum taken directly, undoubtedly, from Jacques de Vitry,[144] indirectly from the *Vitae Patrum*.[145] In *An Alphabet of Tales* it is entitled "Monialis in omnibus debet esse paciens".[146] Sent by her superior to dwell temporarily "for recreacion" with a "gude huswyfe" who had besought the abbess to grant her a nun-companion, the patient nun, who is also "gude buxsom", makes herself the gracious

---

[140] Cf. *op. cit.*, DCCLXXVIII, "*Visitacio personarum religiosarum ali- quando profuit*," 518.

[141] Cf. p. 195, above.

[142] *Op. cit.*, 518-519.

[143] Cf. MS. Royal 7 D. 1, f. 61b (13th cent.), Herbert (2) 479. Cf. *Speculum Laicorum*, Add. 11, 284, f. 89 (14th cent.), *ibid.*, 405. From Peter of Cluny, cf. PL 189, col. 889.

[144] Cf. no. LXV, Crane (1) 26-27.

[145] Cf. Crane (1) 162. "Ambrosius narrat", *ibid.*, 26; "Saynt Am- bros tellis", *An Alphabet of Tales*, 344; Crane, *ibid.*, 162.

[146] *Op. cit.*, 344.

servant of all in "þe howse". At the end of the year, however, the
housewife begs the abbess to remove this nun and to send her
another, "for, sho said, sho mot wyn no þing by hur, sho was so
pacient and so buxsom & so servisable in all þingis, & will nowder
truble hur selfe nor oder folk". The abbess then sends the housewife a nun who is "debatus & passyng angrie & euer chidand, &
alway gruchand agayns hur huswyffe, & wolde flite with hur and
with all þe howse-meneya". The matron keeps this nun with her
all her life, for by bearing with her she has regained the "mekull
mede" she had lost through the "mekenes of þe toder".[147]

VI. *Punishment of Evil*

Many exempla in which the nun is the sole or the most prominent
character have been composed to represent—usually very vividly—
the punishment meted out for the commission of faults and sins.
One of the simplest of these exempla is an incident recounted in the
Speculum Laicorum [148] in which it is said that Alexander Neckam,
to test the temper of an abbess-elect, addresses her as *"Domina
superba"*, and, on her responding angrily, annuls her election.

More detailed is the account of the dreadful fate met by a simo-
niacal abbess as it is related in the tale, "How a monastarye of
Nunnys was destroyed ffor covetise and for symonye". The story
is one that "gevithe cause of grete drede, namely to religeouse
peple" and its moral, "he that shall sayle in the depe sea, hove he
never so gode a shippe and hole; hit avaylith him not". The
abbess and community of some two hundred nuns are exemplary
but for one sin, that of "symonye". They accept members "not
so muche for charite and mercy as . . . for love of monney; ffor
ther myght none entre to abyde in that abbay, but yf she brought
a certayne summe of monney with her". Saint Jerome appears
one night to an aged nun who "gretly abhorryd and hatid this vice
that was amongis theme", warning her to "tell the abbesse and to
the toþer nunnys, that, but thay seasid of thayre syn, they shuld
ffele the sodeyne vengeance of god". The superior and sisters
scorn the old nun's message. A second and a third time the Saint

---

[147] *Ibid.*   [148] No. 447, Herbert (2) 397.

appears and directs the venerable religious to inform the community of their jeopardy. She does so again to no avail, bringing upon herself expulsion at midnight, the hour at which, in obedience to the vision, she had summoned the abbess futilely to beseech her to escape the imminent doom. But " unnethe was this nunne gone out of the durre, but sodenly anone all the monastarye ffell downe on the grounde, sleyng all the nunnys, so that there abode none alyve. . . ." [149]

Another exemplum on this subject states that money hoarded by a nun is found after her death and cast into her grave. The grave being opened later, the money in a molten state pours into the nun's mouth.[150]

Odo of Cheriton explains in a sermon [151] what happened to a certain lazy nun. The devil, he observes in a brief exemplum, came to the bedroom of this religious and whispered to her, " *Dormi, soror, ego sibilabo tibi matutinos*", a message " *quod in lingua Anglica sive Teutonica*", the moralist is careful to add, " *sic sonat,* ' Sleop, suster, sleop, hic wile hwistle þe vhtsanges ' ".[152]

---

[149] Horstmann (6) 356-357, (MS. Lambeth 432. An account of the life and miracles of St. Jerome taken partially from the *Legenda Aurea* and partially from the Epistles of St. Cyril and St. Augustine. *Ibid.*).

[150] Cf. MS. Add. 18346, f. 77, col. 2, 14th cent., Herbert (2) 597.

[151] Cf. MS. Arundel 231, f. 118 b, early 14th cent., *ibid.*, 72.

[152] In the *An Alphabet of Tales* it is an abbess whose love of ease is exposed to impress abbesses in general that " *Abbatissa non debet esse in vestibus et lectis nimis delicata* ". To this end a " fable ", as in the exemplum from the *Sermones Vulgares* of Jacques de Vitry (cf. Crane (1) no. LIX, 23-24), is told, not precisely to explain the punishment of fastidiousness or luxuriousness, but rather to ridicule the vice. The fable is composed of the exchange of experiences between a " lopp " and " þe gutt ". The latter, having, as it tells the former, attacked a poor woman who rose early in the morning to wash clothes in a stream of cold water, almost lost its life from the chill. The " lopp " equally had been harassed almost out of existence by an abbess who, when it bit her, screamed and called her maids to search for it; and when, after quiet had been restored, it bit her again, the abbess had no peace until it was driven out. The " lopp " and the " gutt " decide to exchange places, and, as a result, the " gutt " has a warm, very comfortable place with the abbess, who, at every twinge of pain, wraps herself and the " gutt " in rich coverings and soft furs. *Op. cit.*, 13-14.

Odo of Cheriton also repeats the incident taken from St. Gregory's *Liber Dialogorum*,[153] in which it is related that the devil entered into a nun as she swallowed a leaf of lettuce over which she has neglected to make the sign of the cross.[154] The same anecdote, embellished by details of time, "*tempore ex ordinario*," and place, "*in horto*", serves as an exemplum "*De Gula*" in *Liber Exemplorum*,[155] another thirteenth-century collection. The *Speculum Laicorum* presents the original incident under the caption, "*De crucis virtute*".[156] It is found also in the general continental collections and has place in compilations of religious tales, fables, and similitudes of later fourteenth-century England.[157]

The fastidiousness about food of a certain nun who rejects the conventual diet is punished by her beholding, according to another exemplum, the Blessed Virgin feed all the sisters of her monastery but herself.[158]

Besides the exemplum about the nun and the unhallowed lettuce leaf,[159] the *Liber Exemplorum* [160] contains two other anecdotes also taken practically verbatim from the *Liber Dialogorum,* one [161] warning against unrestraint of the tongue; the other,[162] against folly in speech generally. The first, quoted in the *Liber Exemplorum* literally,[163] explains that two nuns of noble birth but of ignoble mind are threatened with excommunication, unless they correct their incautious and irascible speech. They do not correct it. At their death they are buried in the church. When, however,

---

[153] 1, iv, PL 77. The exemplum is cited also in *Sermones Vulgares* of Jacques de Vitry. Cf. Crane (1) no. cxxx, 59.

[154] Cf. Hervieux, C., 303 and Herbert (2) 69.

[155] *Op. cit.*, no. 153, 93.

[156] Welter, cap. xxii, 34.

[157] Cf. MS. Harley 268, f. 32b, Herbert (2) 568, and MS. Add. 18364, f. 21b, *ibid.*, 610.

[158] Cf. MS. Add. 18929, f. 84b, (late 14th cent.), Ward, 659. The same story is told of a monk in other collections. Cf. *ibid.*, 630.

[159] Cf. first paragraph above.

[160] Cf. *loc. cit.*

[161] Cf. II, xxiii, PL 66, cols. 178-180.

[162] Cf. *op. cit.*, IV, li, PL 77, cols. 412-413.

[163] Orthography and order of words vary in the thirteenth-century version.

at Mass the deacon, as was the custom, calls out " *si quis non communicat det locum* ", the two nuns are seen to rise from their place and leave the sacred precincts. The man of God—St. Benedict in the original and in later redactions—who had menaced the nuns, being informed of the phenomenon, lifts the ban. Absolved, the nuns thereafter rest peacefully in their tombs.[164]

Abridged and converted into energetic Middle English in *Jacob's Well* [165] and in the *An Alphabet of Tales,*[166] the story is told to greater and more pleasing effect. So, too, the other Gregorian exemplum recounted in these three works,[167] in later fourteenth-century collections,[168] in Robert of Brunne's *Handlyng Synne* [169] (1303), and in Mirk's *Festial* [170] (c. 1400). In this anecdote the nun, as Robert of Brunne relates it,

> зede to helle for no þing ellys
> But for she spake ever vyleyng
> Among here felows al ahy,

She has been buried beside an altar before the grill. One night the wardens are startled from sleep at the sound of weeping. They find the nun, out of the grave, being tortured by " fendys " who

> . . . with brynnyng swerdys yn honde
>
> . . . .
>
> clove her mouþe evyn o two.

---

[164] Cf. Little, 78-79.   [165] Cf. " The Two Rebel Nuns ", 64.

[166] Cf. " *Excommunicacio lata in viuum eciam post mortem durat* ", 215-216.

[167] Cf. *Liber Exemplorum,* " *De lucucione bona* ", 107-108; *Jacob's Well,* " *De vanis cogitacionibus, verbis & operibus. Narracio bona contra verba ociosa* ", 232-233; *An Alphabet of Tales,* " *Loquentes multum verba stulta puniuntur* ", 304-305. Cf. also Jacques de Vitry in Crane (1) 113, and *Dial. Mir.* I, Dist. iv, cap. 22, pp. 193-194, where it is told as a recent tale.

[168] Cf. MS. Arundel 506, f. 23b, col. 2, Herbert (2) 550, and MS. Harley 2316, f. 54, *ibid.,* 577.

[169] Furnivall (2a) 56-57.

[170] Erbe, 96-97. *Mirk's Festial* is the volume of sermon literature in which " the exemplum appears to have reached its maximum employment ", as in the religious treatise it will have attained it in *Jacob's Well.* In the *Festial,* moreover, " secular tales mingle in profusion from saints' lives and monkish legends, and though evidently serious in his aims, the preacher has become a teller of tales rather than an expounder of the gospel ".—Mosher, 128, 113.

The lesson is obvious enough here. But, in addition, half her body
is burnt

> before þeauter on þe pament
>
> . . . .
>
> And halvyndele yn her grave lay.

Saint Gregory, the exemplum continues,

> seyþ þat hyt was sygne
> þat half here lyfe was not dygne;
> For þogh here dedys were chaste
> Here wurdys were al vyle & waste.[171]

Mirk's Festial includes the tale in a *sermo brevis, " De Dominica
Tercia Quadragesime "*,[172] addressed to " Good men and woy-
men ",[173] and makes the nun an abbess. Hearing the abbess' cries
in the midst of the torment, two nun sextons, greatly frightened,
yet reassuring each other, approach the burial place. The abbess
herself, in this version, explains to the religious why she is so
afflicted, begs their prayers, and warns them to avoid the same
fate.[174]

In the section, " Of them that ar lyght to speke or to slepe in
tyme of goddes service ", in *The Myroure of Oure Ladye*,[175] and
under the heading, " *Horas canonicas necligenter dicentes puniuntur* in *An Alphabet of Tales*,[176] is another felicitous story of
winsome little maids in a cloister; an attractive exemplum for this
reason, despite the fact that the lesson intended is wholly admonitory. Two little " damysells ", Margaret and Gertrude, both about
ten years of age, dwell in a Cistercian cloister. Gertrude dies, but
shortly after reappears among the nuns at service in choir. Margaret, alone, however, seems to see her little companion as the latter
comes into the church and takes her customary place beside her.
Margaret watches her stay " þer still to sho had said evynsang &
commendacion of our Ladie. And att þe colett she bowed down
vnto þe erthe, & when it was done sho went hur wayis ". When

---

[171] *Op. cit.*, 1548-1550; 1572-1574; 1576-1586.
[172] Cf. *op. cit.*, 96-101.
[173] *Ibid.*, 22.
[174] Cf. *op. cit.*, 95-97.
[175] *Op. cit.*, Part I, cap. xviii, 46-48.
[176] *Op. cit.*, No. ccclxiii, 249, where it is attributed to " Cesarius ".

Gertrude reappears next day at the same time and place, Margaret, according to the abbess' instruction, addresses her:

" 'Gude suster Geretrude, fro whens come þou, & what duse þou now here at vs when þou erte deade?'

" And sho answerd agayn & sayd;

" 'Suster, I come hedur to make satisfaccion, for I rownyd oft sithis with þe in þe where in serves-tyme, & said not oute þe wurdis full. And þerfor, in the same place þer I truspasid, am I commanddid to come & make a sethe. And þer-for be þou war of rownyng in þe where, at þou suffer not þe same payn when þou erte deade.'

" And opon þe iiij day sho said;

" 'Suster, now I trow þat I hafe fulfillid my penance, & fro hyne furthe þou sall se me no mor '.

" And þus sho was had vnto hevyn with aungell-sang." [177]

The application is extended in the *Myroure of Oure Ladye* by the following appendage,

" But take ye hede syth this yonge mayde of ten yere of age was punysshed so for halfe wordes; what shall they suffer that ar of greater age for hole wordes spoken in tyme of place of sylence ".[178]

Stark and gruesome, on the contrary, is the exemplum repeated without mitigation to signalize the punishment meted out to the sin of unchastity concealed in confession. The nun in this cautionary tale is always irrevocably lost. In one version she appears in torment to her aunt who is also her abbess to inform her that she is damned for harbouring evil thoughts.[179] In another she appears to her sister to whom she sings a dire stanza ending with the English line, " For in helle nis no pete ", and adds that she has concealed her sin in confession.[180] The climax of horror is attained, however, in the exemplum, as rendered in *An Alphabet of Tales*. The guilty nun is here represented as appearing in flames and bearing a burning child in her arms before her cousin who has been praying for her. The deceased nun declares to her relative that prayers are futile in her behalf because she had died, having withheld her sins in confession.[181]

---

[177] *Op. cit.*, 250.   [178] *Op. cit.*, 47.

[179] Cf. MS. Egerton 1117, f. 178, col. 2 (end of 13th cent.), Herbert, 471. Cf. also Klapper, 28.

[180] Cf. MS. Add. 11579, f. 117 (early 14th cent.), Herbert (2) 530.

[181] Cf. *op. cit.*, 309 and MS. Harley 206, f. 11 (mid-15th cent.), Herbert

Mild in comparison are two exempla exhibiting the punishment for sin: one, in which a corporal handled by a young girl, who is in sin, displays to the eyes of a nun-sacristan irremovable stains;[182] and the other, in which a sinful nun finds her palm branch withered on Palm Sunday and revives it with her tears.[183]

VII. *The Renegade Nun*

Two illustrative tales found among "Miracles of the Virgin" present a renegade nun. One of these exempla is constructed wholly upon the theme of the foiled nun. It differs only in the added detail of the nun's ultimate departure from the convent. When tempted to return to the world, she passes through the church, intending to leave by the church door. But invariably she pauses on her way to say an "Ave" to the Blessed Mother and as invariably is she overcome with dread at the thought of the step she is about to take, and, consequently, relinquishes the idea. The temptation importunately returning, she seeks an exit along a path upon which she is not inspired to prayer. She thus leaves the monastery and is lost.[184]

The other, based also to a certain extent upon the foiled nun motif, is unique among materials of its kind, because—the exception here proving the rule—the plot, though very simple, has genuine development and the nun, both individuality and character. This narrative, the story of Beatrix, the sacristan, or, as it is sometimes designated, "The Nun who saw the World",[185] has attained, undoubtedly, the most extensive and enduring popularity[186] of all the fictitious narratives of this class of moralizing literature. The striking and elaborate part played in it by the Blessed Virgin, about

(2) 699. Cf. also, MS. Add. 27336, f. 38b (early 15th cent.), Herbert (2) 659.

[182] Cf. *An Alphabet of Tales*, 150.

[183] Cf. MS. Harley 2851, f. 98b (c. 1300).

[184] Cf. *An Alphabet of Tales*, 321. Cf. also Crane (1) 24.

[185] Cf. Ward and Herbert (2) passim.

[186] Guiette, *La légende de la sacristine*, where all versions are cited, 503-532; Watenphul, *Die Geschichte der Marienlegende von Beatrix der Küsterin*. For studies on the legend before 1927, cf. Guiette, 10.

whom most of the " miracles " center, can explain [187] the fast hold of the legend upon medieval literature, the narrative's capacity for romantic treatment, its transferal to profane literature,[188] and its persistence there even into modern times.[189] Appearing first in the thirteenth century [190] and being repeated constantly afterwards in the exempla literature of England, it is retold with a certain degree of simple charm in *Jacob's Well* [191] and *An Alphabet of Tales*.[192]

There was " a nunne ", to quote the exemplum from *Jacob's Well*, the language of which by its directness renders the tale the more realistic and the nun more personal,

> " þat hyȝte Beatrix, sexteyn of here hows, fayr in body, fayrere in soule, meke, mylde, benigne, and obedyent to god, to holy cherche, to here abbesse, & lowly to alle here sustren, devoute in prayerys & in here seruyse, And sche louyd specyally oure lady; often & longe sche was wowed of a clerk, to ben his loue. At þe laste, after cumplyn, sche, so sore temptyd, acordyd to gon awey wyth þe clerk. but ferst, a-forn an ymage of oure lady knelyng sche seyde; 'lady þis temptacyoun may I no lengere wyth-stondyn. haue here þe keyis of myn offyce, ȝif þou wylt; I go my wey '." [193]

The nun leaves; is soon abandoned by the clerk, and as " sche kowde no crafte to lyve þerby ", she falls to the depths. After an absence of fifteen years, her heart full of sorrow and her intention bent upon penance, she returns as a beggar to the convent gate. Approaching the porter, she ventures to inquire,

> ' knowyst þou owȝt swyche a nunne þat hyȝte Beatrix, þat was sexteyn of þis hows xv. ȝere gon and more? '
> þe portere seyde, ' I knowe here wel for a blyssed womman, sche is ȝit here in here offyse, most meke, mylde & obedyente of alle here susterys '.

---

[187] " Marie est le centre des miracles auxquels elle a donné son nom de même que la femme est l'âme des fabliaux et des récits chevaleresques ", Guiette, 443.

[188] Cf. Guiette, 217-398.

[189] Cf. *The Miracle* by Max Reinhardt (N. Y., 1924). Cf. Guiette, 365 ff.

[190] All versions known to Watenphul go back to the Latin version of Caesarius of Heisterbach. Cf. Watenphul, 6. On the legend previous to its incorporation in the *Dial. Mir.*, cf. Guiette, 481 ff.

[191] Cf. *op. cit.*, cap. xliii, " *De pace triplici & obediencia* ", 271-272.

[192] Cf. *op. cit.*, ccccxviii, " *Maria officium servitorum suorum eis absentibus implet* ", 319-320.

[193] *Op. cit.*, 271.

Beatrix, knowing it is not so, turns away weeping, intending, perforce, to continue begging. But on the way Our Lady meets her,

'Beatrix', she says, 'in thy lyknesse and in þi clothyng I haue don þin offyse, syth þou kest to me þi keyis of þin offyse, be-cause þou were meke, mylde, & obedyent. þerfore, go now þou, & do furth þin offyice as I haue don for þe; for no man knowyth þi synne here but þi-self, for alle þi susteryn wendyn of me, þat it hadde ben þou." [194]

Our Lady reinstates Beatrix, then vanishes, and the repentant nun lives virtuously " in-to here ende ".

One version in French, of the mid-thirteenth century, does not mention the Blessed Virgin impersonating the absent nun. But after thirty years in the world, the nun has a vision of Mary, with the result that she returns to her convent and her lover becomes a monk.[195] Another combines the theme of the foiled nun with that of the Beatrix legend. In this Latin exemplum of the fourteenth century, the crucifix bars the passage of the nun intending to depart until she ceases to salute the crucifix and the Virgin Mary. She remains a year in the world, and, returning to the convent, finds that the Blessed Mother has impersonated her during the period of her absence.[196]

A later Latin variant,[197] also a composite of the foiled nun and the sacristan motifs, adds a secondary theme. The nun agrees to elope at midnight with a knight who awaits her at the convent door. The next day and the two following, after the same experience on each preceding night, she is rebuked by the knight for not coming as she had promised to do. She states that she has been unable to find the door. The fourth morning he asks her whether or not she says a prayer to the Blessed Mother on her way. She admits that she does, it having been her custom to say " Mary, for thine yoys fyve ",[198] etc, and five " Hail Mary's " in passing the image of the Blessed Virgin. He instructs her to omit the prayer that evening.

---

[194] *Op. cit.*, 271-272.

[195] Cf. Ward, 723.

[196] Cf. MS. Add. 18349, f. 62, Herbert (2) 604.

[197] Cf. MS. Royal 8 F, vi, f. 21, (mid-15th cent.), *ibid.*, 680. Cf. Guiette, 178-180.

[198] The English in the MS. points to an English origin. Cf. Herbert (2) *ibid.*, and Guiette, 178.

Doing so, she is able to depart. Eight days later the knight is killed. In deep sadness the nun confesses to a hermit, who advises her not even to pray for the slain knight, since his soul is lost. During the night she returns in tears to the monastery. Hearing her lamenting, the nuns ask who she is. " *Ego sum captiva soror vestra* ", she replies and, weeping, humbly implores their forgiveness. The community is greatly astonished, for, as they tell her, her absence has not been observed, the Blessed Virgin having taken her place at the various exercises. But this is not all. The hermit one day during Mass has a vision in which he beholds the Blessed Virgin assisted by angels bearing the soul of the slain knight to paradise, and after the Mass one angel comes to him announcing, *Dominus Deus meus tecum irratus est quoniam non licet iudicare nisi soli deo. Non ergo tu cum nesci finem hominis poteris iudicare illum. Vade et dic sacriste quod in crastino morietur . . ."* [199] The hermit obeys and the next day the sacristan, while among her sisters, falls seriously ill. Suddenly both angels from heaven and demons from hell come to contest for her soul. The infernal spirits claim it, declaring that she had abandoned the cloister and for seven days had dwelt in infamy. Mary then appears with a multitude of angels and she says to the nun, who is still living, " *Veni soror mea electa ut epuleris in convivio meo* ". At these words the nun gives up her soul and goes in the company of the Blessed Mother and the angels to God.[200]

VIII. *Exempla in Which the Nun is Incidental*

Besides the exempla grouped in the preceding arbitrary categories there are others in works of English origin in which the nun is mentioned but incidentally. It is a nun or an anchoress, for instance, who, hearing a death-bed avowal or overhearing a demon rejoice at some conquest, is able either to exonerate an innocent person or to defeat the evil spirit's purposes.[201] To a nun the

---

[199] Guiette, 179.

[200] *Ibid.*, 178-179.

[201] Cf. MS. Royal, 7 D, ff. 70b and 71b (second half of 13th cent.), Herbert (2) 482, and *An Alphabet of Tales*, 261-262. Cf. also " anchoress " in MS. Arundel 407, no. 1, Ward, 655.

eternal punishment of a negligent priest is revealed; [202] by their ultimately becoming nuns the conversion of sinful women is indicated; [203] a nun is entailed in the accounts respectively of an ecclesiastic's sin and release from purgatory,[204] in an account of the evil spirit's warfare against a bishop,[205] and in an account of the conversion of a man and his subsequent remarkable sanctity as a monk.[206] In one version of the Gregory-legend [207] also the queen-mother ends her days as an abbess of a monastery founded by the Pope, her son.[208] With this may be grouped the tale of the virtuous empress who, after many vicissitudes, also becomes a nun,[209] as well as the story of the wife of Apollonius as rendered by Gower in the *Confessio Amantis*.[210] None of these exempla—to repeat—is significant for the study of the nun-type. But with Gower exempla-material—and in this case material in which the nun is found, however incidentally—approaches secular channels,[211] and a little later the preceding exemplum of the virtuous empress [212] emerges in

---

[202] Cf. MS. Add. 15833, f. 122b (14th cent.) from Caesarius of Heisterbach, Herbert (2) 587.

[203] Cf. a) MS. Royal 5 A, viii, f. 144 (13th cent.), Ward, 650; *Speculum Laicorum*, no. 372, Herbert (2) 395; MS. Add. 18929, f. 82 (late 13th cent.), Ward, 658; MS. Harley 2385, f. 58b (early 14th cent.), Herber (2) 524;

    b) *Gesta Romanorum*, no. lxi, 377-379; *Jacob's Well*, " De contricione", 177-178; *An Alphabet of Tales*, " Contricio perfecta . . .", no. ccvii, 143-144;

    c) *Ibid.*, cclv, 178-179.

[204] Cf. MS. Royal, 6 B, xiv, f. 85b (c. 1200), Ward, 638; Horstmann (14) 162 and Horstmann (2) 234-235.

[205] Cf. *Roberd of Brunne's Handlyng Synne*, 241; *An Alphabet of Tales*, 159.

[206] Cf. *ibid.*, " Confusio ", 129.

[207] Cf. Keller, 192.

[208] Cf. *Gesta Romanorum*, Swan, tale lxxxi, 141-154. The Herrtage edition omits the final incident of the queen's entrance into a convent. Cf. tale lxi, 250-261.

[209] Cf. *An Alphabet of Tales*, no. DCLXXII, 447-450. See also the old French version in Miélot, no. xxix, 23-28.

[210] Cf. *op. cit.*, viii, 419-420, 425-426, 430-431, 435-437.

[211] Cf. Mosher, 125, 126.

[212] Hoccleve uses the version found in Herrtage, *op. cit.*, 311-319. Cf. also Canby, 85.

literature proper as the story of Jereslaus' wife told by Hoccleve in the *ffabula de quadam Imperatrice Romana.*[213]

IX. *Summary*

The exemplum, a literary genre which came from the Continent to England and flourished and declined there with the period of popular preaching, represents another phase of later medieval literature which drew copiously upon patristic sources. Among the countless exempla of the epoch, touching upon almost every topic conceivable, those obviously deriving from patristic literature seem most prominent and representative. Although Saints Jerome, Basil, Ambrose, and the author of the *Vitae Patrum* were sources for exempla, Saint Gregory the Great seems to have contributed most to the genre, at least in its English remains. The anecdotes notably of the *Liber Dialogorum,* as well as those in his forty homilies upon the Gospels, become stock and standard exempla. Many of those about the nun are taken from these two works.

Since the exemplum has no aesthetic pretentions and is ordained solely for practical uses, the nun-figure in it is abbreviated according to the demands of the particular exemplum. With one possible exception, she is utterly devoid of a personality, being generally an implausible complexus of the traits useful to the author of the exemplum at the moment. Among exempla about " good and bad bishops ", good and bad clerics, good and bad monks, friars, and hermits—stories concerning churchmen preponderating [214]—comes an exemplum " *de quadam abbatissa* ",[215] " *de quadam sanctimoniali* ",[216] " *de quadam sancta religiosa* ",[217] " *de quadam moniali* ",[218] —a stock figure whose sole reason for being is to represent a glaring vice, a glowing virtue, or the striking intervention of the supernatural. The necessity, moreover, under which the exemplum labors, tersely and unmistakably to bring home the point of a didactic treatise, eliminates ordinarily both development in the narrative

---

[213] Cf. *op. cit.,* Furnivall (13) 164, 166-167, 173.
[214] Cf. Mosher, 7 and note 104, 77.
[215] " *Liber de Miraculis Mariae* ", Crane, 51.
[216] *Ibid.,* 40.
[217] " *Odonis de Ceritonia Parabolae* ", Hervieux, 4; 330.
[218] *Speculum Laicorum,* Welter, 34.

as well as character development in the persons. Hence, the nun in the exemplum is merely the vehicle of the poetic justice which in this type of story, as in the fairy tale, substitutes for both kinds of development.

Whether the nun is represented as persisting in her evil course or as being suddenly, even miraculously, reformed, the taint of ignominy clings to her in these materials. The exemplum-writers seem to be indifferent on this point. The concrete "illustration of the result of obeying or disobeying some religious or moral law",[219] of observing or neglecting some precept or pious practice —this alone mattered. There are, it is true, some exempla on the nun which are not so extreme—four are, in fact, appealingly beautiful. But even in these something of the marvelous, the extravagant, or at least of the uncommon lends unreality and artificiality to the nun.

The saving feature of these exempla is, however, the serious purpose of their author or compiler. To whatever excessive lengths they go,[220] they are intent upon advancing the cause of religion.[221] The end, it would seem, justified the means—means that appear to us at least extravagant and, when touching the nun, in questionable taste.

It is only, then, because constant reiteration kept the nun in this milieu before the popular medieval consciousness that the genre can be considered as an element in the genesis of the literary nun-figure. Familiar as these exempla became by the force of repetition, they must inevitably have modified in some degree the general popular concept of the nun and, in turn, have brought influence to bear upon the formation of the literary tradition. That influence, while palpable, is, however, not a major factor, to say nothing of its being the lone source,[222] of this tradition.

---

[219] Mosher, 8.

[220] Cf. Owst, 243; MME 165.

[221] Cf. Crane (1) xx-xxi; Mosher, 14.

[222] Miss Eileen Power considers the exemplum the "raw-material". Cf. Power (1) 523.

CHAPTER VII

Conclusion

I

To one who can bring to the pages of the literature of Early England the experience of life lived in a convent, the unity of treatment given the nun in that literature is evident from the most cursory reading. The religious didactic treatises, the historiographical records, the letters, the epic legends, the romances, the lesser poetic efforts, the satires, the exempla even, whether in Latin or Anglo-Saxon, whether in Anglo-Norman or Middle English, whether before or after Alfred, whether before or after the Conquest, whether in or outside of the typical medieval continuations, whether in prose or in verse, present the nun with a uniformity in details that becomes the more impressive, the wider the inquiry is extended and the more minutely details are observed. The individual nuns depicted are very few, the passages which treat of nuns do not bulk large in the deposit of literary remains (sequestered lives even in the pre-Conquest centuries could not leave wide furrows on records); but the sameness in accounts of them is something remarkable and it is not to be explained—at least to one who leads the life—by the general uniformity of monastic norms of conduct.

These norms may be presumed to have contributed something—a very remote something—to the sameness that appears. The discipline is penetrating and in principles does not vary. It imposes a common mark upon all who submit to it, a distinctive stamp that sets all religious apart in every place and age despite the infinite variations of personality. This underlying unity, this unchanging outward mold, could have encouraged medieval English writers in their uniform mode of treatment, for whom, as for most moderns until recently, similarities rather than differences in mankind were the peculiar stuff of history. But such facts scarcely serve to explain; for the details of the monotone in which the nun appears could not by any stretch of the imagination be taken as proceeding inevitably from such norms or as imposing themselves necessarily upon the medieval mind. Conceivably nuns could have been associated with other experiences, have been endowed with other personalities, have been characterized by emphasis upon other virtues than those which turn up so faithfully and exclusively in this far-flung literature, even though it be medieval literature. Some force from without—outside the levelling aspect of monastic exteriors and outside England as well—was informing directly the English medieval writers who treated of nuns, or some English writer (or writers) was informing all his fellows, or both factors were working together to achieve the resulting sameness. Let us first survey the English writers themselves for light upon the problem.

II

In all these centuries, from the seventh to the sixteenth, the Norman Conquest is, of course, the great differentiating fact. It is not merely a convenient, it is a justified and accepted line of demarcation in any general survey of pre-Reformation literature. Before the Conquest the two most representative literary forms found in England are the didactic and the historiographical, written in Latin and Anglo-Saxon. After the Conquest five other literary forms are discernible in English literary remains—romance, the beginnings of satire, the exemplum, the ballad, and incipient drama—written in Latin, Anglo-Norman, and Middle English. The dominant forms after the Conquest, as well as before, are the didactic and the historiographical. In both of them throughout these centuries and in three of the five post-Conquest forms the nun appears, and with sufficient frequency and elaboration in each of them to throw some light upon the whole medieval period.

The two dominant pre-Conquest forms are alike instructive, whether viewed by themselves or in relation to one another. Survivals of the didactic significant for our purpose do not happen to begin the earlier in strict chronology, but the first important survivals are found in that form. Aldhelm's *De Laudibus Virginitatis* is the first didactic work extant [1] in English literature which treats

---

[1] I exclude Poenitentials (Cf. Haddan and Stubbs, 3; 176-213) as contributing nothing to the type.

17

of the nun. An examination of it reveals unmistakably the ear-marks of literary exercise, and leads us to suspect an accepted method of procedure and a stereotyped list of topics. Near the conclusion of his long treatise, Aldhelm reveals incontestably that he is facing a theory and not a condition, that his remarks have no necessary appropriateness for the community which he addresses. And he crystallizes his elaborations in a final, concrete portrait of his ideal nun—an excellent device, no doubt, in a work obviously didactic. It is a fact that all the strictly religious didactic works of England down to the Reformation which treat of the nun present her faithfully as Aldhelm presents her in the pages of the *De Laudibus Virginitatis.* Whatever they add to or subtract from the details of his treatise, they do not change in any particular his portrait for the nuns at Barking. And his own portrait is so full, so precise, so carefully thought out that we can well believe that he is reflecting rather than inaugurating a literary tradition.

Not more than three years before Aldhelm's treatise, an anony-mous life of Saint Cuthbert appeared. Shortly after, the metrical and prose lives of Saint Cuthbert by Bede and the life of Saint Wilfrid by Eddius were given to the world. All of them treat of nuns. More epoch-making for our study, however, as well as for English historiography, is the *Historia Ecclesiastica* of Venerable Bede, written about a decade after the *vita* by Eddius and about forty years after Aldhelm's treatise. Bede is more concerned with abbesses, the abbesses of the seventh and eighth centuries, than with simple nuns. Of the twenty-four religious women who appear in the pages of the *Historia,* eleven are abbesses. The abbess, more-over, alone receives elaborate treatment at his hands. She is a plausible, authentic-seeming figure; a responsible, capable religious such as would naturally gain distinction in the discharge of the abbatial office in such times. She is utterly different from, though not contradictory to, the portrait of Aldhelm's nun, but she is the standard portrait of the abbess among writers in England there-after.

It is a remarkable fact, however, that while Bede's abbesses are so distinct, his simple nuns, insofar as they are drawn, embody the ideals given by Aldhelm in his portrait. Regardless of their abbreviation and subordination, every trait which Bede gives **of** them is found in Aldhelm's nun and nothing is said of them that is not to the last detail at one with Aldhelm's figure. And thus the nun of didacticism and the abbess and nun of Bede proceed down the centuries to the Conquest in their respective genres.

When we come to the time of the Conquest, a new development takes place which is of considerable significance to this inquiry. The simple nun in the didactic literature is treated as before, but the abbess and the simple nun of historiography, except in continuations, change. It is no longer a case of merely imposing the qualities emphasized by Bede, in the manner and schema used by Bede, on abbesses and nuns of later times. On the contrary Bede's abbesses and other Anglo-Saxon abbesses and nuns not mentioned by him are treated by historiographers from an impulse that was probably more chauvinistic than antiquarian, the desire to show the newcomers some of the one-time glories of the Anglo-Saxon church in face of the distressing realities which the Normans had to correct. They therefore resurrect Bede's very subjects and other Anglo-Saxon figures but they go beyond his manner. They follow his schema, but they enrich his portraits, and the new elements which they add are at one with the elaborations customary in the didactic genre. The simple nuns treated are thus given in greater detail and Bede's abbesses are endowed with a pre-abbatial career made exactly after the pattern of Aldhelm's portrait. And from now on the two genres, much alike before the Conquest, are less unlike thereafter in treating of the nun. The simple nun becomes in both an elaborate figure; the abbess continues in the historiographical to be the abbess of Bede, although she is now described more fully and she is now revealed to have been a typical didactic nun before her accession to office.

With the coming of the Normans other literary genres develop on the soil of England and three of them are of interest to our inquiry. Arthurian romance, incipient satire, and the exemplum are found in English literary remains from near the beginning of the twelfth century. Each of these presents nuns. The nun in them is bound to reflect the new medium in which she appears—in satire by the antitheses presented to her most characteristic virtues; in the exemplum by the make-shift characterization peculiar to this form; in Arthurian romance by a slight touch of artificiality. Arthurian romance even creates one distinctive nun-figure in the person of Guinevere. But from the twelfth to the sixteenth century the nun in these new genres—even in the case of Guinevere—differs only superficially from her didactic and historiographical sisters. And satire acknowledges the details of the type by its very denial of them in specific instances. The abbess is always the abbess of historiography and the simple nun is almost exclusively the simple nun of Aldhelm and Bede. Even when she is passing from medieval into modern literature, she retains the basic character of the simple nun found first in the religious didactic material of the late seventh and early eighth centuries.

III

All of the didactic literature of all these nine centuries is practically a unit as far as the simple nun is concerned. Historiography throughout this period of many changes—changes that affect monasteries—presents very few exceptions to either the abbess or the simple nun found in Bede. The only change that the latter exhibits in tendency of presentation is a tendency towards greater conformity by combining after the Conquest the elements of Aldhelm's manner with its own. And yet historiography before the Conquest as well as historiography, special records, and episcopal registers after the Conquest show that actual conditions did not always substantiate the literary presentation of the abbess and the nun, facts that could not have been unknown to authors for the most part in close contact with contemporary monasticism and with its unwritten history in England. Not only do standardized characterizations prevail over such exceptions; not only do they ignore many typical monastic traits perhaps as deserving of development as those which they select; but they resist—Guinevere excepted—the high artificiality of Arthurian romance and are implied in detail by the antitheses to themselves presented in satiric materials [2] and in exempla. These facts are extracted from such wide provinces of evidence and admit of such few exceptions, despite the variety of types and the change of outlook, that they impose the conclusion that from beginning to end there was an

[2] For Madame Eglentyne, cf. p. 172 above.

accepted mode of treating of nuns in English literature that only became a tradition more crystallized as the Middle Ages grew older.

IV

How are we to account for these persistent and wide and detailed coincidences, stretching over nine centuries, found in five literary genres, and extant in four languages? We have already considered the levelling effect of monastic discipline as a sustained force for sameness. There is also the habit of repeating or recapitulating one's predecessors so characteristic of medieval historiography and the ingrained tendency toward imitation there as well as in other genres. The saintliness emphasized in earlier accounts would, of itself, earn many repetitions in centuries so devoted to the lives of the saints. If we add the power of taboo against depicting degraded religious figures and the instinctive gallantry that forbids depreciatory accounts of women (inhibitions by no means characteristic of medieval writers), we include all the factors outside of a living tradition itself that could be offered in explanation of the persistence of the nun-figure. Taken together, with no systematic study of origins and without consideration of the organized testimony of the authors in England and of their patristic forbears, these factors alone suggest a plausible reason for the tradition. But they become only auxiliary, secondary factors when the evidence is considered in detail and the nun-type is traced to its origin. Let us recall the evidence briefly.

V

In the quest for origins, the abbess need not give us pause. Undoubtedly she is a type, a tradition in the centuries after Bede and probably she was formed upon the pattern which Bede seems to have made classic for the medieval literature of England. Because Bede is our sole authority for the period before 731 we cannot be too certain about our statements, but what seems to have happened in the case of the abbess is briefly as follows: statesman-like women did, in fact, preside over some of the abbeys of seventh-century and eighth-century England and did play a public rôle great enough to earn large mention in the pages of one of the greatest medieval historiographers. Bede was interested in only certain qualities in them—the qualities that had made them outstanding among the figures of their time, traits which leading abbesses were almost bound to have in common, despite the individual traits which set them off from each other.   On these traits Bede concentrated, and in doing so produced a type, a pattern of monastic executive excellence [3] into which all later abbesses deserving of mention could be made to fit, presuming that any of Bede's successors were critically minded enough to consider the question of such appropriateness.   Either they went through the same process of creation which we have here presumed [4] of Bede, a possibility not at all warranted in their case by our present knowledge of medieval historiography, or there was some tradition afloat, authoritative for Bede as well as for them in treating of abbesses, but lost to us, or they followed Bede in a treatment which, for Bede, was drawn from life, and which they could follow all the easier because the qualities depicted by him almost any abbess worthy of mention might superficially seem to possess.   It is this last possibility that turns into near certainty when we recollect that the traits assigned by Bede to his abbesses were not the only traits that could describe an abbess as a public figure and when we recall the close coincidences between Bede and his successors in historiography.

VI

Though less important in the hierarchy of the monastery, the simple nun is more important for our study, for it is she rather than Mother Abbess who commands much of the attention given in English literature to consecrated women from the Conquest to our own day.   The abbess is too substantial for the growing romanticism.   The simple nun of narrative is repeated faithfully as in Bede down to the twelfth century, when she is merged with Aldhelm's nun.   Outside of the continuations of Bede she appears very rarely in narrative.   So seldom would a simple nun in any age compel historiographical mention.   The simple nun of Aldhelm appears in religious didacticism of eighth-century England

[3] It necessarily included sanctity, to which Bede consistently gave emphasis.

[4] Bede's abbess cannot be identified with that of any preceding or contemporary author on the Continent.   Cf. p. 109, note 338 above.

complete and perfectly defined. But unlike the abbess and the simple nun of historiography, she is an abstraction, an ideal held aloft from the outset of the eighth century in her own genre and dominant and unchanged in all genres after the twelfth century. The simple nun in the literature of Anglo-Saxon, of Anglo-Norman, and of early Tudor England, despite the touch of sentimentality found in romance and despite the degradation and the ignominy attaching to the figure in satire and exemplum, remains forever after the ideal. The fact that the figure as presented in didacticism is as complete at the beginning of England's literature as in the sixteenth century; the fact that its authority remains unimpeached; that it pervades every literary type, and is unchanged by accidents of language, leads one to believe that its source must be sought, first, beyond English beginnings, and second, in an authority beyond the mutations of literary development in England.

We naturally turn for instruction, therefore, to the earliest didactic treatise. It happens to be also the earliest extant work in which the ideal simple nun is found—the *De Laudibus Virginitatis* of Aldhelm. It anticipates, as we have seen, both in outline and in detail of development subsequent didactic works. They exhibit such a striking affinity for and add so little in substance to the elements of Aldhelm's portrait of the simple nun that they either are following him faithfully or are joining with him in reflecting some common source. Aldhelm's treatise and most of the didactic works which follow him are written in Latin; even those of them written in Anglo-Saxon bear unmistakably the impress of Latin influence; all of them, like so many other medieval works, are fond of referring to the Fathers. Such considerations suggest patristic Latin as a possible source of the nun of English didacticism and of early English historiography. It proves to be the fact.

The prototype of the simple nun of historiography is found in the consecrated virgin written of by Saint Gregory the Great in the *Liber Dialogorum* and the *XL Homiliarum in Evangelia, Libri Duo*. The source of the abstract figure, the simple nun of religious didactic literature of medieval England, is also patristic. It is the ideal virgin illustrated and explained in the treatises on virginity written by Tertullian, Saint Cyprian, Saint Jerome, Saint Ambrose, and Saint Augustine. The religious didactic literature of medieval

England from Aldhelm to the fifteenth century adheres absolutely to the figure offered in these works of the Latin Fathers. Not only does the ideal remain the same, but the very expression of that ideal persists unchanged. Medieval churchmen offer the identical model to nuns for eight centuries; they expound the ideal in patristic phraseology. Figures of speech, analogies, symbolical expressions, conventionalized before the literature of England began and associated with the nun-ideal, enter the literature of England at its inception; remain the salient characteristic of one department of that literature; dominate another department, and with a wealth of connotation about the nun, drawn from their patristic source and retained for centuries, make their way with the patristic nun-ideal unchanged, into modern English literature.

VII

The nun-tradition does not arise from historiography, although it contributes the main outlines of the abbess type. Neither does the tradition arise from historical records of monastic abuses. It does not originate in romance, in satire, or in the exemplum. The nun in each of these is herself derivative. Neither is the nun a creation of modern English literature, although the nun-figure keeps recurring in modern English authors. Non-Catholic England, while unwittingly perpetuating in its sublimest poetry (v. g. Milton, Tennyson, Wordsworth) the spirit and the impression created by the patristic nun-ideal, relies upon the external trappings of the nun-figure when it would represent her in definite detail. External trappings are impressive. They convey a certain air of picturesqueness, of aloofness, even of mere oddity. They are ordinarily confused with and mistaken for the essence of the religious character. But they are merely superficial. They are not the source.

Writers about the nun in England simply availed themselves of the tradition. Underlying the sentimental nun-figure of Arthurian romance, the debased nun-figure of satire, and the mechanical nun-figure of most exempla is the traditional ideal nun-type of patristic Latin and of the religious-didactic literature of England. This form it is that issues from the period of literary beginnings in England into modern literature.

The predominance of the tradition indicates the importance of the Latin language in the formation not only of the English language, but also of English literature. It is undoubtedly true that most writers in England before Shakespeare wrote in Latin. Certainly, the majority of religious-didactic authors did so, and " to write in a given tongue is not to be wholly independent of the tradition it carries ".[5] The traditions of the Fathers are those unmistakably carried by Latin into Western Christianity where the language retained an ecclesiastical stamp even while it assumed a somewhat popular character.[6] Insofar as the nun-figure is concerned it was the repetition and popularization by writers in England of the Latin literature, carried over intact from patristic sources, that provided English literature with one of its distinctive if most evanescent of traditions. To know the genuine character of much that is typical of English literature, it is not sufficient even to examine what is ordinarily considered the period of its origin, that is, Anglo-Saxon and Anglo-Norman England. The almost exclusively Christian thought and literature of this era is the mediate source of much in modern English literature. But as the origin of the nun-tradition indicates, students of English literature may well look further [7] and consider the antecedents of the Middle Ages, they may with profit learn " what were the traditions in letters and in thought to which medieval men looked back as to the rock whence they were hewn ".[8]

---

[5] Campbell, J. M., 14.

[6] Cf. Paetow (1) 182.

[7] Although the religious didactic treatises of medieval England provide the ambient in which the ideal nun-figure moves from Latin patristic into the literature of modern England, other genres contribute in part to the nun-figure that appears in modern literature. The abbess type of the *Historia Ecclesiastica* is met in Elizabethan drama and in the modern novel. The abbess of satire, of the exemplum, and even the wicked abbess found here and there in historiography appear in the sensational pages of Gothic romance. Some of the lurid moral lessons of the exempla as well as some of the graphic admonitions of didacticism itself are manifestly the model upon which some nun-figures of modern drama and of the sentimental tale of the seventeenth century are formed. But these are not the English literary tradition.

[8] Rand (2) 6.

INDEX

231